Women Navigating Educational Leadership

Educational Leadership: Innovative, Critical and
Interdisciplinary Perspectives

Series Editors: Jeffrey S. Brooks, Alan J. Daly, Yi-Hwa Liou, Chen Schechter and Victoria Showunmi

The Educational Leadership series provides a forum for books that push the conceptual boundaries of educational leadership and that introduce novel perspectives with the promise of improving, challenging and reconceptualising the field of study and informing practice. Books in the series take a global, interdisciplinary focus and cover educational phases ranging from early years to higher education. They aspire to be field-leading innovations that advance new theories, topics and methodologies. The series will be of interest to those working across disciplines such as educational leadership, school leadership, teacher education, sociology, anthropology, economics, psychology, political science, philosophy and public policy.

Also available in the series:
Educational Leadership and Critical Theory, edited by Charles L. Lowery, Chetanath Gautam, Robert White and Michael E. Hess
The Relational Leader, edited by Yi-Hwa Liou and Alan J. Daly

Forthcoming in the series:
Islam, Education, and Freedom, Melanie C. Brooks and Miriam D. Ezzani
Leadership for Society, Rima'a Da'as and Chen Schechter
Gender and Educational Leadership in Greece, Emmy Papanastasiou
Equity and Influence in the Funding of Schools, Matthew P. Sinclair
Socialisation of School Leaders in Sub-Saharan Africa, Pontso Moorosi and Callie Grant

Women Navigating Educational Leadership

Jana L. Carlisle

BLOOMSBURY ACADEMIC
LONDON • NEW YORK • OXFORD • NEW DELHI • SYDNEY

BLOOMSBURY ACADEMIC
Bloomsbury Publishing Plc, 50 Bedford Square, London, WC1B 3DP, UK
Bloomsbury Publishing Inc, 1385 Broadway, New York, NY 10018, USA
Bloomsbury Publishing Ireland, 29 Earlsfort Terrace, Dublin 2, D02 AY28, Ireland

BLOOMSBURY, BLOOMSBURY ACADEMIC and the Diana logo are trademarks of Bloomsbury Publishing Plc

First published in Great Britain 2024
This paperback edition published 2025

Copyright © Jana L. Carlisle, 2024

Jana L. Carlisle has asserted her right under the Copyright, Designs and Patents Act, 1988, to be identified as Author of this work.

Series design by Tjaša Krivec
Cover image © moodboard / Getty Images

All rights reserved. No part of this publication may be: i) reproduced or transmitted in any form, electronic or mechanical, including photocopying, recording or by means of any information storage or retrieval system without prior permission in writing from the publishers; or ii) used or reproduced in any way for the training, development or operation of artificial intelligence (AI) technologies, including generative AI technologies. The rights holders expressly reserve this publication from the text and data mining exception as per Article 4(3) of the Digital Single Market Directive (EU) 2019/790.

Bloomsbury Publishing Plc does not have any control over, or responsibility for, any third-party websites referred to or in this book. All internet addresses given in this book were correct at the time of going to press. The author and publisher regret any inconvenience caused if addresses have changed or sites have ceased to exist, but can accept no responsibility for any such changes.

A catalogue record for this book is available from the British Library.

A catalog record for this book is available from the Library of Congress.

ISBN: HB: 978-1-3504-0998-9
PB: 978-1-3504-1002-2
ePDF: 978-1-3504-0999-6
eBook: 978-1-3504-1000-8

Series: Educational Leadership: Innovative, Critical and Interdisciplinary Perspectives

Typeset by Newgen KnowledgeWorks Pvt. Ltd., Chennai, India

For product safety related questions contact productsafety@bloomsbury.com.

To find out more about our authors and books visit www.bloomsbury.com and sign up for our newsletters.

*I dedicate this book to women aspiring to and serving in educational
leadership roles
I wish to thank:
The respondents whose stories enrich and shape this book.
My readers, editors, illustrators, and cheerleaders: my father Fred; mother JoAnn;
children Jared, Emma, and Izzy; partner Manny; sisters Ginny, Becky, and Lindy;
dear far-flung friends; and pals from Penn.*

Contents

List of Figures		x
List of Tables		xi
Series Editors' Foreword		xii
Preface		xv
1.	Introduction: A Rising Tide Lifts All Boats	1
	Leadership Story	1
	Overview	2
	Methods	10
	Chapters and Themes	16
	Conclusion	19
	Reflective Questions	20
2.	Leadership Models and Stories: Lean In or Shove Off	21
	Leadership Story	21
	Overview	22
	What Is Educational Leadership?	23
	Leadership Stories and Models	28
	Outmoded and Ineffective Leadership Models	31
	Conclusion	34
	Reflective Questions	35
3.	Purpose, Identity, and Power: What We Stand For	37
	Leadership Story	37
	Overview	38
	Culture and Power	39
	Purpose and Identity	42
	She Persists	45
	Leadership Theories	48
	Gender and Intersectionality	52
	Conclusion	57
	Reflective Questions	59

4.	Navigating Challenges to Women's Leadership: Hummingbird	61
	Leadership Story	61
	Overview	62
	Challenges to Women's Leadership	62
	Bullying, Harassment, Racism, and Abuse	69
	Reflections on Bullying, Harassment, Racism, and Abuse	79
	Transformational Resilience	85
	Conclusion	93
	Reflective Questions	94
5.	Leadership Routes and Areas of Knowledge: Yellow Brick Road	95
	Leadership Story	95
	Overview	96
	Leadership Routes	97
	Knowing and Doing	103
	Reflections on Leadership Standards	110
	Conclusion	114
	Reflective Questions	115
6.	Standards and Dispositions for Women Educational Leaders: The Dance	117
	Leadership Story	117
	Overview	118
	Where Do We Go Now?	119
	Revised Standards' Statements	120
	Dispositions for Women Educational Leaders	138
	Conclusion	162
	Reflective Questions	163
7.	Strategies and Supports: Still Standing	165
	Leadership Story	165
	Overview	166
	A Commitment to Leadership Development	167
	Strategies for Organizations to Employ	168
	Strategies for Individuals to Employ	184
	Conclusion	193
	Reflective Questions	195

Appendices
    A: List of Respondents   197
    B: List of Abbreviations   201
    C: Elements to Support an Audit of Leadership Development Capacity   203

Notes   205
References   219
Index   231

Figures

1.1	Glass Escalator	5
1.2	Approach	10
5.1	Yellow Brick Road	98
5.2	Instructional Leader and Transformational Educational Leader Practices	110
5.3	Dr. Carlisle's Fourteen Draft Standards	111
6.1	Proposed Dispositions and Standards for Women Educational Leaders	119
6.2	Yellow Hat	136
7.1	Strategies for Organizations to Employ	168
7.2	Strategies for Individuals to Employ	185

Tables

1.1	Thirty-Seven Respondents' Profiles	12
3.1	Reasons for Pursuing Educational Leadership	46
3.2	Reasons for Pursuing Educational Leadership (Detail)	47
4.1	Respondents' Experience with Bullying	73
4.2	Respondents' Experience with Racism	75
4.3	Respondents' Experience with Harassment	78
4.4	Respondents' Experience with Abuse	79
5.1	National Policy Board for Educational Administration Professional Standards for Educational Leaders 2015	108
5.2	Council of Chief State School Officers' Model Principal Supervisor Standards 2015	109
5.3	Respondents' Very Important and Extremely Important Ratings of Draft Standards	112

Series Editors' Foreword

Jeffrey S. Brooks, Curtin University School of Education, Australia
Chen Schechter, Bar-Ilan University, Israel
Alan J. Daly, UC-San Diego, USA
Victoria Showunmi, UCL Institute of Education, England
Yi-Hwa Liou, National Taipei University of Education, Taiwan

The history of thought and practice in educational leadership can be conceived as a punctuated equilibrium (English 2008). The arc of the field's history is a steady evolution of traditional ideas centered around management, administration, efficiency, rational decision-making, authority, and power (Beck and Murphy 1993). Heavily influenced by business administration and management literature, the field is also shaped by sociology, anthropology, economics, psychology, political science, philosophy, and public policy. As an applied field, scholarship in educational leadership shapes—and is shaped by—developments in schools, universities, policy making processes, and in other formal and informal education settings (Brooks and Miles 2006). This has meant that there is space in the field both for highly theoretical work and for research grounded in a specific context. Of course, quite a lot of scholarship in the field seeks these aims at the same time as a way of generating relevant knowledge *in situ* while also advancing thought and practice throughout the world (Gunter 2016).

Occasionally, ideas are introduced that compel scholars and practitioners to reconsider the foundations of "what they know" and adopt new ways of thinking about and practicing their work. Among intellectual movements that upset educational leadership's orthodoxy were postmodernism, critical theory, feminist theories, social justice, culturally relevant school leadership, distributed leadership, and more purposeful studies of the relationship between leadership and learning (Brooks and Normore 2017). Each of these domains of inquiry produced novel perspectives on educational leadership (to be sure there are others—we do not pretend this is an exhaustive list) that inform contemporary conceptual and empirical research. Additionally, each of these intellectual movements initiated a paradigmatic shift in the way people engage in the practice of educational leadership, think about their work, and conduct themselves as leaders and followers in formal and informal education settings.

For all this innovation, the arc toward improvement has been slow and often the emphasis on the traditional has subdued the exploration of the radical. This book series seeks to establish a space for research that (1) explores promising concepts at the edges of the field, (2) encourages the publication of new ideas, and (3) critiques contemporary assumptions about educational leadership. Our hope is that the series may play some role in prompting future conceptual and empirical revolutions that will move the field forward via emergent scientific and artistic revolutions.

New perspectives are emerging from across the field and other disciplines that have great potential to influence (and be influenced by) educational leadership scholarship and practice. Among these are exciting developments related to sustainability and climate change, social networking, religion and spirituality, immigration and globalization, student-centered leadership, and innovative contributions to traditional topics such as community-school relations, gender, race, ethnicity, sexuality, diversity, intercultural/cross-cultural studies, globalization, early childhood and adult education, student voice, and activism. To be sure, there are others. While it is easy to point to individual articles or small groups of scholars working in these areas, there is no clear publication outlet for deeper, focused, and nuanced works that explore and challenge such ideas in the detail afforded by a full-length book or highly focused edited volume. Reaching out beyond the field of educational leadership, there are developments in sociology, anthropology, political science, policy studies, psychology, curriculum studies, brain-based research, environmental science, creativity studies, medicine, law, and other fields that have yet to be deeply explored or understood in terms of their possible applicability to educational leadership. We see the series as a place where such disciplines, ideas, and lines of inquiry can come into dialogue and create innovation. We see this book series as a forum for interdisciplinary, innovative, creative, and indeed controversial work.

In addition to providing a forum for such exciting ideas, we aim for this series to also include a diversity of authors and contexts underrepresented in many extant book series. This means diversity of author, geographical context, and perspective. As this is a series of research books, we anticipate the primary audience being academics, but we also anticipate that the topics will be of interest to practicing school leaders, teachers, policymakers, and scholars working across disciplines such as educational leadership, school leadership, teacher education, sociology, anthropology, economics, psychology, political science, philosophy, and public policy. We invite you to join us in the conversation—to share your work and your insights as we explore and extend the field of educational leadership.

References

Beck, L. G., and J. Murphy (1993), *Understanding the Principalship: Metaphorical Themes, 1920s–1990s*, New York: Teachers College Press.
Brooks, Jeffrey S., and M. T. Miles (2006), "From Scientific Management to Social Justice… and Back Again? Pedagogical Shifts in Educational Leadership," *International Electronic Journal for Leadership in Learning*, 4(1), 2–15.
Brooks, Jeffrey S., and A. H. Normore (2010), "Educational Leadership and Globalization: Literacy for a Global Perspective," *Educational Policy*, 24(1), 52–82. doi:10.1177/0895904809354070.
Brooks, Jeffrey S., and A. H. Normore (2017), *Foundations of Educational Leadership: Developing Excellent and Equitable Schools*, New York: Routledge.
English, F. W. (2008), *Anatomy of Professional Practice: Promising Research Perspectives on Educational Leadership*, Lanham, MD: Rowman & Littlefield Education.
Gunter H. (2016), *An Intellectual History of School Leadership Practice and Research*, London: Bloomsbury.
Jackson, L. L., N. Lopoukhine, and D. Hillyard (1995), "Ecological Restoration: A Definition and Comments," *Restoration Ecology*, 3(2), 71–5.
Kensler, L. A. W., and C. L. Uline (2017), *Leadership for Green Schools: Sustainability for Our Children, Our Communities, and Our Planet*, New York: Routledge.
Kensler, L. A. W., and C. L. Uline (2019), "Educational Restoration: A Foundational Model Inspired by Ecological Restoration," *International Journal of Educational Management*, 33(6), 1198–218. doi:10.1108/ijem-03-2018-0095.
Senge, P. M., N. Cambron-McCabe, T. Lucas, B. Smith, and J. Dutton (2012), *Schools That Learn (Updated and Revised): A Fifth Discipline Fieldbook for Educators, Parents, and Everyone Who Cares about Education*, New York: Crown Business.
Stafford-Smith, M., D. Griggs, O. Gaffney, F. Ullah, B. Reyers, N. Kanie, B. Stigson, P. Shrivastava, M. Leach, and D. O'Connell (2017), "Integration: The Key to Implementing the Sustainable Development Goals," *Sustainability Science*, 12(6), 911–19. doi:10.1007/s11625-016-0383-3.

Preface

Women Navigating Educational Leadership is my response to the underrepresentation of women in educational leadership positions and the complicated and veiled routes women take to ascend to leadership. As a practitioner researcher, I include stories from my own US educational leadership career as well as thirty-seven US women respondents to bring life to research-based models, frameworks, theories, strategies, and conclusions applicable to women serving in or aspiring to educational leadership roles. I craft the book as a contribution to women educational leaders and the men who work with, work for, lead, support, mentor, sponsor, and raise these women—allies. I design the book to deliver—in an accessible manner and in one volume—new and existing knowledge, insights, interrelationships, and practices about women in educational leadership. This resource includes a comprehensive equation for women pursuing, and serving as, educational leaders.

Having spent more than thirty years working to transform urban public education for all students, I've served in leadership positions in the not-for-profit, public, and philanthropic sectors—in urban districts and organizations focused on education advocacy, funding, leadership, evaluation, and reform. My titles ranged from Chief Planning Officer to Chief of Staff to Senior Program Officer and Team Leader to Executive Director. I am passionate about leadership and culture. I've observed, and conducted studies on, leaders who were both effective and ineffective. Some of these studies were for clients or partners, some to keep me sane and continuously learning, some for framework or program development, and some for doctoral program requirements. An in-the thick-of-it leadership expert means I've sought to learn how to and how not to lead through self-reflection, study, observation, and feedback.

To test whether my experience was an isolated one and to augment my own story, I fielded a comprehensive survey to a broad network of women educational leaders between July and October 2020. I highlight insights from thirty-seven diverse women from across the United States. In sharing my own thirty-year leadership story—and highlights from respondents—I seek to model reflective, auto-ethnographic, and phenomenological practices. Data collection focused on my own and respondents' experiences with gender and racial bias, resilience, social justice, and leadership strategies and challenges. The thirty-seven women respondents possess different educational backgrounds; reflect different ethnic, racial, and age groups; and inhabit varied roles and organizations—from public school districts to charter school networks to graduate schools of education to partner and support organizations.

I created *Women Navigating* to appeal to practitioners who wish to gain understanding as well as those who teach in graduate schools of education. *Women Navigating* presents a view of what it takes for future leaders envisioning their own journeys as well as insights into what it has taken for women to serve as educational leaders. This book fits into Bloomsbury Publishing's Educational Leadership: Innovative, Critical and Interdisciplinary Perspectives' series, because of its complementary and multidisciplinary objectives and distillation of cross-sector leadership models, theories, themes, standards, drivers, experiences, and support strategies.

Conducting the research and analysis for this book solidified my commitment to continuous learning and reflection, knowledge sharing, and action-based research—one must learn for to teach. It is thus my hope that readers benefit from the ways in which this book:

1. Seeks to build readers' understanding and knowledge of the ways in which power, resilience, social justice, feminism, collectivism, egalitarianism, teaching and learning, and talent management (which involves recruitment, selection, hiring, onboarding, professional development, support, and performance evaluation) influence women's educational leadership practices and success.
2. Proposes applicable models, standards, strategies, and supports vital to women educational leaders and the concomitant leadership equation for women.
3. Presents the ways in which one's identity informs and drives one's leadership approach and purpose.
4. Confronts the persistent barriers women—and those with intersectional identities—encounter even though education is a woman-dominated profession.
5. Highlights the resilience women must and do possess to inhabit education leadership roles and navigate politically fraught educational environments.
6. Includes and defines terms such as manels, bropropriating, and manimization.

When looking back on my career and motivations, I believe my commitment to an egalitarian mission—of ensuring students from all backgrounds have equitable access to, and achieve equitable outcomes from, high-quality teaching and learning—shows up in several ways. First, I seek to advocate for and respect the students and parents on whose behalf I've worked. Second, I try to demonstrate my loyalty to those I've served, those I've led, those to whom I've reported, and the organizations for which I've worked—by incorporating organizational and individual differences, values, and missions into my approach. Third, I'm committed to drawing data-informed decisions and creating rational frameworks. Toward this end, I look through a wide variety of lenses, across leadership models, and across sectors—corporate, philanthropic, non-profit, government, economic, policy, and education—to craft strategies that address calcified and discriminatory systems, structures, and practices. Above all, I rely on humor, passion, collaboration, self-care, and continuous learning.

1

Introduction: A Rising Tide Lifts All Boats

Leadership Story

I stood in the front of an elementary school gymnasium. Parents were agitated. "Why are you considering closing our school? It is a great school and a good place. Why?" They directed their displeasure at me. The district had identified fourteen schools for possible closure and I was meeting with each school's stakeholders. Such closures can help offset budget shortfalls and enrollment declines. Located in one of the more affluent areas of the city, this school's parents had questions about why their high-performing school was on the list of potential district schools to close. We hadn't yet identified academic performance as a criterion.

The prior year's school closure process had run amok and resulted in the superintendent reconsidering several closure recommendations. That process's closure criteria used low academic performance as a criterion and omitted indicators such as a school's role as a neighborhood hub. The process disproportionately singled out schools located in low-income neighborhoods, which had high majority-minority populations and the state had identified as low performing. The process I was leading sought to integrate various proxies for a school's value to the community such as whether the school was used after hours, the number of partnerships underway, and students and families' involvement in the school. The rebooted process placed several high-performing schools on the potential closure list primarily due to their age and physical condition. There was an outcry from the parents sitting in front of me. I also fended off local professors' questions about our methods.

I hadn't wanted to go public with all fourteen schools but was overruled. Our Communications Office felt it would appear more transparent to show the full list and then engage the public in conversations before whittling down the list. So, there I was explaining that "no, academic performance isn't currently one of the indicators being considered." The superintendent surprised me and the parents when he joined me during the question-and-answer session. A parent asked the question again, "Are you going to include academic performance in your analysis?" He said, "Of course!" The parent looked at us, laughed and said, "What is this, good cop, bad cop?"

We went on to shorten the list of schools, fielded accusations of playing politics because the public felt we had disingenuously publicized the initial list of fourteen schools, and closed fewer schools than we intended.

Overview

This vignette highlights that leadership can be imperfect and messy even when one is attempting to be a responsive and transparent leader. This is especially the case when trying to change entrenched practices, systems, and structures. My own reasons for pursuing educational leadership involve improving and enhancing educational access and outcomes for all children, and eradicating educational (and, through education, societal) inequities. I sought work in urban locations and in organizations with missions to improve outcomes for children and families, whom traditional practices and policies had left behind. This chapter's subtitle, "A Rising Tide Lifts All Boats," references my egalitarian perspective—which is not based on a zero-sum calculus or the falsely meritocratic American Dream.

Historically and currently, the US public education has not well served students who are Black, brown, low-income, immigrant, and second-language learners, and those with disabilities. Yet the public school student body continues to evolve and become more diverse. Given this diversity, I maintain that educational settings and educators' workplaces should become fairer and more inclusive. After all, we have children's physical, intellectual, social, and emotional learning, growth, and development in our hands.

This first chapter and the leadership story serve as an introduction—to me, my reasons for writing this book, key themes uncovered, my approach, and the thirty-seven women educational leaders who contributed to the study on which I base this book.

My own path was circuitous. I became an education leader not through teaching or administrating but through political science (my undergraduate degree) and public policy (my master's degree). This education along with on-the-job training served to untether me from any particular sector, position, or organizational type. I didn't always understand this when I was enmeshed in performing consequential leadership roles, but since exiting such roles and when writing this book, I have reflected deeply on my leadership experiences and perspectives. My roles and experiences taught me that attempts at systemic and structural change puts people—in role, in bureaucracies, or when performing previously acceptable practices—on the defensive and on the lookout for threats to power, position, resources, and norms.

While I did earn a doctorate in educational leadership to bolster my education credentials, I believe my political science and policy lenses enhanced my ability to lead. I served in public, nonprofit, and private sector organizations and at the local, state, and national levels. I worked closely with stakeholders to examine, design, and implement new school, service delivery, partnership, and policy models. In my planning roles, I facilitated processes that resulted in state improvement, school improvement, annual, academic, and strategic plans; program evaluations; and grant proposals and awards. I researched the practices and designs of—and then toured—local and national classrooms and schools. I collaborated with stakeholders—from students to teachers to CEOs to foundation leaders to governors to legislators.

I do not highlight these roles or my experiences to imply that I had universal success as a leader. I didn't. Throughout this book, I share the challenges I encountered, opportunities from which I grew and learned, and the ways in which my identity and hardships—which are "adverse situations [that] can teach resilience and integrity"[1]—influenced my leadership. When I look outward to some of my peers, my bosses, or their bosses, I can understand how they may have seen my call to lead, my task orientation, and high energy level as characteristic of someone who is overconfident. That was not the case.

Books tell women to be confident, to lean in, to secure as much education and training as possible, to work hard, to separate work and family, and to demonstrate excellence. Many scholars identify these features as *agentic*—"ambitious, dominant, self-confident, and forceful as well as self-reliant and individualistic"[2]—which are characteristics typically attributed to and acceptable for men. As such, colleagues and supervisors may expect that women present as communal: "affectionate, helpful, friendly, kind, and sympathetic as well as interpersonally sensitive, gentle, and soft spoken."[3]

The academic literature often speaks to women's leadership styles as linked to that of nurturers, advocates, and coaches—not unlike being a mother. Women may gravitate toward enacting leadership that is collaborative, supportive of healthy workplace environments, and inclusive of diverse people, perspectives, cultures, and talents. Women may see themselves as called to leadership for social justice and equitable student learning outcomes. These are not universal truths—undoubtedly there are women who follow different approaches, who may act out of character, or whose behaviors may be at odds with what they believe.

I've appreciated it when people told me that my efforts made a difference to them or a project. I've felt burned when people have questioned my motives or derided my nontraditional background. Regardless of how people perceived me, the unfortunate result is that the desired change for children remains elusive. Together the expertism employed by some in public education (we know what is best), the concomitant belief in the savior myth (we will save you without asking what would be most helpful), and societal inequities serve to erode community members'—and those we intend to help—trust and agency. We so-called-experts haven't always built meaningful participation among those we are entrusted with serving and educating.

The fact that I challenge these default bureaucratic and heroic educational practices contributes to my outsider status. Yet this outsider status isn't just due to my education, experience, and approach but also to my gender. For the decade spanning my mid-thirties to mid-forties, I was also an outsider because of my age, which positioned me as younger than most of my leadership colleagues. Now I'm an outsider because of my age (62). Women are in the minority of people leading organizations in every sector of the economy—even in organizations located in sectors dominated by women such as health and education. As depicted in Figure 1.1, in these cases, women often observe men—of color and white—quickly rise to leadership levels by riding a glass escalator while women remain on, and watch the men ascend from, the lower floors.[4]

To equip myself early in my role as a leader I requested that my employer send me to the Leadership Development Program at the Center for Creative Leadership. There I learned that my colleagues felt I should spend more time chatting with them at the water fountain and tone down my task orientation. A more recent example of feedback involved a boss referring to my work ethic as sick even though he regularly called me at 9:00 a.m. or p.m. on weekends and benefitted from my timely fulfillment of requests. This contradiction—to be pleasant, chatty, and not overly committed to work—has dogged me throughout my career—as I always tried to fulfill work assignments in a thorough, timely, and high-quality manner because this is what women who lead must do to be leaders. We must defeminize and manage how we present ourselves (finding that sweet spot between agentic and communal characteristics such as wearing pant suits and quiet jewelry) and not show dissonance with expected behaviors (such as assertiveness) that align with historical social and gender norms.

Figure 1.1 Glass Escalator.[5]

The National Center for Education Statistics (NCES 2020) documents that women dominate the teaching corps, representing 76 percent of public school teachers in 2017 and made some gains over the last ten years among public school principals, representing 54 percent of all principals in 2017.[6] Yet, women aren't just underrepresented disproportionately in the principalship. They are also underrepresented disproportionately among public school superintendents, representing just 27 percent of superintendents in 2020, according to the

American Association of School Administrators (AASA).[7] Data from the ILO Group's Superintendent Research Project (2022) indicate that not only has there been a significant increase in superintendent turnover during and following the coronavirus pandemic but also that the opportunity for women to serve as superintendents—to fill these vacancies—as a result of the openings has not been realized—"of the 94 women who have left superintendent positions since the start of the pandemic, two-thirds (62) were replaced by men."[8]

What does it take to for a woman to lead in a world designed by and for men? My decades in the field, in academic research, and supporting women leaders and their leadership, suggests that women must work harder, longer, and more excellently than our male counterparts. Women must demonstrate exceptional competence by taking on more learning and projects to be considered as equal to men, including "mastering job-relevant knowledge and being exceptionally well prepared for meetings and negotiations … [and delivering] 'more than people expect.'"[9] Two of this study's respondents—Angela and Zelda who are both women of color—speak about this approach.

> **Angela**: I work harder and research more in order to be seen as equal. However, because I have done that, it has enhanced my educational leadership not just to this group but to the rest of the institution.
>
> **Zelda**: I often feel that I have to prove myself as competent in groups dominated by men rather than it being assumed that I am competent because I am at the table.

Like many women, I was often left standing alone as a singular change agent, on what I learned was a glass cliff. These are situations or positions in which one is expected to take risks, where colleagues don't want to step up, where one is expected to fail because of the associated risks, and where it is okay for that person to fail because she is viewed as expendable and as an Other.[10] An Other is perceived as not meeting certain sets of standards, possessing time-honored sets of experiences, or possessing a historically sanctioned profile of a leader.[11] I knew people who survived and thrived in bureaucracies, staying in their roles through multiple leadership changes, because of their risk aversion, antipathy to innovation, and preference for the status quo. Many times what a survivor said behind closed doors about supporting my or a leader's approach or strategy wouldn't be uttered or reinforced in public. Once, a local pastor approached me after a meeting to indicate that he observed me carrying the ball during a controversial public discussion while my colleagues literally sat on the sidelines. Flying under the radar really does seem to provide cover if not complicity.

My experience confronting, contradicting, or suggesting threatening changes to workplace peers, cultures, and practices has stayed with me. I've come away gobsmacked, because the resistance I experienced belies the ways in which gurus discuss effective leadership—that leadership is selfless, mission driven, and collaborative rather than egocentric, unilateral, Machiavellian, and heroic. My interest in and passion for leadership and culture evolved over time. It is important to get leadership right—and to ensure we also get its associated practices right.

Well-connected, savvy, and supportive mentors and sponsors, and access to stretch assignments and professional networks, are valuable tools for development. Stretch or developmental assignments are those that challenge one to grow, are visible, are consequential, prepare someone for the next promotion or role, and depend on clear goals and objectives for both the individual and assignment.[12] Sponsors "are successful people who understand how to develop effective relationships and networks with other successful people. They understand politics within their professional area and have a degree of power in influencing others."[13] Sponsors provide access to, and advocate on behalf of their protégés for, specific roles. Networks can be local, regional, and national in nature and can stem from areas of interest (such as sororities, synagogues, and churches), professional groups or associations, graduate schools, and alumni groups.

While I benefited from such supports and found the work rewarding, within the educational organizations I worked I frequently discovered myself standing alone to fight daily battles simply to do my job. I worked tirelessly. I sought to mediate, navigate, reflect, manage undercurrents, deflect, and adjust. I learned to read my audiences, peers, communities, and leaders. I developed mettle because of a myriad of early life, work, professional experiences, and relationships with partners, colleagues, classmates, friends, and family. During especially difficult and personally challenging spells, I wore a Wonder Woman T-shirt under my suit blouse. I once left it at my father's home and he called to ask if I could wait for him to send it. It takes more than passion, commitment, support, and expertise to be a singleton change agent; it also takes resilience and grit. While I was alone during many of these experiences, I've come to understand that I was not alone in experiencing them. Unsurprisingly I've concluded that successful leaders and change agents require allies.

For many years, colleagues, family members, and classmates urged me to write about my educational leadership experience. I delayed the undertaking because I was enmeshed in work, child-rearing, marriage, and continuing education. Then, I was concerned it wasn't the right time to write about women given that the United States was (again) in the throes of simultaneous social justice and civil rights' reckonings. Yet I know women are the primary caregivers, caretakers, and educators at home and in workplaces. I also know women are our households' primary consumers. Women start half of new small businesses. Women graduate at higher levels from four-year colleges and universities than men. Women thus possess tremendous influence at home, in the economy, and in educational organizations.

Upon these reflections, I began documenting women's educational leadership experiences and the challenges they faced and overcame. The reckonings catalyzed (but not originated) by the Me Too, Times Up, and Black Lives Matter movements demonstrate that workplaces, society, and high-level leadership roles are still places where women (but not only women) can encounter various forms of harassment, micro-aggressions, and bullying, and a dearth of leadership opportunities and support. If one is an other, they encounter even more biased treatment such as Double Jeopardy, which is when women of color "suffer the effects of both gender and racial prejudice."[14] Such compounded biases can also affect others, including those who don't affiliate with traditional gender binaries. Thus, when reflecting on these women's experience, it can help to employ intersectional approaches—seeking to understand them/themselves as women as well as those who are Latina, first-generation college graduates, immigrants, nonbinary, or trans; those who possess a disability; and so on. Intersectionality "assumes that identities, including gender, are multiple, fluid, in part self-constructed; that a perspective on a single characteristic such as gender risks active harm in encouraging the 'appalling effects of the miniaturization of people' and in research terms unhelpful in privileging one characteristic over another."[15] This study relies on diverse experiences, backgrounds, and profiles of the thirty-seven respondents and to place intersectionality at the fore.

The reckonings and movements are synergistic. They concern fair and equitable treatment, opportunities, and outcomes. Addressing them together can benefit everyone. Our workplaces are not microcosms of society—they are society. Gender discrimination doesn't supplant other racial, gender, and social justice reckonings nor vice versa. Nonetheless, I possess a privilege (as a white cisgender woman focusing on gender bias) that women of color don't possess because they must simultaneously navigate—and confront—their multiple identities, including race, ethnicity, and gender.

We are disappointingly observing regular and systemic backlash, against gender, racial, and social justice undertakings—powerful people and groups can distort and erase these reckonings' rationales, legitimacy, and impact. It is truly unfortunate that personalized instruction for, welcoming cultures for, and a commitment to educate all students—regardless of background, neighborhood, or gender—are political hot potatoes central to the education culture wars of today. Change is threatening. And changes to educational and workplace access, opportunities, and outcomes for one group imply that those who currently possess the most power and privilege will, at a minimum, need to learn to work differently and make room for other perspectives and people.

This book is my own story, which the thirty-seven cisgender women respondents and a robust literature review inform. I did not intentionally exclude women who don't identify with the gender society assigned them at birth. While my sample is comprised of cisgender women, they are not the only women or others to whom this book's findings and lessons can apply. I examine respondents' experiences to see if the tricky waters I navigated were an anomaly. They are not. I insert respondents' insights to broaden, deepen, and diversify examples, explanation, and strategies. Like me, the thirty-seven respondents desire to give back to the field of educational leadership.

Although we possess different backgrounds and identities and thus ways of experiencing and interpreting our professional experiences, many aspects of my leadership story and lived experience parallels those of the respondents (or vice versa), as well as the trends identified in scholarly and lay sources. Because of their different ages, backgrounds, and professional experiences I highlight differences between, among, and with the respondents. In sharing our stories, I hope to make scholars' findings accessible to women educational leaders and their allies. Scholars often delve into a specific element of the equation, which comprises women's leadership journeys, practices, and impact. As such, scholars may study a single component or sometimes many components of women education leaders' equation—from promotion to culture to bias to sexism to networks and more. Such studies help to isolate and test specific components of this leadership equation.

However, I did not find in a single current source—other than educational leadership handbooks with single chapters dedicated to unpacking a specific element—a synthesis of the entire equation for women wishing to navigate educational leadership. My contribution is to share, in an accessible manner

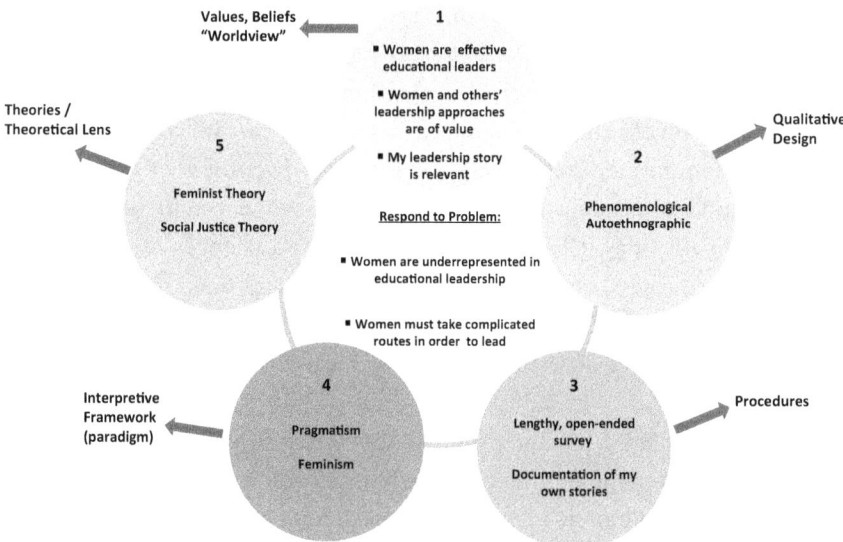

Figure 1.2 Approach.

and in one volume, new and existing knowledge, insights, interrelationships, and practices with women educational leaders who are practitioners.

Methods

Here I describe the approach I took for this book (see Figure 1.2). First, I sought and received Institutional Review Board (IRB) approval for aspects of the study that included the respondents and for chronicling my own story.[16] In the most basic terms, this means an accredited body deemed that I—as a practitioner researcher unaffiliated with any particular university or scholarly lens—outlined a sound and an ethical proposal and approach.

Second, as depicted in the center circle of Figure 1.2, I address two problems: the underrepresentation of women in educational leadership positions and the complicated and veiled routes women must take to ascend to leadership. Throughout this introduction—and book—I share concepts about leadership, social justice, and feminism. These concepts are foundational to my worldview, which is "a basic set of beliefs that guide action"[17] and manifest my beliefs that women can and should lead; women and others bring unique and diverse gifts to leadership; and my own and the thirty-seven respondents' leadership careers can teach others about leadership.

Third, as depicted in the top (#1) circle in Figure 1.2, the foundational concepts for my survey's design included the following:

1. Women feel they must demonstrate higher levels of competence than men.
2. Women feel they may only demonstrate confidence in ways that society and men recognize.
3. Women feel they must be resilient to overcome personal and professional challenges.
4. Women encounter a variety of microaggressions and macro-aggressions in the workplace.
5. Women's unique leadership style tends to focus on communication, collaborative decision-making, social justice, and teamwork.
6. Women feel they must learn and integrate their learning at every step.

Here my foundational reading drove my inquiry and the respondents'—and my own—contributions led to the coding, which informed my analysis and the framework and findings I share in this book. I asked respondents about their definition of educational leadership and the importance of specific knowledge domains for women educational leaders. I also queried them about their rationales for pursuing educational leadership; their experience with racism, sexism, harassment, and abuse; and the strategies they felt were most helpful to combat workplace bias and succeed in leadership roles.

Fourth, to secure the thirty-seven diverse women respondents, I reached out to my own networks from LinkedIn to doctoral program alumnae. Many respondents forwarded the survey to their own networks, which was essential to diversifying and broadening my sample and somewhat akin to snowball sampling—which is "a recruitment technique in which research participants are asked to assist researchers in identifying other potential subjects."[18] The findings I share—and suggestions for strategies, standards, and models—appear to have consistency—from me to the literature to respondents and from the literature to me and the respondents. This could be due to my bias in interpreting the data and information or due to my network, which is as I am, older, whiter, and educated with graduate degrees. The people who forwarded the survey—expanding my network and respondents—may not be similar in their age and background but rather in possessing similar values, missions, and approaches. This is something for me—and you as a reader—to keep in mind. While I do introduce women who fall outside some of the approaches I promote and to which I ascribe, they may or may not be complete anomalies. We all possess strengths, weaknesses, and varied approaches, which our environments, roles, and backgrounds influence.

Table 1.1 Thirty-Seven Respondents' Profiles

Answer Choice	Demographic Responses	Answer Choice	Age Responses	Answer Choice	Degree Level	Answer Choice	Hispanic or Latino
White or Caucasian	22	25–34	8	High school	0	Hispanic or Latino	8
Black or African American	8	35–44	8	Bachelor's	2	Not Hispanic or Latino	29
Asian or Asian American	2	45–54	7	Master's	15		
Mixed	2	55–64	9	Doctorate	20		
Other	3	65+	5				
Total	37	Total	37	Total	37	Total	37

Briefly, I describe the thirty-seven cisgender women respondents. They possess different educational backgrounds—two possess a bachelor's degree, fifteen a master's, and twenty a doctorate. They represent different ethnic and racial profiles with eight identifying as black, twenty-two as white, two as Asian, five as mixed and other, and eight as Latina/Hispanic (overlapping with other racial areas; see Table 1.1). They represent different age groups—eight indicated they are between twenty-five and thirty-four; eight as between thirty-five and forty-four; seven as between forty-five and fifty-four; nine as between fifty-five and sixty-four; and five as older than sixty-five. Their work status varies. Their titles include charter school principal or leader; traditional public school principal; professor or adjunct professor of educational leadership; curriculum coordinator or supervisor; special project manager; strategic planning director; content area coach; assistant superintendent; superintendent; education nonprofit or association leader; state education department leader; assistant or deputy independent school leader; finance or business officer; education consultant; and retiree.

Fifth, as depicted in circle #2 of Figure 1.2, this book is a type of auto-ethnography and phenomenology. In academic terms, an auto-ethnography is a method for an individual (me) "to dig deeply into their [my] own experience."[19] A phenomenology is a description of "what an experience means for the persons who have had the experience and are able to provide a comprehensive description of it [the phenomenon]."[20] Both of these approaches are qualitative in nature. Qualitative approaches are:

> A means for exploring and understanding the meaning individuals or groups ascribe to a social or human problem. The process of research involves emerging questions and procedures; collecting data in the participants' setting; analyzing the data inductively, building from particulars to general themes; and making interpretations of the meaning of the data.[21]

My procedures drew on my own stories and lengthy open-ended survey questions and resulting responses—some of which included page- or paragraph-length responses and others, single-sentence responses (see circle #3 of Figure 1.2). I selected this latter type of procedure because I launched this project during the lock-down portion of the pandemic, desired to include a variety of voices, and was diverse and creative in my approach. Note that, although the study commenced during the pandemic, this is not an inquiry about leadership during the pandemic.

I derive the ethnographic component of the study from my recollections about past encounters, roles, experiences, and situations. As I read the literature—and the respondents' narratives—I considered what applied to my own story and vice versa. I first wrote dispassionate examples—descriptions of what occurred such as one would when looking down from one thousand feet up. I then, over numerous iterations, interjected how I felt, why I felt that way, and what I took away. I see my own, the literature, and the respondents' stories and vignettes as circular in nature—opportunities to reinforce and deepen the reflections and the experiences. Each story sparks a recollection; a recollection sparks an insight; an insight sparks a theme; and the theme then sparks another story.

Sixth, an academic research framework typically includes an articulation of one's paradigm, which can overlap with the theories one uses to study an issue. A paradigm is "a set of very general philosophical assumptions about the nature of the world (ontology) and how we can understand it (epistemology), assumptions that tend to be shared by researchers working in a specific field or tradition."[22] As I depicted in circle #4 of Figure 1.2, I identify pragmatism and feminism as the two paradigms on which I draw. Pragmatism "focus[es] on the outcomes of the research—the actions, situations, and consequences of inquiry—rather than antecedent conditions ... Pragmatist researchers look to the 'what' and 'how' of research based on its intended consequences—where they want to go with it."[23] I want this project to result in practical implications and steps for aspiring and current women leaders as well as those who support them. Feminist researchers "expose the ways that **gender** operates as a social construct to effectively oppress women by limiting their access to power and certain resources."[24] The respondents' stories, the literature, and my own stories address women's leadership and experiences in relation to male dominance—whether it be deliberate, incidental, or the result of structural, societal, or other factors.

I also identify theories relevant to my research framework specifically social justice and feminist theories as I depict in circle #5 in Figure 1.2. These are critical theories that focus on critiques of unequal power relations in society, seek change, and forward equity.[25] This means I analyze my own story, the literature, and the respondents' contributions through feminist and social justice lenses. In regard to race, class, and gender, among other oppressed groups, these theories highlight groups' lived experiences.[26] "Feminist theory emphasizes the shared experiences of women across the divisions of race, class, age, and/or culture ... [and] frames the gender/power dynamics in political, social and organizational lives."[27] Critical feminist theory "describe[s] how organizations privilege men and marginalize women."[28] In Chapter 3, I discuss feminist leadership and critical theories along with their shortcomings—they can inadequately represent people with intersectional identities. Social justice theory envisions "democratic life as offering the greatest potential for social justice,"[29] building toward agency and meaningful participation.

Eighth, I apply a reflexive lens to uncover my own approach to leadership. Leaders and researchers can use reflexivity to evaluate and understand the ways in which they navigate their own and others' backgrounds, interpretations, assumptions, and expectations. It is a process through which one can "reflect about their biases, values, and personal background, such as gender, history, culture, and socioeconomic status, and how this background shapes their interpretations."[30] I kept this reflexivity at the forefront when coding the respondents' contributions using critical feminist and critical social justice lenses and the desire to give back to the field (pragmatism). When I interpret a situation, a theme, or a term I do so from my own perspective—a sixtyish, white, upper middle-class woman who possesses a doctorate and someone with a long and varied career who experienced a range of professional challenges, environments, and colleagues. There is always a risk of bias toward my own interpretation and example selections. Yet I am one individual researcher who draws conclusions from experiences and data while I seek to be as reflective and unbiased as possible.

Ninth, I include aggregated responses to highlight themes, based on responses to a handful of close-ended survey questions, which I juxtapose with my own experience, findings from the literature, and responses to open-ended survey questions. For the closed-ended survey questions, I disaggregate the data by age, ethnicity, race, and level of education and compare my own responses to those of respondents. However, I share the closed-ended question data predominantly in aggregated form given the small sample size and lack of statistical significance. These data appear in tables in several chapters.

For the open-ended survey responses, drawn from fourteen questions, I used inductive qualitative coding (i.e., allowing groupings of data and concepts to emerge[31]) to identify initial patterns that helped me begin to make sense of the literature, my own experience, and respondents' contributions. To interpret literature sources and participant responses, I broadly grouped the data and information. After rereading—numerous times—my notes from the literature (which I captured in a program called Zotero) and respondents' comments, and continuing my literature review, I further refined the data into twelve categories. The categories ranged from make invisible to power to environment or organization climate to frameworks to supports to talent management, which I define. Then, using a social justice and feminist theoretical lens, I identified areas of overlap, resorted the data, and refined the broad categories into fourteen themes, which include subthemes such as power, routes, characteristics, and leadership development. I also considered their relationship to each other—that is, how may one's calling affect one's leadership approach? I didn't use a software program to help me capture and group the data into themes and at many points felt like I was drowning in data. I manually captured and grouped respondents' comments (which amounted to 29,000 words spanning thirty-seven rows and sixteen columns of a database) into chunks of data. I arrayed them into a huge spreadsheet that I could use to track quotes, separate by category, and eventually by theme. I did the same for the literatures—first separately and then in one large file grouped by theme. While rudimentary, conducting old-school coding facilitated my familiarity with each respondent, their cadence, and my ability to identify discrepancies or errors. The respondent sample, though small, provides a rich array of insights and opportunities for further inquiry. The respondents' contributions informed and augmented the themes. Like a tapestry with a plaid pattern, the literature and the respondents' and my contributions created a pattern for this book to follow.

Tenth, the lay and academic literature include tens of terms to describe the experience of women and marginalized groups. I capture these idiosyncratic, sobering, and humorous terms—which describe bias, discrimination, racism, sexism, and workplace encounters—and define them for use here and in a stand-alone glossary. Many of these—from an angry woman to someone who self-silences—embellish descriptions in chapters.

Chapters and Themes

The themes I identify, and italicize, provide a structure on which I base the chapters and analyze the ways in which women end up in, navigate, and are thwarted from ascending to, leadership. Descriptions about convoluted *routes* to leadership include the use of *metaphor*, from labyrinths to jungle gyms to ladders (often with broken rungs). Numerous *leadership models* and *definitions* serve as guides for presenting leadership types and examples. Definitions of system-level, supervisor, and structural *barriers* and *challenges* shed light on women's leadership experiences. Challenges include bias, bullying, harassment, culture and environment, norms, the absence of social capital, someone making women invisible or stifling their voices, and presenting against leader type (or fit). References to *power* and *identity*—individual, economic, societal, and political—are prevalent. For implementation at the individual and organization levels, the book delivers a synthesis of success *strategies* and necessary *supports*. These include networks, sponsors, mentors, talent management, leadership development, and individualized navigational tactics such as gaining superior task knowledge. *Leadership standards* along with *characteristics* encapsulate what women educational leaders need to know and demonstrate and can inform existing lists. Unlike anger as a catalyst, the *drivers* for women desiring to move into educational leadership appear to indicate that many women pursue leadership to accomplish specific goals or serve their values.

In Chapter 2, which has the "Lean In or Shove Off," subtitle I tackle what it means to lead. The subtitle implies that women hold a poisoned chalice—if they lean in to become leaders, then the onus is on the individual to progress despite biased systems, structures, and practices. If they shove off, whether because of a culture that perpetuates bias or one that doesn't provide necessary support, then they've given up and it's their own fault. The leadership models lay the groundwork for women leaders' dilemmas and styles. In this and in every chapter, I share a leadership story to highlight themes—here, *leadership models* and *leadership definitions*. First, I share the models of leadership that I follow, including collectivist, cultural, feminist, and social justice approaches. Next, I introduce aspects of Instructional Leadership or Leadership for Teaching and Learning and provide insight into the ways the respondents define leadership. Then I share profiles of effective leaders and align these people with the model(s) they practice(d) such as adaptive, authentic, contextual, distributive, ethical, implicit, resonant, servant, and transformational leadership. Examining less-effective leaders, I conclude that their espoused and enacted visions of leadership are discordant; they may believe they practice distributive leadership but instead they fall back on administrative or transactional models. I use these models of leadership to describe less effective leaders.

Where women follow their callings and identity toward leadership models—predicated on benefitting children and adults—they may lean toward including others in decision-making and solution formulation. In Chapter 3, which has the "What We Stand For" subtitle, after sharing a leadership story linked to this chapter's focus, I examine what compels women to lead in educational settings (their *drivers*) and the role of *identity* and *power*. I share how I believe my own identity and worldview formed based on my birth order, sisters, single mother, egalitarian beliefs, and scrappy nature. I introduce the ways in which dominant organizational and personnel norms and cultures can reinforce and preserve themselves and the ways in which identity, power, and hardships define my and respondents' call to lead. I synthesize many reasons for women's educational leadership pursuits. Respondents emphasize the following reasons for leading: (1) forwarding social justice/improving educational outcomes, (2) improving teaching and learning, (3) making changes to bureaucratic management and leadership structures and approaches, and (4) diversifying perspectives. Theories in this chapter serve as lenses for understanding women's leadership and leadership in education. The theories also contribute to the tapestry's pattern.

Knowing about one's purpose and identity isn't enough. In Chapter 4, whose subtitle is "Hummingbird," I introduce *barriers* and *challenges* to women's leadership and discuss bullying, harassment, abuse, racism, and sexism. Here the female Hummingbird's plumage, when evolved within a species to mirror male birds, serves as a talisman for avoiding harassment. Among my respondents, women of all ages, education levels, and races and ethnicities encounter a variety of unwanted verbal and physical microaggressions and macro-aggressions from their colleagues—including other women. Twenty-eight separate women experienced bullying—the most reported form of discrimination respondents experienced. Racism was the next most prevalent with nineteen separate women having experienced racism. Sixteen separate respondents experienced harassment and eleven experienced abuse. I speak to strategies for and reflections about handling such situations.

My understanding of leadership standards, or knowledge domains, is that they highlight best practices. In Chapter 5, which is subtitled "Yellow Brick Road," I introduce leadership *routes* and *standards*. I use the Yellow Brick Road to convey that I took an unfamiliar and unclear path to leadership. I share educational leadership frameworks from the National Association of Independent Schools (NAIS), the Council of Chief State School Officers (CCSSO), the Leadership Academy, and the National Policy Board for Educational Administration (NPBEA). After presenting standards I drafted based on these national models, my own experience, and a client project, I share which standards are of greatest importance to the respondents. Respondents assign the highest level of importance to Communication (thirty-one respondents); People and Relationships (thirty respondents); Culture and Vision (each with twenty-eight respondents); Resilience (twenty-five respondents); and Teamwork (twenty-four respondents).

I propose that these current frameworks are insufficient to address the needs of women educational leaders. In Chapter 6, with "The Dance" as a subtitle, I propose that women educational leaders should have their own set of leadership standards and dispositions. I use the dance to convey that like a well-executed dance—based on choreography, skill, and verve—women educational leaders can benefit from following a roadmap and acquiring competencies to become great leaders. I want scholars and experts to use these standards and dispositions as a baseline and for leadership development programs and graduate schools of education to incorporate them into their courses. I maintain that, to forward equitable teaching and learning outcomes for all children, women educational leaders must apply skills and knowledge in specific areas that speak to their unique leadership needs. This chapter presents eight priority standards and seven priority dispositions (*characteristics*) ranging from Competence to Equitable Culture to Political Savvy to Professionalism and Ethics.

The implementation of standards geared to women education leaders and key leadership development strategies can help women lead. Chapter 7, which is subtitled "Still Standing," includes organizational and individual leadership development *strategies* and *supports*. The chapter subtitle conveys that having a planned path and tailored supports allows women to move from thinking about leading to securing roles to achieving leadership success. Strategies include on-the-job support such as mentoring, sponsorship, and networks. Additionally, women can benefit from stretch assignments, ongoing performance evaluation, coaching, transparent and fair talent management practices, and 360° feedback—which is when a cross section of colleagues including supervisors, peers, and direct reports contribute to someone's performance evaluation or growth plan. This last chapter draws on the standards and dispositions from Chapter 6 to highlight the ways women may better access critical organizational supports: women—through collectivist, cultural, feminist, social justice, and teaching and learning means and ends—can thrive in educational leadership roles. I don't intend to place the onus for combatting workplace toxicity on women. Instead, I wish to put them in control of their careers. I revisit the importance for women leaders to build their knowledge, skill, and mettle—by drawing on all of the standards and dispositions—and because of the systemic and structural nature of the barriers undergirding the organizations in which women work and lead.

Conclusion

Women—like myself and respondents—have much to share and learn about navigating leadership. The stories, experiences, and strategies speak beyond age, gender, race, ethnicity, and intersectionality. This book provides lessons about and from women in education-focused workplaces, and shares workplace practices, which unfortunately remain dominated by systems and structures developed by and for white men. Some of the vignettes, highlighted responses, and literature excerpts may be difficult or frustrating to read; all are difficult to ignore. The perseverance of these women leaders is palpable. Their, our, and my ability to ascend to and navigate through leadership roles delivers more than frustration, difficulty, and perseverance. They, we, and I provide you with insights into their, our, and my motivations and core drivers, and expose their, our, and my most vulnerable selves. There is humor. There is reflection. There is advice. There is commitment. Importantly there is a cabal for aspiring and serving women leaders to join. Take what in your professional life may feel messy and opaque and use their, our, and my stories and lessons to achieve clarity and growth.

Reflective Questions

1. What story about your own leadership journey would you want to tell?
2. If you were to conduct your own study of women educational leaders, what would you want to know and why?
3. Consider your own affiliations and networks.
    a. Who would you approach to augment your own networks?
4. In what ways do the themes resonate with you and why?
5. Consider what you hope to learn about and take away from this book.
    a. Which chapters do you think will be most relevant and why?

2

Leadership Models and Stories: Lean In or Shove Off

Leadership Story

George is a mid-fifties former school principal and African Methodist Episcopal (AME) pastor whose mother emigrated from Jamaica. The elementary school he led was in a city sector that the superintendent sought to transform by tackling uneven educational outcomes through health, socioeconomic, and employment interventions among others.

The superintendent identified this area based on its students' below-average academic performance (the state named the schools as "in need of improvement" due to poor test scores). Poverty, unemployment, health issues, and population density exacerbated these academic concerns. I initially turned down the project's leadership, because I understood I shouldn't lead it given my employer's reputation with these families and my profile as a white woman in a position of power. The superintendent asked me a second time and I acquiesced.

In addition to George, the superintendent assigned a handful of others, all of whom enjoyed a long history with this neighborhood and without whom I'd have been sunk. They schooled me about community dynamics and distrust of public organizations. Sometimes I felt bruised by their counsel. Yet they were more supportive of me than were my leadership team colleagues who seemed pleased I was off doing that "community stuff." This team was loyal and mission driven. We bonded—they'd slap their heads in mock frustration when encountering my ignorance. They taught me the meaning of "on the down low" and couldn't stop laughing when I thought I heard "download," and interpreted the term to mean downloading something on a computer rather than implying discretion.

They taught me to hang back, listen, and lead from behind. We strategized about community planning; identified sector and neighborhood co-leads; determined a way to compensate neighborhood members for participating; secured community-based vendors to provide food for meetings; and used community-based sites for meetings. We built trust, commitment, ownership, and agency. I convinced the nascent board to take an asset-based, inclusive approach; to identify community members to serve on the board; and to eventually relocate the project outside of the district.

George took me to my first AME church service. I finally understood the meaning of "call and response!" I took him to his first funder meeting held at the local community foundation's headquarters in a tony old mansion. When we walked out of that meeting, George looked at me, thanked me for taking him, and said, "I've never been in a room or meeting like that in my life."

Overview

Leadership can reflect power, official authority, influence, and access (to resources and to people). And leaders may base their practice—and understand that their performance is evaluated—on their visions, abilities, characteristics, commitments, knowledge, and results.

As the short leadership story seeks to convey, one's leadership approach can evolve over time and educational leaders may choose to pursue their leadership in a selfless and mission-driven manner. Such educational leaders may seek to create and ensure that structures, practices, and cultures are fair and of high quality. They may seek to advocate for all children, provide equitable access to learning, deliver equitable learning outcomes, and rely on collaboration and partnership. Further, these leaders may endeavor to equip faculty and staff with the tools, resources, supports, and culture essential to placing every child at the forefront of their work—attending to children's physical, intellectual, social, and emotional learning, growth, and development. I strive to emulate these leadership tenets.

This chapter tackles what it means to lead. Its subtitle implies that women hold a poisoned chalice—if they lean in to become leaders, then the onus is on the individual to progress despite biased systems, structures, and practices. If they shove off, whether because of a culture that perpetuates bias or one that doesn't provide necessary support, then they've given up and it's their own fault. Leadership scholars and gurus spend their professional lives parsing leadership definitions, tenets, implementation, and impact. I know I have. As a result, there is a plethora of ways to examine, frame, prepare, and screen for effective leaders. In this chapter, I thus highlight *leadership models* and *leadership definitions*, which should provide a foundation for women leaders' pursuits.

High-level leadership roles are risky. My and respondents' careers reflect this. To evoke leadership models, I describe many of my experiences. I intentionally avoid naming organizations or people because the point of the portraits is to inform and show how people influenced my evolution as a leader. First, I share the models of leadership that I follow, including collectivist, cultural, feminist, and social justice approaches. Next, I introduce aspects of Instructional Leadership or Leadership for Teaching and Learning. I present respondents' educational leadership definitions. Then I share profiles of effective leaders and align these people with the model(s) they practice(d). Examining several less than effective leadership models, I conclude that the leaders don't seem to connect their espoused and enacted visions of leadership; they may believe they practice distributive leadership but instead fall back on administrative or transactional models. I discuss outmoded models of leadership using leaders whose profiles align with administrative and transactional approaches. This and the next chapters provide a foundation for the chapters that follow and is instructional—I hope to encourage readers to reflect on their own and others' motivations, approaches, and impact to inform their practice.

What Is Educational Leadership?

Team members like George—along with myriad neighborhood members, school principals, and partners—influenced my practice of collectivist, cultural, and social justice models of leadership. My analysis of the literature, contributors' responses, and identification of themes enable me to share descriptions, frameworks, and models.

I was fortunate to work with and on a variety of cross-community, cross-organizational, and cross-sector projects. I absorbed the importance of involving and learning from experts and community members. I discovered value in and results from working as part of diverse teams comprised of people committed to realizing positive change. Such strategies align with Collectivist Leadership, which emphasizes what happens in relation to the external context, with stakeholders, and within unofficial times, spaces, and places. This involves the "relationships, events, and activities—particularly the unstructured intra- and interorganizational ones that contribute to the organizational direction setting and goal achievement that all organizations operate in relationship to their external environments"[1] as well as drawing on collective knowledge and ideas to arrive at a decision or direction.[2]

Next, I include Cultural Leadership as a key part of my leadership pattern. John Collard (2007) describes Cultural Leadership as requiring leaders to be aware of their self-concept; mitigate the transmission of a "monocultural reality"; to "mediate between groups"; attend to diverse cultural values, identities, forms of privilege, and norms; consider ways "to harness diverse forms of cultural capital"; explore different "institutional frameworks to discover forms appropriate to particular communities"; and share leadership.[3] In short, cultural leadership involves "Assessing Culture (One's own and others); Valuing Diversity; Managing the Dynamics of Difference; Adapting to Diversity; and Institutionalizing Cultural Knowledge."[4]

As a teenager, I became aware of my belief in recognizing people's individuality and their a unique set of experiences, contributions, and backgrounds. When people identify differently from me, I endeavor to treat them as individuals and respect and draw on what they bring to the table. I try to interact with people in this way not because I believe in the fatuous notion of color blindness, neoliberalism, or neo-feminism. Such terms imply that detrimental impacts—which affect those with racial, societal, or gender difference—are not attributable to systemic or structural discrimination; that such profile differences do not matter; and that it is up to each individual to personally (not as a group) confront such issues.[5] I maintain that differences absolutely do matter and individuals require allies to change systems and structures. Allyship is:

> A strategic mechanism used by individuals to become collaborators, accomplices, and coconspirators who fight injustice and promote equity in the workplace through supportive personal relationships and public acts of sponsorship and advocacy. Allies endeavor to drive systemic improvements to workplace policies, practices, and culture.[6]

I view diversity as a vital part of this country's schools, workplaces, society, and history and that diversity of thought, background, and experience make personal, professional, and social relationships rich and varied. We live in a global society. I thus found Cultural Leadership an essential thread in my leadership tapestry.

My commitment to diverse, cultural contributions—along with my belief that education in this country is a right and not an economic or neighborhood-based privilege—drew me to Social Justice Leadership. I pursue my work to affect positive change for those shut out of the American Dream, which is a meritocratic rather than egalitarian notion—the American Dream espouses that when one works hard and seizes opportunities, they can succeed. As quoted in a

2021 *New York Times* article, National Education Association (NEA) President Becky Pringle (2021) maintains that social justice leadership in education is about "reclaim[ing] public education as a common good, and transform[ing] it into something it was never designed to be: racially and socially just, and equitable."[7] Social justice leadership speaks to the moral obligation of giving back to a cause or community, to children or families, and to leveling the societal playing field between and among all groups. It also suggests that prekindergarten through twelfth grade (PreK-12) educators and staff should possess a willingness, ability, and commitment to identify and change embedded racist, ableist, classist, and sexist educational structures, practices, and cultures to benefit all students. There is also the objective of positive change (in one's community, circumstances, or organization) and a commitment and ability to navigate differences and create meaningful participation among those who are marginalized or less powerful.[8]

Feminist Leadership is the final thread in my leadership tapestry. From the age of twelve, my single mother raised my three sisters and me. I started babysitting when I was twelve and working in a formal job at sixteen. As the youngest daughter, I fought strenuously for my position in the family and for my voice to be heard at home and in school. I also experienced—starting with my first job as a sixteen-year-old movie theater concessionist, then as an eighteen-year-old store clerk, next as a twenty-year-old waitress, and well into my early fifties—on-the-job paternalistic treatment, inappropriate comments, as well as improper and unwanted touching which included pinching, grabbing, hugging, and kissing. Feminist leadership is a reaction to, and an attempt to redress, the male domination of society and its gendered organizations, the corresponding privileges granted males, and the legacy systems created by men. Feminist leadership is both a goal and a style.[9] Feminist leadership is a shared social justice process that challenges and leads to change for social injustices such as "racism, sexism, homophobia, classism," through collaboration, learning, inclusiveness, common values, relationships, honesty, hearing and engaging diverse views, teaching, reflection, and education.[10]

> Feminist women who aspire to and end up in leadership positions bring to these positions values and characteristics that shape how they lead, but they are also shaped by the environments in which they find themselves [and the context from which they come]. Based on feminist principles and values, it is a goal of feminist women that they apply these principles of collaboration, egalitarianism, and inclusiveness to leadership and to the positions of leadership in which they find themselves.[11]

When I asked the respondents to consider how they define leadership in an educational setting, their most oft repeated focus includes a commitment to students—specifically equitable opportunities and outcomes for students. Respondents also emphasize honoring student and stakeholders' backgrounds, ensuring the quality of the learning experience, and developing the whole child. The respondents focus on motivating, inspiring, and creating conditions to ensure stakeholders and their backgrounds are considered and supported, and to involve stakeholders in, and focus them on, educating all students. Many respondents cite the importance of educational missions and visions.

> **Bonnie**: Leadership in educational settings is the act of bringing together multiple and varying stakeholders to focus on what is best for students.
>
> **Dionne**: Leaders in education have an expert background in multiple domains such as curriculum, instruction, assessment, child development, culturally responsive classrooms, teacher pedagogy, technology education, leading adult professional development, how to lead teams, servant leadership, budget discernment, and emotional intelligence etc.
>
> **Ellie**: Educational leaders empower teachers/students and give them the resources they need to achieve their academic potential while being mindful of and supporting their mental and physical needs.
>
> **Jaimie**: Leadership in education settings should be focused on growing instructional leaders who will ensure success and equity for all students.
>
> **Joan**: Leadership is the way you choose to intentionally show up for students in the work that you do.
>
> **Karin**: Leadership is finding the right balance between compassion, empathy, and practical solutions that leads to equitable opportunities and outcomes for all students.
>
> **Lara**: I define leadership in an education setting as both formal and informal responsibility for the health, well-being, climate, and culture of systems and structures that govern and impact those within the learning community.
>
> **Michelle**: Education leaders know the research, have many years of experience, and are a role model in their fields … Education leaders are dedicated to their community and constantly seek resources and supports that will lead to improvement. The goals education leaders seek to achieve are understood and embraced by the team. Education leaders are persistent, inclusive, advocates of diversity, and seek equity

in all opportunities. The heart of education leadership is ensuring that each child can reach his or her full potential.

Natalie: Educational Leadership is the ability to listen, hear, and act to support students, teachers, and families in creating transformative experiences for students while developing agency and collaboration among and between these groups.

Reese: Leaders have to be connected to the communities they serve in authentic ways. Building trust and relationships is just as important as leading initiatives with a strong vision and plan.

Sonja: Leaders are people who are able to make progress forward for their team/school, organization/district, or the larger education landscape. "Progress forward" means doing right by kids to provide them a high-quality education that is historically honest, pushes critical thinking, and empowers kids to be active in their own education.

Tang: I define leadership in education settings as the capacity to garner support for decisions that lead to institutional or networked change in order to improve equitable educational experiences for students.

Wilma: Leadership is influence. It involves inspiring a shared vision among those that you work with, building relationships, and collectively sharing in the decision making and problem-solving processes that drive change forward.

I equate these, and other, respondents' educational leadership descriptions with two educational leadership models: instructional leadership and leadership for teaching and learning. Instructional Leadership focuses on delivering teaching and learning—particularly teaching and learning that results in improved student achievement for each student. Individuals practicing instructional leadership are steeped in educational research and knowledgeable about effective teaching—pedagogy, curriculum, data, technology, and professional development. Instructional leadership incorporates the establishment and monitoring of high standards for students' academic achievement and growth and the creation of positive school learning cultures. Instructional leaders typically possess a passion for education, students, and teachers; demonstrate significant experience with classroom teaching; and provide professional supports and development.

Leadership for Learning (or Leadership for Teaching and Learning)—though initially a response to short-term, accountability-based objectives—focuses on what happens for the students as well as for the educators working in environments dedicated to teaching and learning. The dual emphasis places importance on building the support for, capacity-development of—and the dexterity required of the environments, students, and educators—along with leaders' prioritization of student learning.[12]

Leadership Stories and Models

This subsection introduces leaders and aligns them to leadership models, focusing on the leaders I've encountered who were constructive. First, is an early sixties white man, who I call "Jeff," and who led a national nonprofit seeking to change PreK-12 educational outcomes—particularly by linking secondary and postsecondary pathways. Jeff could have practiced Authentic Leadership. He demonstrated knowledge about himself and his organization. Jeff was methodical in gaining support for, conducting, and then implementing strategies aligned with our international educational comparisons. He used this support to garner funds for several new strands of work. Authentic leadership is represented by the ways in which a leader governs them self and acts on their values, their individual and organizational truths, and self-identity. In short, the leader must be true to them self and the organization when making choices and decisions.[13] Having hired me during my master's program, Jeff supported the organization's novices through exposure to national leaders and effective strategies. He didn't pigeonhole us into menial roles based on age or gender; he assigned and entrusted us with consequential work. The novices' stretch assignments included project management, stakeholder engagement, research, writing, public policy, and marketing. I accessed facilitation, communication, and teamwork training. A savvy networker, thought leader, fundraiser, and strategist, Jeff's own and the organization's mission drove him.

Another leader, an early sixties' Black man, whom I call "Matt," was someone with whom I worked closely when developing a graduate education program, its program standards, and its degree pathways. Matt was dean of a local education school and a former state education leader. He was confident, professional, and committed to his college's work, to educating all PreK-12 students, and to delivering high-quality graduate education. Matt took care of himself, cared for those around him, and treated others respectfully. He served on my doctoral review committee. After flying—at his own expense—to my university's locale, Matt provided me with invaluable feedback the night before I defended my dissertation successfully. While a variety of models could describe Matt's leadership practice, because of his strong moral compass, he likely practiced forms of Ethical Leadership and Resonant Leadership. Ethical leadership relies on actions guided by "a set of moral precepts that define right and wrong ... [Such leaders] take on leadership roles because they have a duty and responsibility to do good for others."[14] Ethical leadership tenets include moral compass, collaboration, inclusion, consensus orientation, and transparency in one's communications.[15] Richard Boyatzis and Annie McKee (2005) describe Resonant Leadership as predicated on service to a cause or purpose, engagement, inspiration, empathy, compassion, trust, mental clarity, self-care, mindfulness of approach, impact, and emotional intelligence—with emotional intelligence including "the competencies of self-awareness, self-management, social awareness, and relationship management."[16]

An artful leader—to whom I reported and call "Rafael"—was a mid-fifties Hispanic male. Charismatic, strategic, mission-driven, and knowledgeable, he held numerous leadership positions both within and outside of the organization. Rafael sought to create and deliver a cross section of systemic changes to benefit students and the community. He supported my professional development by assigning me to visible stretch assignments, providing release time to attend a doctoral program, and ignoring those who wanted him to reassign me. Rafael could've practiced servant, implicit, contextual, situational, adaptive, and transformational leadership.

Servant Leadership relies on stewardship of others. It involves leading with legitimacy, moral authority, and directional clarity while seeking to serve others and act on their behalf.[17] One respondent speaks to these sentiments.

> **Leslie**: Leadership is servitude. Leadership is doing what is best for the community you serve. It encompasses learning about the students, the parents, and the community. Then making decisions, based on their specific-identified need.

A former student government and cross-country team leader, Rafael could've modeled Implicit Leadership, which applies when one embodies leadership—whether through alignment with organizational behavioral norms or possession of the competencies needed to tackle an organizational challenge or crisis. Such leaders meet the ideal leader expectations.[18] Contextual Leadership implies that a leader may modify their behavior based on the setting or situation.[19] Others may refer to this as Situational Leadership, which also looks to tailoring one's leadership approach to where the leadership is occurring.[20] I often saw Rafael switch tactics, styles, and messages when interacting with students, the business community, the board, parents, community-based leaders, or city government.

Rafael seamlessly helped people to understand—and moved them to support—an idea, a program, or an initiative.

His approach depended on the topic, purpose, audience, and situation. Adaptive Leadership brings different contributors into decision-making, solution formulation, idea generation, and problem resolution. This approach involves flexibility, relationship orientation, collectiveness, and dynamism. Adaptive leadership allows for uncertainty, conflict, divergent ideas, and change.[21] At times Rafael was combative and stubborn. I was once so frustrated that I left a meeting to walk around the block. Upon my return, Rafael arrived at a compromise.

Transformational leadership uses passion, support, strategic resource allocation, encouragement, teamwork, empowerment, and a clear vision and set of goals. With these tools, the leader motivates, inspires, provides direction, and drives innovation, change, and success. This model employs shared ownership, followership, and confidence in, trust in, and loyalty to the leader and, as such, is entity based.[22] Rafael possessed an uncanny ability to develop and communicate a vision, translate it into programs and strategies, convince others to embrace and implement visions and plans, and navigate political waters with constituents. He allocated resources, people, and time to a variety of stakeholders—from teachers to politicians to parents—and worked with followers to achieve common organizational goals.

Another leader, "Gabriella," modeled Distributed Leadership, which implies that leadership evolves and is distributed based on circumstances, inputs, and players. She shared ownership for leading, delegated to her department chiefs, and entrusted others to carry out the organization's agenda. Her philosophy evolved around giving people autonomy, sometimes too much so. Yet she provided pointed, constructive, timely, and regular feedback, supported others' contributions, and credited staff members. Jeffrey Brooks and Lisa Kenslar (2011) describe distributed leadership as fluid as it:

> Emphasizes the way that leaders and followers interact in situations, how various artifacts mediate these interactions, and how the behavior of leaders and followers evolves over time … [It] recognizes and accounts for the idea that in certain situations, a person might be a leader and in another situation, that person may practice a follower's role.[23]

Culturally Responsive Leadership is yet another educational leadership model. The Leadership Academy (2021) defines culturally responsive leadership as focusing on racism and systemically racist systems and structures in schools and school systems—it combines both the leaders' "impact of institutionalized racism on their own lives and the lives of the students and families they work with and embraces their role in mitigating, disrupting, and dismantling systemic oppression."[24] Its four core practices are "a strong foundation of cultural understanding," "the academic success of all students," "cultivating and deepening the cultural competence of themselves and the adults they lead," and "the cultivation of sociopolitical consciousness."[25]

Many of the core practices in this section and the prior subsection are associated with leadership attributes, skills, and practices that many effective and competent leaders may master. While I may also practice, or embody, aspects of these positive leadership models, I identify with collectivist, cultural, social justice, and feminist models because they speak to my calling. Chapter 5 covers the core areas of knowledge and competency effective educational leaders may practice, and Chapter 6 shares areas unique to women educational leaders.

Outmoded and Ineffective Leadership Models

This subsection shares leader profiles linked to models I—and scholars—now associate with less effective leadership. The leaders who align to these models are people who likely shouldn't have served in their roles, because they didn't seem sufficiently equipped for them. Maybe it was due to poor selection, hiring, and retention practices. Maybe it was because traditional educational certification programs focus on administration rather than leadership and management. Maybe these leaders weren't evaluated or didn't receive ongoing mentoring, coaching, and consequential feedback. Perhaps they were burnt out. Some didn't appear to be mission driven (or, if they were, their egos, insecurities, or politics seemed to prevent them from carrying out their missions). Perhaps these leaders didn't, couldn't, or weren't willing to see the disconnect between their espoused (what they claim to want to do) and enacted (what they actually do) visions of leadership. They couldn't walk the talk or weren't aware of the knowledge they lacked.

I had at least two supervisors, one forty-something Black man (whom I call "Bill") and one mid-fifties white man (whom I call "Bob"), who could've practiced Heroic Leadership while affecting support for the distributive leadership model. Heroic Leadership is a traditional form of leadership that relies on a single, charismatic person who holds a leadership position, through which this person derives organizational and decision-making authority, holds power, and benefits from enthusiastic and trusting followers.[26] Very little is delegated in this model and it has traditionally been defined in terms of a single often white male (this is also called an entity-based model because it focuses on an individual) who is viewed as a great man or a hero.[27]

Bob and Bill gave lip service to supporting my autonomy when I was a senior organizational leader but departed from what they espoused when they led and managed. They called into question and overrode, in very public ways, my and others' decisions and authority. Neither Bob nor Bill took me aside and discussed what they would've preferred I do, provided me with constructive feedback, or listened to me to seek to understand my rationale for a decision. As someone who takes her work and commitments very seriously, I find it deeply unsettling when a boss or a colleague publicly overrides or undermines my decisions, questions my integrity, or assumes that I acted with malintent. With these two leaders, my awakening snuck up on me—it started with a feeling of foreboding, moved to walking on eggshells and muting my voice, continued with me questioning every one of my actions, and then turned to disbelief.

With Bob, after closely collaborating, he began tamping down on my own and direct reports' areas of assigned autonomy and responsibility. Bob did so after my team restored the organization's depleted funds and reestablished its purpose. We were running a statewide campaign and leading a coalition of like-minded organizations. A funder approached my team to manage a new undertaking. Bob was aware that I would eventually transition from the organization because of a mutually developed and board-approved plan, which didn't yet have a specific timeline. He began to micromanage what I said, how I shared information, and what my staff did and then abruptly changed the terms of my employment by offering me a consultancy. I chose to walk away. It was time to live in the same time zone of aging parents. Yet to this day, because Bob never took the time to provide feedback or tell me why the timeline became that day, I remain clueless. I served in my leadership role as an at will employee.

Bill, another supervisor, actively recruited and regularly relied on me. He provided me with the highest evaluation rating among his leadership team members and gave me visible assignments and glass cliff projects aligned with his agenda. I've learned that women and people of color—who are seen as others—are often given glass cliff roles (whether so assigned deliberately or not), which are precarious, high-risk positions with high a likelihood of failure because the assignee is viewed as expendable.[28] Bill had clearly defined my role but didn't himself interpret my role the way he defined it. There was one decision I made, which didn't have a negative consequence for him or his agenda, but which caused him to conclude that I purposefully acted in direct violation of his wishes. Prior to having made this time-sensitive decision, I attempted to reach him, consulted with another leadership team colleague, and requested a briefing from the person overseeing the department requiring the decision. I made what I concluded was an informed and appropriate decision. After Bill returned, he berated me loudly in front of other people and stormed away. I immediately pivoted to an on-camera interview during which I delivered unwavering support of his agenda and attributed credit to him.

Bill then told me I needed to find another job. Shortly thereafter he left, on my desk, a letter terminating my contract, texting me to say it was there, and later saying he expected me to come to him to negotiate the terms of my retention! (I only learned about this expectation in our exit conversation.) Whereas someone with less bruising, fatigue, and experience with misogyny may have attempted to remain in the organization, I simply didn't possess sufficient reserves to do so and didn't believe anything I did would change the situation. He'd already fired two of my direct reports, overridden my selection of another, and caused one person to leave after two months, who as she was leaving cautioned me to "watch out." I was the person left standing (sort of). At the time, I was experiencing a long period of power stress, which is a chronic form of stress attributed to leaders who deal for long stretches with complexity and ambiguity.[29] I'm not alone. Others have also made difficult choices.

> **Mathilda**: My ethical stance has prevented me from getting promoted as I refuse to do something that is unethical. There was an instance where my supervisor wanted me to lie about a non-bid contract. When I chose not to lie, I was then formally reprimanded with a letter. Had I stayed, I know I was going to get fired/moved out of the position ... I had another similar experience where male supervisors wanted me to take on a different leadership position. I spent 6 months "proving" I could do it to only have them then wanting to promote me without additional pay for the added responsibilities. I turned them down and went back to my previous job. They were appalled that I did that.

Additional leadership models prevalent in bureaucracies and traditional public school districts include administrative and transactional leadership. I see these as running counter to social justice and feminist approaches and having far-reaching and systemic consequences. The behaviors of a particular former male organizational leader whom I will call "Bud" align with these models. With Administrative Leadership one uses rules, procedures, and common practices to maintain the status quo and govern one's own and others' work. Bud, a white male colleague, was the consummate holder of bureaucratic power because he knew—and likely made—all the rules and policies in the organization. He followed them to a "T" and employed them to his advantage. Bud had negotiated labor contracts, had once headed a union, possessed budget authority, and served in the organization for years. He knew people and legacy issues inside and out. I also observed Bud deploying an extreme interpretation of Transactional Leadership, which focuses on exchanges between employees and supervisors. Everything for Bud was a quid pro quo; he never ceded his ownership of or knowledge about something unless he received something in return.

When I left the organization where I worked with Bud, no one on my leadership team came to the going-away party though numerous direct reports, community members and leaders, and other organizational personnel attended. One former principal and union leader sent me an email expressing his gratitude for what I accomplished, along with his dismay and acknowledgment about, my perseverance despite the lack of internal support. When I announced to my doctoral cohort that I was leaving that role and organization, the entire class applauded and gave me a standing ovation.

Conclusion

Each day and over their careers, leaders practice many models. I draw on four and practice aspects of others! Effective leaders adopt what works based on their identity, experience, mission, and more. Their contextual choices aren't free of gender or societal norms. While leadership choices may be accidental, effective leaders are deliberate—they study and reflect on leadership models and situations. Each of this chapter's leadership models and leader profiles hint at a leader's style, power, benefits, and harms. Some leadership models may seem so lofty that they appear impossible to practice.

The leader profiles and model descriptions I reference include a myriad of elements on which a leader may draw. To a lesser and greater extent, leaders may elect to embody aspects that range from authentic to collaborative to transparent. Leaders may also consider levels of authority, work conditions, community context, organizational culture, and symbolism. Do leaders share or distribute leadership? Are they directive, fixed, or independent in their leadership or do they motivate and influence others? To what extent do leaders take professional and personal responsibility? One may practice adaptive leadership and contextual leadership together or one may be a transformational leader. However, when there is a fire in the building and everyone must get out, the leader may—appropriately—exercise components of more directive leadership models.

These short descriptions and stories inform the extent to which a leadership model addresses the who (for whom and by whom); the why (the rationale, the benefits, the impact); the how (the values, dispositions, qualities brought); and the what (the steps the leader takes). There is also the where and when leadership occurs. Is the school's context aligned with a grassroots movement or located in a conservative, affluent district? Is the leading occurring in a blue state or red state (or city or county)? Is the leadership taking place in the midst of anti-Critical Race Theory (CRT) legislation or book bans of Black or indigenous authors? Or, is the leading happening when the first Black (or Asian, or Hispanic, LGBTQIA, or woman) leader has been appointed? Context and timing matters.

The next chapter examines challenges having to do with bias, discrimination, and stereotype that women regularly confront and the ways respondents and I addressed and navigated our circumstances without compromising ourselves.

Reflective Questions

1. Which leadership models and which of their components resonate with you and why?
2. In what types of situations might employing elements of what I've called the less constructive or more outmoded leadership models be appropriate?
3. How can you inform your practice by naming—and knowing about—the models you follow?

3

Purpose, Identity, and Power: What We Stand For

Leadership Story

My mother—who became a single parent around my twelfth birthday—waitressed while earning a graduate education degree. Although she kept a jar of tips under her bed, our household was defined as middle-class (we had a dishwasher). Yet it was always clear that I could attend college and choose my desired career path. This assumption came with living in a "middle-class" household and parents who held advanced college degrees. My parents believed their four daughters should pursue further education and our dreams. I felt empowered to question authority, push back against harassment, and envision myself as whatever I wanted to become. My parents raised me at a time when women thought they could have it all. Studying dance—primarily ballet—for fifteen years contributed to my determination and focus.

I observed my single mother teaching urban physical education, facilitating special education for severe emotionally and physically disabled students, waitressing, and serving as a district-level special education administrator. I saw her—a first-generation, college graduate, and advanced-degree-holding woman—work diligently, overcome hardships, and ascend to educational leadership. Bullying and harassment from male supervisors was just part of her experience. Despite the odds stacked against her, my mother fulfilled her mission to educate prekindergarten through twelfth grade children.

I saw that working in public education was draining—physically and emotionally—and required an all-consuming commitment. Thus, when determining my career route, I pursued political science and initially avoided public education. When I later pursued a master's in public policy, I argued with my peers about which social policy lever—housing, employment, transportation, energy, environment, health care, food security, education, etc.—would evince positive change for all children. I zeroed in on the promise of public education as a social policy lever, because, when we deliver public education in an egalitarian fashion, it provides great opportunities for social mobility and self-sufficiency. My calling became clear.

Overview

My call to education is attributable to the promise of public education. A promise for all children to realize social mobility, political access, global citizenship, and civic participation. A promise to develop children's full potential. A promise to transfer knowledge and build agency for learning. A promise to reinterpret and transform the unequal systems and structures that maintain our outmoded societal hierarchies and entrenched inequities. A promise to affect positive change. A promise to ensure that no one child is shortchanged by the education to which they have access.

This chapter addresses women's rationales for leading and the way *identity*, *power*, and *culture* shape women's leadership approaches. To inhabit an identity as a leader, it can help for women to believe they belong among other leaders, see themselves as leaders, and observe and relate to other women leaders. This chapter also considers the *drivers*—one's calling, purpose, or mission—that motivate women to pursue educational leadership. Consequential to the realization of one's leadership is the interplay of their own identity—and that of others—with their own and other's access to and use of power. Research elevates power as a key factor in leadership—who possesses it, their profiles, their rules, and their decision-making, selection, and promotion practices. I thus address dynamics surrounding dominant power structures prevalent within leadership and institutions.

I share how I believe my own identity and worldview formed based on my birth order, sisters, single mother, egalitarian beliefs, and scrappy nature. I introduce the ways in which dominant organizational and personnel norms and cultures reinforce and preserve themselves and the role power plays in perpetuating bureaucratic and hierarchical dynamics. The respondents' comments, coupled with my own anecdotes, highlight the ways in which identity, power, and hardships define our call to lead in educational settings. Respondents emphasize the following reasons for leading: (1) forwarding social justice/improving educational outcomes, (2) improving teaching and learning, (3) making changes to bureaucratic management and leadership structures and approaches, and (4) diversifying perspectives.

Again, I use vignettes about the people and cultures I encountered to highlight how such experiences affected my sense of self, response to various forces, and evolution as a leader. I discuss how having a moral code coupled with knowledge about their own and others' identities can enable women leaders to navigate through difficult situations and take advantage of positive ones to forward their core purpose. I introduce educational *theories* that women leaders can use to better understand the ways in which leadership models and definitions, coupled with their identity and drivers, can inform their practice.

Culture and Power

It's not enough for someone to want to lead, want to change things, or hold power. A woman leader can also benefit from "know[ing] one's values and deepest commitments, to identify[ing] one's 'non-negotiables' and to understand[ing] one's culture, and how one connects to others in the wider community."[1] District, network, school, and organization culture contribute to shaping educational leadership approaches and identity, due to education's myriad and interconnecting contexts. These contexts—from that of the broader community to individual schools to the entities working in and governing them—define the culture. Culture implies that there are norms, values, expectations, and shared meanings, which together affect both identity creation and presentation along with leadership creation and presentation. Culture also establishes the tone and parameters for the ways in which power is secured, maintained, and wielded and the extent to which it results in changes to societal, workplace, educational, and political systems and structures.[2]

Organizational culture has historically been associated with a dominant culture, which the Leadership Academy (2021) defines as "an artificial, historically constructed culture and refers to socially accepted dominant language, religion, behavior, values, rituals, and social customs. These traits, such as those of white, heterosexual, Christian, able-bodied, cis-gendered, English as a first language, U.S.-born, etc., are often seen as the norm for society as a whole."[3] The Leadership Academy also speaks to white dominant culture, which privileges the thinking, backgrounds, and experiences of white people over those of people of color. Such historical and common structures, practices, norms, and cultures result in organizations being "imbued with masculine values, sometimes including displays of competitive masculinity, especially among executives."[4] Closely aligned to the role of dominant cultures is that of dominant power, which is used by those in power to keep those in power in power and which drives decision-making, solution generation, and resource allocation.

Organizational social structures can preserve and reproduce power. This is at least one reason why change, even if attempted, may not stick. I consider the bureaucratic forces operating for or against change as mirroring an old pinball machine—the ball acts as the attempted change and the existing structures, practices, and cultures are the levers that shoot the ball back to the start. The people merely follow the ball. The individual examples from Chapter 2—which highlighted transactional, administrative, or heroic leadership—explicate this aversion to change and the intransigence of workplace practices. They also encapsulate the roles that power and culture can play. DeDee, Jean, Lottie, Lydia, and Sonja address their attempts to overcome similar dynamics.

> **Dedee**: [Race and Ethnicity] is one of the core "checks" in my work—as a leader, if the decisions we are making do not attend to equity issues brought about by race and/or ethnicity, then we are not leading for equity or for each/all students.
>
> **Jean**: As a white woman, I believed I had an obligation to learn about racial and ethnicity issues that affected students and families in a large, extremely diverse school system. I carried that learning into my work with national nonprofits as well.
>
> **Lottie**: I believe that putting yourself in another one's position is important to understanding where they're coming from in a particular situation.
>
> **Lydia**: Race mattered [in my school district.] As the regional superintendent of the largely minority region, quite often, I was cognizant of my white privilege. I learned a powerful lesson, and that was to listen to students, teachers and parents and to learn from their stories and not to tell people what to do but rather work collaboratively to seek a resolution to issues.
>
> **Sonja**: As someone who works with schools that serve predominantly black and brown kids, I know that my instincts or understandings aren't always comprehensive enough to reflect the lived experience of someone who is not white, who is not born in the US, whose first language—or only language—is not English, etc.

The literature comprises myriad rationales and explanations for the perpetuation of hegemonic practices and structures—with Hegemonic described as "how groups of people are subjugated by other groups of people through meta-messages of what is normal."[5] Leaders and employees alike continue legacy practices and structures through repetition, reinforcement, and legitimization. Resistant to evolve, power structures and practices prevail in part due to their influence over organizational preferences, rules, and regulations; decision-making norms; and individuals' levels of autonomy. Who in an organization possesses power can also be associated with an individual or a group's perceived competence and access—from resources to relationships to identity to social, economic, cultural, and political privileges. Charles Dwyer's (1992) distinctions between power and authority shed light on why I wasn't viewed as possessing such authority, or as I acquired power, why others seemed to want to usurp or undermine that power:

> Power is the ability to use your behavior to tap into the resources of an organization and get your values served. Authority, on the other hand is nothing more than an organizational privilege extended to you by someone in the organization to engage in certain behaviors in the expectation of being supported in those behaviors ... Every increase in authority is accompanied by an increase in responsibility, and the latter almost always outruns the former in magnitude. The all too frequently experienced gap in between one's authority and one's responsibility has to be filled with one's power ... Power has unlimited potential.[6]

You'll hear more about the effect of power dynamics on me (and respondents) in the following chapter.

In most workplaces, power, culture, and organizational practices influence leadership, leadership identity, and individuals' beliefs and behaviors—there is implied or required consensus about leader appropriateness and even guidelines and rules that follow or reinforce the male leadership norms.[7] Such contexts can affect identity formation. One's sense of self-worth, self-awareness, and self-concept—including one's gender, race, ethnicity, religion, and physical and mental abilities—shape identity. Identity is also formed based on one's sense of others, public presentation, public reception, and leadership style. Acceptable historical, societal, workplace, and political norms, influencers, and expectations are incorporated through a leader's interactions with others and others' reactions to a leader's presentation of themself. If the leader norm is male, "Then women are immediately perceived as 'other' or 'deviant' [so that women need] to work to maintain a sense of coherence between the incongruity of playing in two conflicting roles, such as the respectable female and the credible leader."[8] The prevalence of agentic (rather than communal) approaches reflects this conundrum. I know colleagues and supervisors have misperceived my own confidence and work ethic as competitive or off-putting and I've struggled with the negative connotations of me possessing self-confidence and a strong task orientation.

Autumn Tooms, Catherine Lugg, and Ira Botoch (2010) share a description about the way school communities interact dynamically with individual and societal identities to affect continuous adjustments and negotiations—which are based on one's own perceptions, the validation of others, and particular contexts and associated norms.[9]

> The community, which ultimately governs a school, sets the parameters of acceptance of school leadership through discursive interaction as to how an administrator is to be and not to be in terms of both role and identity … Ultimately, school leadership candidates blend multiple aspects of themselves into social selves that shift discursively to context, situation, and desire.[10]

Purpose and Identity

I made a deliberate decision to pursue educational leadership because I wanted to make a difference in children's lives and I felt I could. Such leadership pursuits may be conscious or unconscious choices. For example, unfettered access to leadership may affect men's reasons for pursuing leadership. Reasons may also include men's upbringings, embodiment of prevalent leadership traits, and affiliation with agentic/androcentric leadership models. Scholars suggest that women leaders may elect to link their pursuit of leadership to a purpose (driver), which aligns with their personal values, identity, and goal achievement. Herminia Ibarra, Robin Ely, and Deborah Kolb (2019) describe the role of purpose for women and its impact on leadership as follows:

> Anchoring in purpose enables women to redirect their attention toward shared goals and to consider who they need to be and what they need to learn in order to achieve those goals.[11]

> Effective leaders develop a sense of purpose by pursuing goals that align with their personal values and advance the collective good. This allows them to look beyond the status quo to what is possible and gives them a compelling reason to take action despite personal fears and insecurities. Such leaders are seen as authentic and trustworthy because they are willing to take risks in the service of shared goals.[12]

Authors Karen Longman and Debbie Lamm Bray (2017) define purpose as:

> Viewing leadership as the opportunity to fulfill one's purpose in broader spheres of influence, or for the benefit of those serving in the workplace, can engender tenacity and motivation for women to navigate or even counter the effects of a challenging male-normed organizational environment. Beyond its connection to purpose, awareness of calling is also inextricably aligned with identity development, both of which contribute to confidence.[13]

Many respondents' comments highlight the importance of women's motivations to lead.

Billie: There is no doubt that my childhood experiences in a home with parents actively committed and working toward social justice, racial equity and inclusive practice formed the mission I chose to undertake. As a young child I was the only Caucasian participant in a number of youth programs and quickly recognized that race, gender and disability were barriers that needed to be addressed as a matter of justice and equity.

Bonnie: Black and brown students throughout the country have been underserved in public education—my work has been devoted to improving urban districts for the last 20 years.

Joan: "MY WHY" [is] the belief that I can be a catalyst for change and reform in education. The belief that I am capable, prepared and have what it takes to lead effectively and to build an infrastructure for justice in education view in, rooted in equity, access to resources and to a high-quality education for all students in the United States. My belief that being Hispanic is an advantage and a privilege, not a disadvantage.

Karin: As a white woman, I have thought a lot about the way to both empower people of color within my organization, as well as be the voice of others who may not yet have "a seat at the table."

Lydia: If you can determine your why then you can move mountains. BTW my why is to create schools good enough for my children. I have since modified that why to include my grandchildren. Every decision I make has to end with, will this create a school good enough for my own children?

Michelle: My education leadership efforts are always focused on making a positive difference in children's lives. I can see the faces of many of my past students and remember their stories and their needs. I know that I have to have strong shoulders because many people are counting on me, and I made my choice to take on this work.

I was struck by Jason Feifer's (2022) *Entrepreneur* article about the late-night host and comedian Jimmy Fallon and Fallon's rationale for and understanding of why he does what he does. Feifer's insights about purpose are captured below:

> People talk endlessly about the things they do at work, but they don't always reflect on the reason they're doing it. What motivates them? What gives them purpose? What is their measurement of success, and what will guide them when things go wrong? You could call all of this a person's why—it is the reason for anything they do, and the core of who they are … People who know their why are people who never feel lost … The late-night job came naturally because he [Jimmy Fallon] was making people happy. And when he looked back at his life, he saw that same instinct: "At the time I was too young to realize it, but I just wanted to make people happy." … He had his realization. 'I think my why is, Can it make people happy?' … Now that is something on which you can build a career. It isn't following a path. It isn't doing something just because. It is a mission. A purpose.[14]

Would it be that we could all have the purpose of making people happy! I love making people happy as a purpose and that there is someone as gifted as Fallon with this mission. I also know that Fallon's background—as a white cisgender male—facilitated his ability to make choices and experience life to become what he is today. This is not to say he didn't work hard and overcome hardships.

One's purpose, identity, possession of power, and ability to navigate different contexts and organizational cultures form a coil. To lead effectively using these elements, such leaders may practice self-awareness, humility, continuous learning, and a growth mindset. Carol Dweck (2006) defines growth mindset as "the belief that your basic qualities are things you can cultivate through your efforts, your strategies, and help from others."[15] Dweck also says that, for leaders with a growth mindset, "success is about stretching themselves. It's about becoming smarter … success is about learning."[16]

I equate possession of self-awareness with engaging in a continuous reflective practice. The Council of Chief State School Officers (CCSSO 2015) articulated the need for transformational education leaders to "re-examine their practices and dispositions habitually in order to develop the 'wisdom of practice' needed to succeed in pursuing new and more effective approaches."[17] This definition emphasizes continuous knowledge acquisition about oneself, one's setting, and stakeholders; the ongoing practice of mindfulness; and reflection about oneself, one's impact, and one's stance. Mindfulness is defined as "living in a state of full, conscious awareness of one's whole self, other people, and the context in which we live and work. In effect, mindfulness means being awake, aware, and attending—to ourselves and to the world around us."[18]

I know I haven't always led with aplomb. I realize it would've been ideal to have had the opportunity—like football players do in their game postmortems—to review each situation and identify what worked, what didn't work, and what impact I had. Instead, I created my own survival strategies. I listened to people's whose feedback and support I trusted such as George and the team I profile earlier. I sought to learn from, rather than ruminate over, the snarky comments, personal attacks, and misgivings my detractors delivered. Considering all feedback—such as gleaning lessons from the most persistent and negative blogger who shows up to complain at school board meetings—can shed light in areas unseen: one's detractors may be saying something that requires addressing and one's supporters may simply be telling you what they think you want to hear.

She Persists

Women's reasons for pursuing educational leadership are varied and specific. Motivators can include making changes to male-dominated and bureaucratic leadership structures and approaches. Pursuit of a leadership role in educational settings may also focus on improving teaching and learning, forwarding social justice, or increasing collaborative decision-making practices. Another reason may be to diversify leadership ranks and practices. Other motivators could include a boss or mentor guiding a person into leadership and positive role models. Some may not even deliberately choose to lead.

I asked respondents to share their reasons for pursuing an educational leadership route or position. Applying a four-point scale of not important, somewhat important, important, and extremely important, contributors identify their four most important reasons for pursuing educational leadership. Those they prioritize as important and extremely important are (1) forwarding social justice/improving educational outcomes, (2) improving teaching and learning, (3) making changes to bureaucratic management and leadership structures and approaches, and (4) diversifying perspectives.

Whereas Table 3.1 doesn't include my ratings for pursuing an educational leadership career, my responses are consistent with most respondents. My primary—and only extremely important—reason for pursuing an educational leadership career is forwarding social justice/improving educational outcomes. I also rate the following reasons as important: improving teaching and learning,

Table 3.1 Reasons for Pursuing Educational Leadership

Reasons	Respondents Imp/Ext Imp
Forward social justice/improved educational outcomes	36
Improve teaching and learning	32
Make changes to bureaucratic management and leadership structures and approaches	29
Diversify perspectives	26
Increase collaborative decision-making practices	24
Was guided or promoted into leadership	21
Make changes to male-dominated leadership structure	11
Did not consciously choose to go into leadership	7

making changes to bureaucratic management and leadership structures and approaches, diversifying perspectives; and increasing collaborative decision-making practices.

Notably just twenty-one respondents indicate, when important and extremely important are combined, that they were "guided or promoted into leadership." I myself also didn't rank the choice as important or extremely important. However, when examining just the extremely important ranking, being guided into leadership ranks as the fourth most extremely important reason based on thirteen responses. Perhaps the other respondents were scrappy like I was (see Table 3.2). I persisted even when an employer told me I wasn't management material.

Influencers to respondents' professional goals, aspirations, and perseverance are myriad. They comprise supervisors or organization leaders who showed faith and possessed confidence in respondents' abilities and provided opportunities, growth, encouragement, access, and connections. Other respondents say they had supportive colleagues, mentors, professors, college advisors, and family members—fathers, mothers, and grandparents—who provided encouragement, role modeling, belief in one's abilities, and expectations. Respondents mention mentors (male and female) from within and outside of education. Numerous combinations of external influencers—from Rhiannon to Michael Fullan to God—reflect respondents' values. My influencers range from my graduate school peers and network to my father to my children to mentors to team members.

The responses to why one pursues a leadership career also show that respondents did, in large part, make a conscious choice to pursue leadership—just

Table 3.2 Reasons for Pursuing Educational Leadership (Detail)

Reasons	Important	Extremely Important
Forward social justice/improved educational outcomes	12	24
Improve teaching and learning	12	20
Diversify perspectives	11	15
Was guided or promoted into leadership	8	13
Make changes to bureaucratic management and leadership structures and approaches	17	12
Increase collaborative decision-making practices	13	11
Make changes to male dominated leadership structure	7	4
Did not consciously choose to go into leadership	4	3
Total respondents	37	37

seven respondents indicate, via their important or extremely important ratings, that they did not make a conscious choice to pursue leadership. I further address influences in Chapter 7 discussion on strategies and supports, which I propose so that women see themselves, and succeed, as leaders. The majority of respondents say they didn't pursue leadership because they want to change male-dominated leadership structures (eleven respondents indicate this was the case). However, twenty-nine respondents indicate they pursued leadership to change bureaucratic structures and practices. This response difference represents a conundrum given that those who created the power structures and associated rules undergirding bureaucratic organizations are men. And, men continue, for the most part, to reign in bureaucracies and perpetuate organizational structures, practices, and cultures that benefit men.

Seven people added suggestions that ranged from a parent figure guiding her into leadership to giving back to one's community to ethics to the dearth of women of color inhabiting human resource roles.

Dionne: Give back to the profession.
Lara: Women of color in the education leadership space are too often relegated to principalships, a few superintendents' roles, even rare roles on the national scene. I saw an opportunity to influence personnel development which is largely dominated by white men and women, in the union world, definitely dominated by white men.

Lottie: I believe I was guided into a leadership by my Dad. … My Dad was a single parent, raising seven girls and one boy on his own. He depended on me for so much. … I was a single parent …. I went to college to improve my lot in life, not to be a leader. I believe it was just a natural part of who I am.

Mathilda: Ethics—I see many educational leaders who lack ethics, so it is my responsibility to rise up in leadership positions to foster integrity.

Patty: Improve community and school relations and partnerships.

Sonja: Do the work that wasn't being done in service of schools when I was a school leader.

Wilma: To work towards creating systems that more equitably serve all young children.

Because of the study's sample size, the respondent subgroups—demographics, age, and education levels—are too small to examine for statistical significance. However, after clustering all non-white respondents into a single group, one purpose among women of color arises as a potential area for further study. Fourteen out of fifteen respondents of color indicate via an important or extremely important rating that they pursued leadership to diversify perspectives. Three points are relevant. First, this is a potential area for further exploration and is not statistically significant. Second, I merged women of color respondents into one subgroup, which runs counter to the tenets of intersectional approaches. People of different ethnic and racial backgrounds experience—and confront—the world and racism differently. Third, the Hispanic women respondents are part of both the white respondent group (with four Hispanic respondents affiliating as white) and respondents of color (with four Hispanic respondents affiliating as Black, mixed, or other). Combining the responses into one group thus isn't an ideal approach, but it generates a desire to diversify perspectives as a possible area for further study when unpacking motivators for women of color. Such a reason is consistent with social justice, Black feminist, collectivist, and critical approaches.

Leadership Theories

Theories contribute to the framing of leadership and explanations about identity and purpose. This subsection introduces theories designed to explain who assumes leadership roles and why (and often, how) they become leaders.

Such theories can orient and frame examinations of women in leadership. John Maxwell (2005) defines theory as follows:

> Theory is a coat closet ... A useful high-level theory gives you a framework for making sense of what you see. Particular pieces of data, which otherwise might seem unconnected or irrelevant to one another or to your research questions, can be related by fitting them into the theory. The concepts of the existing theory are the "coat hooks" in the closet: they provide places to "hang" the data, showing their relationship to other data.[19]

Feminist theory and social justice theory are critical theories, which seek to critique unequal power relations in society with an aim of achieving equity. Feminist leadership is not complete without an understanding of critical feminist theories and the relationship to other critical theories. One of those, Social Justice Theory, or Critical Social Theory, focuses on a leader's drive to address a shared social cause, positive community or organizational change, and meaningful participation among marginalized groups.[20] Practicing critical leadership involves "meaningful dialogue"—it educates others who lead (whether or not they are official), brings about transformational "social change," and involves ethical and communal practices.[21] Critical leadership is an extension of Critical Theory, which "is a philosophical perspective that critiques unequal power relations in society with the goal of seeking change and creating equity."[22] Women and marginalized groups sometimes criticize critical leadership because men developed and applied it.

Feminist Leadership is core to my practice. Feminist leadership opposes hierarchical approaches. Women's historical activism and confrontation of oppression—from "emancipation, suffrage, teacher's rights, and unionization efforts"—undergird feminist leadership.[23] Feminist leaders may seek change and to "enact policies that will improve women's lives" from childcare to equal pay.[24] Critical Feminist Theory views organizations as:

> Sites where major societal conventions and norms, ways of doing, and knowledge manifest in ways that have crucial, often economic consequences for groups who have had little to do with the organization of society whole ... Organizations were by and large developed by men, so "neutral policies" are in fact ways in which organizations privilege men's experiences or that of their ideal worker image. The primary aim of critical feminists is to illuminate such biases.[25]

Whereas feminist theory tends to espouse the importance of shared experiences among and solutions for all women, white, middle-class women have typically led and benefited from feminism. Thus, Black feminism—as well as

Critical Race Theory (CRT) and Intersectionality—are tools people of color and allies employ to unpack and seek changes to dominance, oppression, and power.

Intersectionality "assumes that identities, including gender, are multiple, fluid, in part self-constructed; that a perspective on a single characteristic such as gender risks active harm in encouraging the 'appalling effects of the miniaturization of people' and in research terms unhelpful in privileging one characteristic over another."[26] Women who are white, middle-class, cisgender, and educated possess multiple privileges. These privileges, regardless of one's level of awareness or acceptance of them, shape how they view the world, how they communicate and lead, how the world views them, and where on a societal hierarchy they sit. In the next subsection, respondents share their experiences with intersectionality.

The role of Black feminism and Black Feminist Leadership involves taking action, making change, providing direction, and giving voice (to black women) at the intersection of race and gender. Black feminism views gender as insufficient to understand the black woman leader. Women who identify as people of color—whether Black, Asian, Latino, Native American, Pacific Islander, mixed race, or other—are not unidimensional; the disparities, prejudices, and oppression they face are not singularly focused on their race, ethnicity, or gender.[27] Black feminism involves the importance of considering and using social location, which is "a construct that embraces gender, race, and social class as well as the elements of historical place, time, and culture."[28] In her book *Hood Feminism*, Mikkie Kendall (2021) argues that, "mainstream white feminism often fails to show up for women of color … [and often involves the] complete erasure of issues most likely to impact those who are not white."[29] Her feminism, Hood Feminism, addresses the needs of marginalized women and roots itself "in an awareness of how race and gender and class all affect my [her] ability to be educated, receive medical care, gain and keep employment, as well as how those things can sway authority figures in their treatment of me [her]."[30]

Following the summer 2020 Black Lives Matter protests and public discourse about the insufficiently addressed discrimination against people of color, CRT entered the national dialogue. Since then, CRT has been misappropriated—becoming a conservative lightning rod. It need not be. CRT maintains that organizational structures, practices, and cultures are racist because they were developed by and favor white people—those in the dominant culture. CRT contends that to rectify the legacy racist structures and systems, people of color should be the primary focus and drivers. For those who are uncomfortable with the recent discussions about a continuum of privilege and agency—with white privilege and legacy systems that oppress being on one end (the right one) and equitable and fair structures, practices, and cultures being on the other end (the threatening one)—even the notion of CRT is a sticky wicket. When applying CRT to societal and organizational racism, the focus is less on individuals and more so on the systems they comprise. The point of CRT is not that people in organizations are overtly or knowingly racist. Rather the system itself is prejudiced—it is the target for change. Similarly, critical feminist theorists frame such embedded societal and organizational biases as favoring and protecting men and excluding (not just) women.[31]

Some assume effective leaders possess in-born traits while those lacking such traits aren't presumed to be of leader quality. Historically white men have led; thus, many equate maleness and whiteness with leadership. We now refer to these traits as agentic and as part of one's personality. Alice Eagly and Linda Carli (2007a) discuss how role theories view women and men leaders differently:

> Two connotations predominate in people's associations about women and men: the communal and the agentic. Communal associations convey a concern with the compassionate treatment of others. Women elicit communal associations of being especially affectionate, helpful, friendly, kind, and sympathetic as well as interpersonally sensitive, gentle, and soft spoken. In contrast, agentic associations convey assertion and control. Men elicit agentic associations of being especially aggressive, ambitious, dominant, self-confident, and forceful as well as self-reliant and individualistic. These associations about agency and communion form the basis of gender stereotypes.[32]

Women do not fit the mold because of the roles they've played over the course of their lives. Savita Kumra (2017) explains that,

> Women seeking advancement to executive levels are impacted by the effects of social stereotypes in two ways: firstly, they are perceived as too feminine for leadership roles; and secondly the very fact they seek such roles undermines their femininity … [Social Role Theory posits that] behavioral gender differences are endorsed by socialization from a young age, where males are rewarded for achievement-oriented (or agentic) behavior, while females are rewarded for their emotional (or communal) orientation.[33]

Trait Theory "developed from the belief that ability arises from innate, internal traits that some possess and some do not. Through this approach, critical leadership traits can be isolated and people with such traits can then be recruited, selected, and inducted into leadership positions."[34] A trait approach "identifies the personality characteristics of a leader"[35] and explains that "certain traits are directly related to leadership ability [and that] people perceive certain traits as being related to leadership."[36] Trait theory "suggests that you can identify a potential leader by examining the personality traits of the person and matching them to the characteristics that effective leaders possess. It also suggests if a person possesses the correct combination of traits, he or she will be able to lead."[37] A woman leader who possesses characteristics like ambition, confidence, charisma, and competence runs against type. While male leaders are viewed as demonstrating such characteristics, women leaders should not or, if they do, they should strategically soften such approaches. Women regularly confront damned if you do and damned if you don't situations—double binds in which "highly communal female leaders may be criticized for not being agentic enough. But female leaders who are highly agentic may be criticized for lacking communion."[38]

Social Role Theory, or Role Theory, depicts the ways in which we form, present, and influence leadership characteristics. Role Congruity Theory explains gender differences as influenced by how children learn to behave starting in childhood. Still, this theory focuses on the constraints women face—in other words, women's profiles are incongruous with and less favorable to the leadership roles they may seek.[39] Similarly, Synergistic Leadership Theory (SLT) looks at interactions between and among various forces affecting women in leadership. Beverly Irby, Genevieve Brown, and LingLing Yang (2013) developed this multifaceted theory, with four components explicitly described and tested, to be uniquely feminist and relational rather than linear. These authors describe SLT as comprising the following four factors: "leadership behavior, organizational structure, external forces, and attitude, beliefs, and values."[40]

Gender and Intersectionality

While I employ critical feminist and social justice theories, the additional leadership theories I share facilitate how I examine women leaders—particularly the impact of gender and intersectionality. Let me explain. I attempt to balance my own privileged perspective by, at a minimum, identifying it and respecting that I cannot know or understand others' lived experiences. Even so, I have misstepped and blundered. I try to avoid making assumptions and I seek to win each new person's trust. Cultural competence falls into this quagmire; while no one can fully be competent in another's culture, they can seek awareness.

Respondents share how and in what ways the intersection of gender affected their educational leadership. Across ages and employers, respondents describe feeling overlooked, under-promoted, and underpaid for roles they felt went to less qualified men. Their responses hint that white males and patriarchal expectations still dominate respondents' organizations. Even respondents already in leadership positions express the continuous need to prove themselves. A broken rung describes a promotion pathway broken at the start for women: "Women are promoted to manager at far lower rates than men, and this makes it nearly impossible for companies [organizations] to lay a foundation for sustained progress at more senior levels. Additionally, the gains in representation for women overall haven't translated to gains for women of color."[41] Consider:

> **Avril**: Over the years there were times when I felt excluded from important discussions, as I wasn't part of the "boys' club." Luckily, looking back, this was not a pervasive theme through my career, but associated with one supervisor.
>
> **Catrina**: When I first started in education, there may have been 1 female on the site administrative team, but no female principals. The same was true in district leadership. No females were in the superintendency. I was one of the first female principals in our high school district. Learning how to navigate through a male dominated organization proved challenging at times.
>
> **Dedee**: Gender was my first lens on equity in education and educational leadership. It was personal, and it was the lens that then cracked to help my perspective across many other equity issues.
>
> **Jaimie**: Gender has impacted my educational leadership because often times based on data, experiences, education pedigree, I have experienced many men promoted into leadership positions without proper credentials etc. and I was not given a chance but instead the second in charge and still expected to perform his duties, despite him getting the lead position over me.
>
> **Joan**: Sexism is big in this work. At the administrative level, the large majority of leaders are white males … Males also progress and get promoted a lot faster than women in education. It is a hard reality to grasp … I have been perceived and mistaken multiple times as being the secretary in groups of men who I work with, who are older than me, when in fact I am the person leading the meeting! Sexism is real in this industry and it is felt harder the higher you move up in this work.

Kelly: I believe society still primes women as emotional or emotionless and men as practical/impartial and in the Ed space when decision making happens, I see these arguments subliminally surface.

Natalie: Gender is an issue and I believe as we deal with the twin pandemics, we have sometimes lost sight of the intersectionality between race/ethnicity and gender. In my privilege as a white woman, I do not think about my race daily, but I certainly think about my gender. I need to continue to stand and point out when gender is used as a barrier. People don't like it and get defensive, but I can't be silent anymore.

Nola: Gender has had an impact on my movement into leadership. My rise to my current position seemed to have been slowed by the fact of my gender. There have been males moving into leadership positions on an advanced trajectory who were less qualified and demonstrated fewer skills than I at the time.

Reese: I'd say my own awareness of gender in the workplace has increased tenfold since I went to grad school in 2013 and met an incredible group of women who I'm still friends with. I think it's where I became a feminist and began to interrogate the implicit biases that women face at work. I strive to be a leader that can sit in the same room as men, but not emulate their leadership styles … I want to be the type of leader that facilitates growth opportunities for women and that values the unique strengths and skills that women bring to the workplace. Most workplace cultures—non-profits included—are still very driven by white, male-dominated corporate culture norms and in my growing awareness of what these are, I am becoming more comfortable naming them and working in ways that counteract.

Sharon: White, male, privilege is alive and well. It seems that the dominant culture is very threatened at this time and many appear to band together to protect their position of privilege in ways not as visibly obvious as they are now. It makes me sad and feel I live in a very unsafe society.

Sonja: It was shocking to me that the patriarchal norms forced on me in a male-dominated space were also present in the education space.

Wilma: Many (particularly white men that I speak to) can identify being a leader as early as 14 or 15 years old. They were doing the same things I was in high school (holding leadership roles, serving on ASB, being president of clubs, etc.), yet I never felt the same sense of leadership that my male colleagues felt. This brings me back to the feeling of having started late in my development as a leader … It isn't until now that I can add that title [of leader] as a part of my identity. As a young woman, that title would have probably done wonders for my self-esteem and for feeling a sense of belonging ... I think about how many other young Latinx women don't realize their full potential because that world of opportunity isn't opened up to them through affirmation and mentorship.

Respondents share their experience with micro-aggressions, which are "the everyday verbal, nonverbal, and environmental slights, snubs, or insults, whether intentional or unintentional, which communicate hostile, derogatory, or negative messages to target persons based solely upon their marginalized group membership."[42] We return to these topics in Chapter 4 when further examining challenges to women's leadership. Several respondents indicate that, in meetings, their supervisors and colleagues overlooked, didn't acknowledge, or failed to hear their contributions whereas the men who made the same or similar points were heard and recognized. Respondents say they moderated their stance, approach, and impact to accommodate how colleagues perceived them if they came across as too confident, competent, or self-assured.

Respondents share how, and in what ways, the intersection of race and ethnicity affected their educational leadership. Providing complex and individualized responses, some respondents said people misidentified them because they are light-skinned or white in appearance but identified as Latinx, mixed, or Asian. Given their ambiguous appearance, they sometimes sought to demonstrate their commitment to, and elevate the voices of, underserved, minority, or immigrant communities. Other respondents mention that their personal mission is to educate underserved, marginalized students. Most white women recognize and note their white privilege and sometimes their frustration with not receiving a promotion (which some attribute to their whiteness). Women of color express the strain of balancing their roles and associated expectations with their race and ethnicity as well as their gender.

Many women of color also indicate a desire to be role models for others like them, prove their worth and qualifications, and modulate their communication style and impact depending on the setting. They also seek to address equity issues, advocacy, and training even if it cost them reputational chits. They weather the consequences of their advocacy with weathering connoting psychosocial hardships—including discrimination—which can lead to "worse wear and tear effects" on mental and physical health including premature aging and depression.[43]

Angela: [In] my current place of employment, I am the only woman of color … As far as being the only woman of color, I have to be very strategic in how I present myself when I want to be heard and not dismissed.

Diedre: While my ethnicity is Latinix, I look white and have benefitted often from looking white … In schools and in districts, we were often making decisions for people instead of including them to be part of the decision-making. It was not out of malice. When I mentioned it, people were always agreeable, but did not necessarily know how to organize it effectively.

Georgette: As a black female leading a suburban predominantly white district and all white leadership team, I was very much aware of my communication style, cultural competence in my interactions and made adjustments when and where needed.

Joan: I have been discriminated against and perceived as less prepared or less competent for being Hispanic and for having an accent even though I speak English very well and I am usually some of the most prepared/qualified people in the room for my role and compared to others with less preparation and bigger titles than mine … I have also been compensated less than my white peers holding the same job title and having more education and experience than them.

Lara: I continue to be "one of" or the "only" Black woman in many spaces in the [association] role. I still have to push my way into spaces and conversations.

Leslie: Professionally being a black female administrator has to be the toughest job on the planet. Years of institutional racism, bias, micro-aggressions, and sexism can wear you down.

Lottie: I seldom mention my credentials. On some occasions, I've had to do so to convince others that I was qualified to do a certain job. I find it sometimes necessary when there is a question regarding my skills that I truly believe are due to my race and gender. I have had to prove myself over and over again … [and have been] told I was "too good to be true."

Michelle: I became a cultural role model and had to learn as much as possible about the needs and issues of the Latinx population as well as all other underserved and lower achieving populations. I continued to grow in my own knowledge and expertise (MA in bilingual ed, principal and superintendent certifications) and these efforts helped me progress in my career. I also connected with colleagues across the country by joining professional organizations, presenting at conferences, and so forth.

Reese: On the one hand I think that the White and slightly older members of our staff often are the same people who commit micro-aggressions without even knowing. How do you force them to self-educate and doing the internal reflective work to reverse some of those ingrained reactions or behaviors without making them feel singled out?

Tang: My identity as a woman of color, specifically a Vietnamese American woman, has both facilitated and hindered my ability to implement leadership practices. My social identities have created pathways for me to connect with other people of color in the field. Similarly, my social identities have resulted in having assumptions or stereotypes projected on to me—these stereotypes either close doors to potential opportunities (for instance, when decisions are being made to create a task force) or limit others' ability to see that they can turn to me for advice or decision-making.

Tanya: As a Black woman, seeing my peers who look like me struggle and being told by older men that my contributions were minute if at all essential made me strive to prove them wrong. I see the power of Black women and have always believed in our impact on society, so I wanted to become a part of proving ignorant people wrong and help those that I can along the way.

These and other responses speak to the current debates surrounding Diversity, Equity, and Inclusion (DEI), misapplications of CRT, and defensiveness—and misunderstandings—about privilege and access. Consider the current-day battles over reading materials, educator training, curriculum, access to public school funding, and the profile of leaders and elected officials. It is helpful for women educational leaders, particularly those with intersectional identities, to understand dynamic contexts and draw from a variety of leadership approaches.

Conclusion

This chapter presents information about why women pursue leadership in educational settings and the role culture, power, and identity play in shaping leadership approaches. These examples reinforce the view that women may indeed pursue leadership to serve a purpose and that their rationales for doing so track with the reasons and models scholars have attributed to women in educational settings. My own and the respondents' dominant reasons for pursuing educational leadership focus on forwarding social justice, improving educational outcomes, improving teaching and learning, making changes to bureaucratic management and leadership structures and approaches, and diversifying perspectives. Women-of-color respondents appear more likely than white respondents to pursue leadership to diversify perspectives and increase collaborative decision-making.

The theories help frame and undergird leadership models and their implementation. This chapter suggests that women leaders can benefit from being aware of and navigating their leadership identities and values as part of their leadership approach. They can do so alongside the contexts in which they lead and the stakeholders on whose behalf and with whom they lead. Gendered and hegemonic cultures and organizations affect women's leadership identity, workplace experiences, and access to the power, authority, and positions that allow them to follow their callings.

My identity drove my rationale for pursuing, and formed my approach to, leadership. Shaping my identity are my birth order, gender, early (and ongoing) experience with on-the-job harassment, hard-working mother's leadership experience, and family's involvement in education. The contexts in which and people with whom I worked, along with the ways in which they wielded power, also molded my leadership approach. Respondents' backgrounds, profiles, experiences, and influences drove their identity formation and approaches as well. They tend to lead to improve the lives of children and improve working conditions for people like them. Environments, colleagues, and leaders buffeted them along the way, but these respondents remain true to their missions and demonstrate that is it unnecessary to wield power in hegemonic ways. I choose to lead with and for people rather than to obtain credit and accumulate power. Sometimes I have garnered or sought power—typically through collaborative means and influence—to move people and practices.

The next chapter examines challenges having to do with bias, discrimination, and stereotype. I also share the ways in which respondents and I addressed and navigated our circumstances without compromising ourselves.

Reflective Questions

1. Which of the rationales for leading, if any, appeal to your reasons for leading?
   a. Why?
2. Who or what influenced your decision to pursue leadership?
   a. How?
3. What compels you to (want to) lead?
4. Who have you encouraged to lead?
   a. Why and how?
5. In what ways can knowledge of different theories help you understand your own—and others'—approach(es) to leadership?
6. How can the tenets of feminist and critical race theory help you navigate your own context?
7. In what ways can the discussion about gender or intersectionality inform your leadership approach and context?

4

Navigating Challenges to Women's Leadership: Hummingbird

Leadership Story

During the lockdown portion of the coronavirus pandemic two of my three adult children stayed with me. While they struggled with not being among their own things, we made memories. They donned fake Mom tattoos for Mother's Day. We ran outside in pajamas to see the orange moon, tie-dyed socks and shirts, baked cookies, and watched Dolly Parton, Lily Tomlin, Jane Fonda, and Dabney Coleman in "9 to 5." They'd never seen the movie and we laughed until we cried. This iconic 1980s movie portrays the overt harassment Dolly's character, among other women in the office, endured—until they didn't—from their male boss played by Coleman. It made plain the outrageous situations women encounter in their workplaces.

Every parent wants to leave their children well set for an equivalent if not better life than the parent experienced. The challenges parents experience and overcome suggest that some future betterment will result. When contemplating my own future, it never crossed my mind that I couldn't have it all. Work. Marriage. Love. Children. A Career. Good health. Naively I didn't expect the harassment my mother experienced, when waiting tables while putting herself through a master's program and then when in a district leadership position, would repeat itself in my own life or in my children's lives. I cannot believe that my mother and others who fought for the right to vote, equal rights, reproductive choice, civil rights, or Title IX imagined that their children, grandchildren, and great grandchildren would need to continue such fights or be denied such rights.

While laws and the courts are supposed to be on the side of protecting civil rights, overt and subtle, forms of discrimination persist. As such, women's voices are muted; clothing is androgynous; jewelry is modest; hair is dyed, ironed, tamed, and bobbed; pay is inequitable; choices are limited; concerns are dismissed; and bodies, ambitions, contributions, discomfort, and clothing are ridiculed—all while women's chores, work ethic, reproductive burdens, and education levels increase. Women's hands remain tied in a double bind.

Overview

Throughout this book, I reference specific *challenges* and *barriers*—encounters with racism, sexism, bullying, and harassment, as well as discrimination and bias. In this chapter, I specifically study bullying, harassment, abuse, and racism. A *New York Times* article about hummingbirds titled, "Female Hummingbirds Avoid Harassment by Looking Like Males," evokes the female hummingbird's plumage, which when evolved within a species to mirror male birds, serves as a talisman for avoiding harassment. The article's hook statement claims, "Among white-necked Jacobin hummingbirds, those with plumage that resemble males get harassed less."[1] I also speak to strategies for and reflections about strategies to help women combat toxic workplaces, cultures, and situations. My intention is not to place the onus for combatting workplace toxicity on women but rather to provide them with navigation tools. I seek to shed light on 2023 workplace practices and strategies similar to those Betty Lehan Harragan provided in 1977 with *Games Mother Taught You: Corporate Gamesmanship for Women*.[2]

Challenges to Women's Leadership

Women confront numerous challenges to their recruitment for, selection for, and appointment to leadership positions. Many of the respondents in this study chose to walk away from a role or were blindsided by someone they trusted. I know I have been and walked away. Barriers combine to result in hiring committees selecting a dearth of women to serve effectively as leaders. Unconscious bias is "the automatic categorization of people based upon ascribed characteristics such as gender."[3] It is often used to stereotype, evaluate, assign appropriate organizational norms, and establish guidelines for selecting candidates who mesh with the organization's and hiring team's definition of fit. "Within the context of organizational leadership, unconscious bias manifests not only as a barrier to entry, but also as an obstacle one must continuously grapple with once in a position of authority."[4]

Second generation (or implicit bias) is another shrouded form of bias, which "erects powerful but subtle and often invisible barriers for women that arise from cultural assumptions and organizational structures, practices, and patterns of interaction that inadvertently benefit men while putting women at a disadvantage."[5]

Similar to definitions of biases are "blind spots," which are socially constructed "bits of knowledge" that contain a "large set of biases," and which result in one's lack of awareness of their hidden biases.[6] These blind spots often result in mindbugs; "ingrained habits of thought that lead to errors in how we perceive, remember, reason, and make decisions."[7] Everyone is fallible. A hidden blind spot is just that—mindbugs and blind spots can influence recruitment, selection, and advancement. I once thought I was doing the right thing by hiring two Black women to fill roles on a community project. While I was doing the right thing, I was blind to the obvious differences between inner city African Americans and African immigrants, whose families had sufficient assets to study in America and become citizens.

The practice of seeking and selecting someone who fits is typically akin to reproducing the dominant culture and power structures within organizations, and in the case of schools and districts, to replicating the school board's and community's structures and cultures. Fit "is about how one group can decide and perpetuate whichever values (and therefore reality) they choose under the guise of crafting who best 'fits' as a leader."[8] Fit, or a historically acceptable background, comprises styles, traits, behaviors, skills, and experience. The use of fit in education extends beyond embodiment of organizational norms to encompass how that leader duplicates community norms. Tooms et al. (2010) report that, "in educational administration, the community has decided which person represents what they believe a school leader should look and behave like" and those in leadership ascribing to the paradigm of finding people who fit are likely to perpetuate the selection of leaders who are male and charismatic.[9]

Gatekeeping can rely heavily on one's fit. As I share in Chapter 1, women experience disproportionately low representation among superintendents when compared to their teaching presence. Possibly, due to supervisors viewing them as communal and nurturing, women represent the majority of elementary school principals. For whatever reason, elementary roles and academic or curricular roles do not hold the same advancement opportunities and visibility when compared with someone who has served as secondary school principal and/or coach to an athletic team.[10] Society historically views men as the district leader prototype. A majority of superintendents are white males, many of whom may have coached teams, taught at the secondary school level, or served as a secondary school principal.[11] Coaching can be a precursor for district leadership—it is after all about strategy, teamwork, and motivation. Board of education and community members likely view secondary schools as more complex organizations than elementary schools and thus more appropriate training for future superintendents. Robert Maranto, Kristen Carroll, Albert Cheng, and Manuel Teodoro (2018) maintain that,

> High schools are typically larger institutions with bigger budgets, more staff and students, larger facilities, more differentiated structures and missions, and (partly due to athletics) far more community visibility. Further, the size of high schools requires principals to play stereotypically masculine roles leading and managing adults, rather than stereotypically feminine roles building relationships with individual young children.[12]

Christy Glass and Alice Ingersoll (2017) indicate that the known or unknown reproduction of the status quo is "the tendency of incumbents to reproduce their demographic composition in new hires or recruits."[13] Homosocial reproduction causes hiring teams, who when comprised of like-minded and similarly profiled people, to draw on their limited networks and to select people like them. Glass and Ingersoll conclude that, "the emphasis on conformity makes it difficult for members of the out-group to penetrate positions of leadership. The challenges outsiders face in gaining access to positions of authority monopolized by the dominant group can be used to demonstrate the lack of leadership competency in the subgroup, resulting in justification of homosocial reproduction among elites."[14]

When men dominate educational leadership roles, the formulation of decisions, policies, and processes may be prejudiced against women in favor of benefitting men.[15] In their ground-breaking meta study about leadership behavior, effectiveness, and prejudicial evaluations, Alice Eagly and Linda Carli (2003) describe prejudice as consisting "of unfair evaluation of a group of people based on stereotypical judgments of the group rather than the behavior or qualifications of its individual members."[16] Their conclusion was that,

> When people hold stereotypes about a group, they expect members of that group to possess characteristics and exhibit behavior consistent with those stereotypes ... These stereotypic inferences yield prejudice against individual group members when stereotypes about their group are incongruent with the attributes associated with success in certain classes of social roles. This incongruity tends to produce discrimination by lowering evaluations of such group members as potential or actual occupants of those roles.[17]

In addition to having hierarchical, bureaucratic, and old-boys-club practices, arcane rules can still govern positions in bureaucratic and public sector organizations. In the past, many of these rules prevented others from accessing roles under the guise that the others did not meet certain sets of standards or possess time-honored sets of experiences. Civil service rules and other types of credentialing tests have served as gatekeeping mechanisms to keep others out—to create barriers to entry. An example of this is my attempt to study in an education doctoral program without having served in an instructional role inside a school district.

John Powell (2017) maintains that, "othering is not about liking or disliking someone. It is based on the conscious or unconscious assumption that a certain identified group poses a threat to the favoured group ... Overwhelmingly, people don't 'know' those that they are Othering."[18] Othering is closely related to tokenism, which refers to placing a singular person of a certain profile in a position and then considering that the person represents their entire group. Such tokens also possesses less social status, which includes less power and access to resources, and which can perpetuate inequality. Therefore, by putting one such person from a marginalized group on a hiring committee, that person has an undue burden to represent a different perspective from that of the status quo.[19] "In many settings, it is a breakthrough to appoint even one woman, and such first steps are important. However, because token women receive extra scrutiny, it is essential to move beyond token representation. Token women are often subjected to intense performance pressures."[20] Tokens' status encompasses one's numeric representation among the majority population. Glass and Ingersoll (2017) define tokens as:

> Members of a group who represent 15 percent or fewer of the individuals within a rank, position or organization; "solos" are defined as individuals who are the sole members of their group within the rank, position, or organization. Compared to members of the numerical majority, tokens and solos have lower status, prestige, and influence within the organization. Tokens experience a variety of challenges as a result of their under-representation such as heightened visibility, performance pressures, and negative evaluation bias.[21]

Michelle Ryan and Alexander Haslam (2007) suggest that benevolent sexism can apply to situations where "women are assigned (and rewarded for taking on) roles that can be represented as attractive (e.g., as 'challenging') but are actually problematic."[22] They go on to explain how these situations and assignments can be problematic:

By providing women with these "challenges," those who appoint them may feel that they are doing women a favor (at least in contrast to hostile sexists, who would be opposed to appointing women to senior positions altogether). The sense that they are being done a favor may imply that women feel unable to refuse such offers (lest they be accused of "looking a gift horse in the mouth"). At the same time, by appearing to support women but actually giving them inferior positions with limited opportunities for development, those in power can deny charges of overt discrimination while ensuring that any change does not dramatically challenge the gender-based status hierarchy or rock the organizational boat too hard.[23]

I recall a situation when an important client granted me a contract because of my leadership capabilities in talent management, crosscutting school issues, and board-approved policy development. After I submitted recommendations about how each type of the client's handbooks—staffing, policy, and human resources—could reinforce each other while also serving different purposes, a male organization leader, who I will call "Stan," grilled me about why I was making these recommendations. Stan hadn't bothered to look at my background and didn't believe I could possibly know about the subject. This was a good way to reject any suggested improvements or changes and he didn't forward or adopt any of my recommendations.

Respondents expound on the ways in which identity, power, and culture arise for women leaders and those with intersectional identities. Many share anecdotes and experiences highlighting the identity challenges they confronted—from having one's ideas usurped to experiencing an excessive burden of responsibility to showing up for one's community to experiencing more than one type of discrimination simultaneously. These challenges can trivialize women's contributions, undermine their ability to present themselves authentically, and mute their voices. Such challenges can also create stressful if not toxic cultures that women leaders must navigate.

Several respondents provide insight into what it feels like to experience bropropriating, manimization, and hepeating situations. Bropropriating is "a man taking a woman's idea and taking credit for it."[24] Manimization is "a man's minimization of a woman's thoughts or ideas which, upon the man's further reflection, leads to the man's perception of the validity/intelligence of the thoughts or ideas which more often than not eventually lead to bropropriation."[25] Hepeating is when a woman's ideas, suggestions, or contributions are dismissed, trivialized, or ignored and then that same idea is repeated or commandeered by a man whose idea, suggestion, or contribution is then heard, applauded, and acknowledged.[26] The "Mathilda effect" is a moniker coined to define situations when a woman's "discoveries and research [are credited] to male peers."[27]

> **Jean**: As a woman in the central administrative office of a large school system, headed at the time by a male Superintendent, I often felt that I needed to be assertive and clear in order for my perspective to be counted. Often I would make a statement at a meeting that would be ignored. When my male colleague reiterated what I said, he was heard. That was frustrating! That behavior was more typical of the superintendent than of my immediate male supervisor.
>
> **Lydia**: Very early in my career, I had an experience in which a colleague took credit for my work. It set me back on my heels and made me second guess all of my decisions so that I would 'get the credit' I deserved. It certainly got in the way of future decisions. Like all experiences, I learned that being so invested to get the credit was counter to the mission of serving children well.
>
> **Natalie**: I work in a suburban public school system that is progressive in thought. As a woman, I am hyper-aware of my gender and it can be frustrating to see ideas dismissed or have to strategize around how to approach a situation. There is also the annoying question how much I can take on while I work on my doctorate. Men also working toward their doctorate have had children and been promoted while I have been told to take it easy and focus.

Kelly discusses both the burden of, and opportunity stemming from, community expectations. Collective endorsement "refers to the process whereby an individual's leader identity is recognized by the wider community. Thus, leadership is about the construction of a relationship or relationships."[28]

> **Kelly**: As a Latinx leader in education, my background is both a positive and negative it feels. I know inherently I occupy space that very few people of my background are in and I want to expand that space and I also acknowledge the toll that role has. Especially when your decisions have ripple effects on communities that you have deep ties to. Having to balance the objectivity of the role (focus on the goals/project) vs thinking how will this be received, what are the long term impacts, will hurt be caused by this … sometimes feel like there is no right answer.

Double jeopardy is when Black women "suffer the effects of both gender and racial prejudice … according to this perspective, black women are often marginalized or ignored because they are not seen as prototypical members of both their racial group, where black men are prototypical, and their gender group, where white women are prototypical."[29] The following two respondents express this challenge.

> **Jaimie**: Race has affected my leadership, because many times despite me being the leader, I was still seen as being in a subordinate role (despite my knowledge it appeared that my Caucasian colleagues would get credit for my work and ideas) … My salary was also affected due to race, gender and ethnicity. My white male colleague who held the same position as me with less leadership experiences, education and degrees was paid more than I was for doing the same job … I also believe that stereotypes of black women have affected my leadership, when I speak up for equity, high expectations, inclusive practices, and justice for all students' families in the school district, and "leaned in" to ensure students received what they needed to succeed, it was met with the "angry black woman stereotype" or I was seen as "trouble."
>
> **Lara**: As a Black female, I am met with double discrimination by men and women, definitely by Black and white men, even more by matriarchal white women.

A good woman equates with "not being demanding, loud, or expressing her own needs"[30] and as I share earlier, a double bind "requires women to be communal and to avoid directive and assertive behavior. So, a dominant manner places women at risk of being disliked and can undermine their ability to wield influence."[31] Sharon and Tang remark about such leadership dilemmas.

> **Sharon**: As a woman, I must be impeccable in my practice at all times and my voice has been marginalized in conversations and decision making throughout my career. When I have gently pushed back or "leaned-in," it has been viewed as being difficult. This marginalization has been both by men and women.
>
> **Tang**: As a woman, I feel that I can't be perceived as being overly confident or overly competent, otherwise I'm not received as being trustworthy. There is a delicate balance for me, as a woman. For me to be effective, I need to balance intelligence and competence with a good dose of humility and vulnerability. Again, knowing which cards to play is important; otherwise, you run the risk of being misunderstood as a leader and potentially become a scapegoat unnecessarily.

Ellie and Wilma share their experience with imposter syndrome, which is "characterized as insecurity about their abilities, and feeling less competent, prepared, and accomplished than their peers."[32]

> **Ellie**: I am a White, first generation, Cuban American, who has always dealt with feeling imposter syndrome.
>
> **Wilma**: Growing up, I never considered myself a leader because I didn't see others that looked like me in leadership roles. I figured that, if I was a leader, someone would tell me. No one ever really did … As a result, I feel like I got a late start on my conscious leadership journey.

Perceptions about women include their soft approach. Stacey Vanek Smith (2021) describes the overuse of softeners as "'all the extra words and qualifiers and smiley face and apologies women tend to use when communicating' and … may cause people to be less 'inclined to take your softened ideas seriously, even if they do listen to them.'"[33] Angela spoke about this dilemma.

> **Angela**: In my current position and in a majority of leadership fields I have worked in, being a woman has always been a challenge. I am often seen as incompetent or too soft to make decisions. When in actuality, I am simply respecting everyone's opinion.

For me, continuously balancing myriad forces required me to interpret, navigate, mediate, and adjust my own affect and impact. I was—and am—perpetually in a learning and an adapting mode, which can itself be taxing. I balanced my identity along with the responsibility, authority, and power I possessed. This balancing act was required whether I was in state, national, urban school district organizations.

Bullying, Harassment, Racism, and Abuse

Among my respondents, women of all ages, education levels, races, and ethnicities indicate they encountered a variety of unwanted and uncomfortable verbal and physical micro-aggressions and macro-aggressions from their colleagues—including other women. Twenty-eight separate women experienced bullying—the most reported form of discrimination respondents experienced. Racism was the next most prevalent with nineteen separate women having experienced racism. Sixteen separate respondents experienced harassment and eleven experienced abuse. Respondents indicate whether they experienced such forms of discrimination and also the agent of the action—a male peer, a female peer, a peer group of two or more peers, a senior level male, a senior level female, or senior-level group.

I define bullying as intimidation, threats, belittling comments about ability or appearance, microaggressions, and jokes made at someone's expense. Harassment includes sexual innuendo, sexual jokes made in one's presence, overt sexual requests, comments about appearance that were sexual in nature, forced physical contact one interpreted as sexual in nature, or quid pro quo (sexual) requests tied to workplace opportunities or promotion. For this survey's purpose, I define racism as racial or ethnic innuendo, racial or ethnic jokes, overt racial or ethnic comments that were derogatory in nature, or racial or ethnic threats. I define abuse as verbal abuse that created fear for one's physical safety and forced physical contact interpreted as physically threatening.

These and other forms of discrimination link to power dynamics and workplace cultures that may tolerate—if not enable—such treatment.[34] Similarly, when the notion of such treatment is viewed as an individualized experience, rather than one endemic or attributable to a system, it can result in the recipient of the discrimination feeling that they them self must address the situation or the perpetrator rather than the onus for change residing with an organization's leadership team. Respondents and my own experiences highlight some ways in which women mitigate their own discomfort, humiliation, frustration, confusion, guilt, and hurt. A recipient may feel powerless to change the situation.[35] Soraya Chemaly (2018) speaks to the role of power and its link to hostile and toxic work environments:

> Harassment is never an issue solely of individual experiences. Environments that tolerate harassment are, almost always, more broadly hostile and toxic. People who harass in the workplace are not sex addicts or people with poor dating skills; they are abusers of power and of people. They badger and cajole, joke and flatter, trade in unnerving hints and innuendo. They rely on gender-role expectations, silence, and status gaps, as well as their targets' economic and professional needs, to ensure a lack of consequences. Mainly, however, they leverage widespread social tolerance for their behavior and their ability to flip the switch on multiple overlapping networks that institutionalize perpetrator perspectives: the law, religion, media, and schools.[36]

Another prevalent barrier is the stress women experience in leadership roles. Stressors can involve balancing work and family, navigating constant scrutiny, and attempting to monitor and mediate the impressions one makes. Women leaders may experience a lack of belonging as they navigate bias and harassment, maintain different identities simultaneously, make career compromises to accommodate their male partners, and sacrifice time needed to care for themselves. They also might strive for perfection at home and work and feel guilty about time at work away from family or time with family away from work. They may blame themselves for structural and systemic discrimination or for being too confident or not confident enough, while others may blame the women for holding themselves back and not leaning in sufficiently.[37]

It was my hope that my experience, primarily with bullying and harassment, would be an exception among women leaders. It is not. Respondents' answers daylight situations that belie the intent of civil rights' laws and human resource policies designed to protect women and marginalized groups from unwanted, inappropriate, illegal, and discriminatory attention and practices. Again, twenty-eight separate women experienced bullying, nineteen experienced racism, sixteen separate respondents experienced harassment, and eleven experienced abuse. These respondents' and my own experiences underscore incidences of workplace toxicity and negativity even in female-dominated workplaces.

Angela, an independent school leader, Jean, a former school district leader, and Sharon, a superintendent, address this dilemma:

> **Angela**: I made the decision to file a formal complaint against my former boss to HR knowing that my job could also be at risk. My job thought giving me a new boss would stop my former boss from harassing me, but it didn't stop. I endured 6 years of this bullying and I had enough. The impact it made was significant!
>
> **Jean**: When I was harassed or bullied I moved away, changed the subject, ignored, and/or reasserted my position—depending on the situation … When I pushed back against verbal bullying by a female supervisor, she would not acknowledge her behavior and basically indicated that if I didn't like it, I could leave. I did. Ultimately I left the school system position when I was tired of being mistreated by a female supervisor … I should have more directly said a firm "No" to the superintendent for inappropriate touching (of my neck), instead I would quickly stiffen and move away … The organization ignored everything … The organization could have made clear to all employees—professional and nonprofessional—that there were policies and practices in place to protect them from abusive behavior of any kind and very overtly welcomed people coming forward to report in appropriate, abuse behavior.
>
> **Sharon**: Oppression, bullying, harassment, and abuse of women has been a regular part of everyday experience and I have tried to educate offenders

and most recently removed a popular white male principal for these behaviors. The blow back publicly, especially by white men and some women, who received advantages and privileges by this male leader, was intense and there is still a faction of white male politicians that want to "take me down" in town ... No matter how much I advocate or stand up against the injustices faced by minority populations, it seems like I am often left standing alone when collective action and visible push back is necessary.

Many of the respondents mention handling something themselves, which is laudable. But why is it that the recipient of bad behavior and malintent must address it them self? It is exhausting, which is why I believe several respondents—along with myself—chose to depart toxic workplace environments and colleagues. I could suggest that we leave all toxic workplaces behind, but then I doubt many of these environments would change. Zelda addresses this issue.

Zelda: Is it my job to address other peoples' ignorance when I'm the target of their ignorance? Sometimes I'm not in a place to put up a fight and often I don't have the energy to try to change their mind.

Recall the definition of weathering, which depicts one's ongoing experience with psychosocial hardships—including discrimination—and can lead to "worse wear and tear effects" on mental and physical health including premature aging and depression.[38]

Women shouldn't feel unsafe when they daylight inaction or penalized when they express a concern or lodge a complaint about macro-aggressions and micro-aggressions. Organizational leaders, leadership teams, and those responsible for organizational culture can better equip themselves to address such complaints, become allies, and recognize when a structure, practice, culture, or person is unfair to a particular individual or group. These situations may be murky such as the case with bullying, microaggressions, or a "he said/she said situation." Yet all such situations require fair and confidential investigations and consistently applied strategies so that one coworker or group of coworkers cannot cause another coworker or group of coworkers to feel uncomfortable, unsafe, thwarted from contributing, or closed out of opportunities for growth and advancement.

Bullying

Respondents report that bullying is the most frequent form of workplace discrimination they encountered. Unfortunately, bullies may be those with whom we work and are often expected to build collegial relationships. Reese speaks to this issue.

> **Reese**: There's a small handful of individuals who commit micro-aggressions fairly frequently … our organization's response has been tepid at best. I don't think we know how to handle the instances of 'light' bullying in the form of micro-aggressions … I have been belittled/bullied by a slightly more senior-level female who is White. They mostly show up as a micro-aggressions and little slights that are passive-aggressive.

In regard to bullying, not unlike my own workplace experience, twenty-eight separate women report they experienced bullying inflicted by one or more of their coworkers—a male peer, a female peer, a peer group of two or more peers, a senior level male, a senior level female, or senior-level group. At least one third or more of respondents say they experienced bullying by a male peer (thirteen), a female peer (thirteen), a more senior-level male (fifteen), or a more senior-level female (sixteen) (see Table 4.1). Six of the eight women who identify as Hispanic note they experienced bullying. Of these respondents, two also identify as white, one as Black, and three as other. All five of the women who identify as mixed or other experienced bullying; six of the eight women who identify as Black did so; both of the women who identify as Asian did so; and fifteen of the twenty-two women who identify as white experienced bullying (two of them also identify as Hispanic).

As Dweck (2006) maintains, "Bullying is about judging. It's about establishing who is worthy or important."[39] Bullies often possess a fixed mindset. Dweck discusses why people with fixed mindsets are also bullies: "for those with the

Table 4.1 Respondents' Experience with Bullying

Reasons	37 Respondents	Dr. Carlisle's Response
By a male peer	13	1
By a female peer	13	1
By a peer group (two or more)	6	1
By a more senior-level male	15	1
By a more senior-level female	16	1
By a more senior-level group (two or more)	5	1

fixed mindset, success is about establishing their superiority, pure and simple."[40] I mention earlier in the book that I encountered bullying in both staff-level and leadership roles. Recall Bud, who was also an underminer and blocker of colleagues, his own supervisor, and the collective agenda. He knew all the organization and its individuals' secrets. Consistent with someone who follows the transactional leadership model, I equate underminers with possessing zero-sum approaches—another's position, project, success, contributions, or new initiative become a direct threat to the underminer or their own sense of self, position, or power level.

They may disparage, block, backstab, question, calculate, contradict, gossip, and position and not want things to change—particularly the power, position, or recognition they possess; and their own identification with, and narratives about, the organization or their past organizational accomplishments. When initiating a change, I seek to convey that we wouldn't be where we are today, if we hadn't experienced what came before. Thus demonstrating how the change builds on existing practice(s). There are things Bud said in front of groups of his direct reports about our boss that were patronizing and discrediting. Bud also acted as a saboteur when not complying with grant agreements and disproportionately allocating resources and assigning students thus ensuring a project's failure. He also spread negative information about the rationale for and likely success of a new initiative and deliberately withheld vital information and resources from colleagues and organizational leaders. When I communicated with him, I rewrote my emails multiple times and asked a colleague to read them to ensure I was dispassionate (this after losing it—much to my chagrin—over email with him a couple of times). When an in-person negotiation was necessary, I envisioned a rope bridge that extended from my office to his (on the other side of the building) and traversed along it to reach his office. During this time, I peppered my computer passwords with terms like bully or jerk.

Bud—given my outsider status and the relational power I held—often targeted me. I recall my first undermining (and bullying) experience with him, which was when an organizational leader charged me with the redesign of a consequential and cross-departmental process. I was still new to the organization and not yet serving on the organization's leadership team. A critical component of this process involved me facilitating a large cross-departmental committee to develop and reach consensus on a new process. Bud and another of his long-term colleagues sat in the back of the room interrupting me, contradicting me, and making jokes. They laughed and belittled. It was tough to keep my composure as someone new to the organization and charged with a very public and difficult assignment. I laughed. I redirected. I built consensus among the others. We were all embarrassed.

Racism

Racism is the next most prevalent form of discrimination that respondents report encountering. Overall, nineteen separate women say they experienced racism inflicted by colleagues or supervisors. Thirteen respondents indicate they experienced racism by a male peer, sixteen from a female peer, ten by a more senior level male, ten by a more senior level female, and six by a more senior level group (see Table 4.2). Five of the eight women who identify as Hispanic experienced racism. Of these respondents, two also identify as white and three of as mixed or other. All five women who identify as mixed or other experienced racism; five of the eight women who identify as Black did so; both of the women who identify as Asian did so; and seven of the twenty-two women who identify as white (two of them also identified as Hispanic) experienced racism.

I cannot personally speak to how a person of color experiences the negative impact of racism, its prejudices, and its stereotypes. I am however aware of and knowledgeable about its systemic and structural consequences, which are societal, political, physical, psychosocial, environmental, educational, and economic. A white, affluent, college-educated male, who I call "John," challenged me about the very notion of white privilege—he said, "I'm not privileged." I tried to explain that just because he possesses privilege; it does not mean John did not work hard for what he's achieved. It means I said, that our privilege grants us higher status, greater access, and a far greater likelihood of achieving the American Dream than is the case for people of color, people who speak a language other than

Table 4.2 Respondents' Experience with Racism

Reasons	37 Respondents	Dr. Carlisle's Response
By a male peer	13	0
By a female peer	16	0
By a peer group (two or more)	8	0
By a more senior-level male	10	0
By a more senior-level female	10	1
By a more senior-level group (two or more)	6	0

English at home, people who have a disability, people whose parents did not attend college, and immigrants. I understand that my privilege encompasses my whiteness, my upper middle-class status, my upbringing with two parents who earned advanced degrees, and my own possession of an advanced degree. Such factors position me among a very small percentage of the population. Yet I spent most of my career trying to affect positive change for students of color. This placed me in environments where I can easily be perceived as an outsider—as someone who lacks an understanding of the complex web of circumstances that marginalized students and families encounter.

Admittedly, I spent a significant part of my career promulgating neoliberal policies, which apply private market principles to educational change making. Neoliberalism implies that it is up to the individual to change their circumstance rather than the system (laws, regulations, policies, and practices).[41] While my mission is steadfastly focused on eradicating these inequities, I recognize that many of my own, my colleagues, and my organizations' efforts lacked their desired impact due to the structural and systemic nature of the educational inequities. Many of the reforms didn't adequately involve those whose circumstances we wished to change or help. The recipients' true lived experiences weren't typically incorporated into solutions. We did not dismantle biased structures. Nonetheless, I continue to try to move these systems and structures and seek to do so from various vantage points, to continue learning, and to employ a reflective practice.

Seven white women respondents report that they experienced racism. While I feel uncomfortable identifying anything that a white person encounters as racism, I know I experienced what could be referred to as backlash. Once, when presenting to a board of education, a Black school board member who also served as a community leader, said, "I don't believe we should be leading this initiative and I don't believe a skinny white woman should be representing us." I took a deep breath in part because I'd voiced my own concerns about the district leading such a broad community initiative and my appointment to lead the initiative. I also took a deep breath because of the collective gasp from other board members, audience members, and the superintendent. I gestured to the superintendent not to intervene, said to the board member, "Thank you for letting me know how you feel," and finished my presentation. Such situations are frustrating and uncomfortable. This frustration is present even with my awareness of and knowledge about systemic and structural racism, its effects, and the need for organizations dedicated to fairness and social justice to demonstrate their commitment through tangible action. My discomfort stems from my awareness of the complex nature of, and my commitment to, allyship. I'm committed to social justice, I'm taking direct action, and I'm an ally—albeit someone who occasionally blunders by presupposing that marginalized people understand that I operate with good intent.

Harassment

In earlier chapters, I share examples related to mediating one's—and my own—femininity while presenting as a leader but not one who is either too agentic or too communal such that I would rock the boat. I rocked it anyway (I can still hear the splashes). Often this balancing act involved moderating my dress, hair, jewelry, posture, and tone of voice—all adjustments designed to deflect unwanted male attention and female hostility. Yet, for the most part I was nice, which saddled me with its own pros and cons—just because I'm nice and respectful toward others and have a sense of humor does not mean I seek unwanted physical attention or wish to insinuate myself into someone's good graces to gain power.

Harassment for me started at a young age and continued through to my leadership roles. The first time I experienced harassment was at sixteen when working at a movie theater. The married thirtyish manager regularly pinched my bottom. He kissed me after pushing me up against a projector in a production booth. My coworkers surrounded me when he was near in attempts to shield me from his unwanted advances. They were my allies. I doubt there was any recourse for me other than quitting. From there, I continued to encounter various forms of harassment—from a sixtyish manager putting his arm around me when he wanted to give me feedback to a cook putting his hands around my waist when he squeezed by me in a tight space to a colleague on a leadership team asking me if we would share a room on a retreat. This doesn't encompass the bullying that typically followed when I spoke up for myself. The cook did not like it one bit when my nineteen-year-old-self told him to "get your fucking hands off me." By that stage in my short work life, I was disgusted. He threw every order back at me for illegibility. The leadership team colleague—who suggested we share a room at a retreat, put his arm around my waist, and often broke into my personal space—belittled me in meetings.

Sixteen separate respondents state they experienced harassment. Eleven respondents indicate they experienced harassment by a male peer and eight by a more senior level male (see Table 4.3). Four of the eight of the women who identify as Hispanic experienced harassment; three of the five women who

Table 4.3 Respondents' Experience with Harassment

Reasons	37 Respondents	Dr. Carlisle's Response
By a male peer	11	1
By a female peer	3	0
By a peer group (two or more)	2	0
By a more senior-level male	8	1
By a more senior-level female	4	0
By a more senior-level group (two or more)	3	0

identify as mixed or other did so; three of the eight women who identify as Black did so; one of the two women who identify as Asian experienced harassment; and nine of the twenty-two women who identify as white experienced harassment (two of them also identify as Hispanic). Michelle comments on her experience harassment:

> **Michelle**: [I] was in a meeting where I was the only female and one of the males made a sexual-innuendo joke. I told the leader of the meeting that the joke made me uncomfortable and was not appropriate. He asked if I wanted the issue to be reported to HR and I said no, that first the individual needed to be spoken to and have explained to him why that kind of conversation should not have occurred.

She is not alone.

Abuse

When compared to the other discriminatory practices, the fewest number of respondents report they encountered abuse. I ask about abuse in large part given the *Me Too* movement. Whereas my definition includes unwanted touching, which I encountered, none of it seriously threatened my position or safety. I chalk the unwanted touching experiences up to harassment.

Nonetheless this category is the most egregious offense one could encounter on the job, in the gym, or in the doctor's office. Overall, eleven separate women say they experienced abuse. Four respondents indicate they experienced abuse by a male peer and six by a more senior level male (see Table 4.4). Just one of the eight of women who identifies as Hispanic—and as other—indicates she

Table 4.4 Respondents' Experience with Abuse

Reasons	37 Respondents	Dr. Carlisle's Response
By a male peer	4	0
By a female peer	1	0
By a peer group (two or more)	0	0
By a more senior-level male	6	0
By a more senior-level female	3	0
By a more senior-level group (two or more)	3	0

experienced abuse; two of the five who identify as mixed or other (one of whom also identifies as Hispanic) did so; two of the eight women who identify as Black experienced abuse; none of those who identify as Asian say they experienced abuse; and seven of the twenty-two women who identify as white share they experienced abuse.

Reflections on Bullying, Harassment, Racism, and Abuse

Many of the respondents who experienced or observed bullying, abuse, harassment, or racism say they addressed it—via confrontation, reporting, education, or legal means—inadequately at the time. They report they'd do so in a timelier, calmer, more strategic, or different manner in the future. Some express regret for not directly addressing the behavior. Still others feel their race, gender, position, or the organization's structures, practices, and culture negatively influenced their willingness to step forward. They didn't possess the power or wherewithal needed.

If respondents were on the receiving end of the offense, many report that they employed tactics such as ignoring the behavior, avoiding the person, and talking to peers about it. Several also stuck to their convictions when the offense was about an action they'd taken (such as advocating for students of color, for themselves, or their voice to be heard), or ultimately left the organization. If they observed the offense, the ways in which some respondents indicate they took direct action included addressing the person privately or offering support to the offended person (allyship). They also elevated the concern especially when it occurred more than once, documented it, reported it, and even dismissed a leader popular in the community and then suffered public consequences. Several respondents report experiencing loss of respect or promotional opportunities because of speaking up.

I chose to complain to my supervisor about my bully. While my supervisor spoke with Bud on several occasions, he downplayed the negative dynamics between us as a Jana–Bud problem and I did not bring the situation to human resources. Others also encountered such situations.

> **Dionne**: Bullying can be difficult to prove and the culture did not always deal with it.
>
> **Kelly**: When I was in the position of being bullied, I shared with a few of my close colleagues and tried to find ways to mediate it on my own. I did not feel comfortable sharing the incident with my manager given how the organization viewed the bully and they [the bully] were constantly praised for their results.

Respondents indicate that leaders and organizational responses ranged from discouraging the respondents from reporting a complaint to requiring the individual to navigate the bullying herself to brushing off the complaint to actively pitting people against one another. Other responses included actions like forming committees or allocating resources to a remedy—such as to the provision of education and training or the dissemination of information. Some respondents report cases where upper management was party to the microaggressions while others indicate that actual investigations and consequences were undertaken. Unfortunately, there were more instances of dissatisfaction with the organization's response than there were instances of satisfaction.

Respondents identify methods—some of which were welcome and some seen as inadequate—for navigating such situations with agency, confidence, and integrity. Respondents note the impact of organizational culture, leadership, action, and allyship on these issues. Some indicate they spoke up. Others express guilt over their own inability to act and self-silencing behaviors. Others tried redirection, modifying their own behavior, or removing themselves from the situation. Others left their organizations. Still others describe the impact of positional power.

> **Diane**: Part of the reason I never bought it to the organization is because they did not have a good track record in addressing issues like this. I am unsure if I felt safe to bring it to the organization.

Diedre: In most of the cases, calling people out, in a private and respectful way, generally caused the person to reflect and see why this was not okay, but there were often the people who felt I was "PC" and now they had to "walk on eggshells around me" … In my personal example, had my concerns not been brushed aside, I think fewer people would have had to suffer from this colleague's behaviors. After I left, there was a suit brought against the district and the district had to pay damages. That could have been addressed earlier … In the cases where I personally experienced it, I talked to the offender and then when it persisted, to our supervisor/superintendent. It was not taken seriously at the time … The supervisor has since admitted it should have been taken more seriously and they feel badly they did not do anything to address it, realizing the person created a reign of terror bullying and harassing people across the district. No one had ever brought it to the superintendent's attention before. It wasn't until the superintendent was retiring that people came and shared other examples of the behavior. Where I have witnessed it happening to others, it was with peers. I have spoken to the offender and offered to be an ally to the offended if they wanted to report it.

Dionne: As a department chair, I had a principal bully me … He wanted a "yes" person and not someone who was willing to innovate, try new things and ask questions … Honestly I am not sure what I could have done. I saw a pattern of abuse that this person was able to perpetrate at no costs to their livelihood and they got promoted while colleagues had concerns. At the end of that school year, ironically, my principal was moved to another building. This was not due to my encounter. The organization saw the lack of leadership and need for change. Instead of dealing with it head on, they just moved him to another building.

Jackie: I believe our principal pitted people against each other, which was wrong. He also sort of let the teachers fend for themselves and hash it out. As an administrator, he couldn't really involve himself in the formal decision-making process … The issue shouldn't have been an issue for so long. It seems like discussions dragged on and on and people became more and more angry. It was not good for students.

Jaimie: Verbal abuse [came from my] immediate Supervisor [who] wanted me to take responsibility for something unethical and I refused, so he came to my office and yelled at me it was so loud that the HR manager came to my office to check on me.

Joan: I have not always taken action when the bullying is directly towards me. I have chosen to report it sometimes and others I have just decided to leave the organization.

Leslie: I wish I could have reported the individual without having to wait for others to go first. Unfortunately, I did not feel that my claim would be taken as seriously due to my race and position. SADLY, I knew that white women "sounding the alarm" would cause concern and generate action.

Lottie: I recall one instance when an HR Director was abusing [someone applying to become] a VP. This situation was addressed by the CEO, although not entirely to my satisfaction. This person was not promoted to a VP because of the HR Director; instead he was promoted to an Associate VP because the CEO was not strong enough to confront the HR Director for her bias towards this individual.

Mathilda: Educational organizations are so bureaucratic that you feel helpless when you are in it. There's also so much ambiguity around these terms that it's hard to prove … In some instances, I have just let it go … In some instances, I have confronted the senior-level people by having a private conversation with them. When I have taken this action, I have been put in a position where I am not afforded job interviews for positions where I know I was the most qualified candidate and was labeled as not being a "team player." There was also one instance where I went to HR and was told, "the person is your supervisor and she can do whatever she wants" I ended up leaving that organization … More times than not they go through a checklist of acting like the investigate it, but it has been my experience that most times there is no finding and the behavior continues with no hope of addressing it.

Rachel: [I] spoke up to parties that were directly involved and documented incidents that were inappropriate to those who could remedy the situations … Unfortunately, most times situations were not adequately addressed and colleagues brushed off experiences or just dealt with them.

Sonja: I was explicitly told by my managers to not file a grievance because it would not result in anything other than trouble for me, based upon the previous history at our organization of folks who have issued grievances against people in higher-up roles.

Tang: In the past, I silenced myself and attempted to ignore the interaction when it was too painful to deal with at work. Avoiding it and oppressing my feelings was how I learned how to manage my feelings.

Tanya: I spoke up on behalf of the person, confronted the person doing them harm and reported the situation to those who could help more than I could. I also followed up to assure the person got the aid they required.

Wilma: Honestly, I don't think I ever handled it directly. If I did address such issues, I did it in a very passive-aggressive manner because that was all I knew at the time. I did things like going behind a superior's back to do what I felt to be right, despite being told not to do so. I also would talk to others in the workplace about what was happening to me, in the hopes of rallying support. I can't think of a time when I directly addressed an issue that I experienced. What would happen is that I would eventually get tired of dealing with the situation and I would find a new job and move on.

Zelda: It was not addressed because the people who were the leaders are the ones who often did not recognize their own micro aggressions.

It upsets me that so many respondents describe female-dominated (or any) work environments as hostile. Respondents suggest that human resource departments should proactively clarify their role, structures, practices, reporting steps, and common definitions for issues and complaints relating to abuse, bullying, harassment, and racism. While some of these suggestions may seem like common—and even best—practices, which should already be in place, organizational leaders should ensure they implement such practices with fidelity and significantly bolster them. Carolyn Shields (2017) speaks to the importance of addressing the misuse of power, which she says requires:

> Tremendous moral courage, for it often means going against the norms of the group within which one was raised or with which one is living or working ... Moral courage that enables leaders not only to critique inequity but also to move forward, ensuring the promise of a better future for all ... To exhibit moral courage, one must often be explicit. It is not enough to simply work quietly to address racism, homophobia, or other inequities. One must be seen to take a stand and to be making progress.[42]

All this tells me that leadership teams and human resource departments should work harder to create—and be more accountable for creating—safe, trusting, and transparent environments for people from all backgrounds and profiles. In addition to clearly defining and enforcing policies, behaviors, and consequences regarding bullying, harassment, racism, and discrimination, leaders can allocate adequate resources for supporting implementation of antidiscrimination strategies and for monitoring implementation effectiveness. Respondents make note of organizational strategies as follows:

Billie: I think that additional deep professional learning about these topics, and a clear focus from the very top of the organization are critical.

Jaimie: They should have promoted a culture of inclusion, created goals and followed through around the issues, have courageous conversations, have a culture of no-tolerance for such behaviors and project that everyone mattered and needed to treat each other like human beings each other for the success of the district.

Lara: [The organization should have] had an Ombudsman dedicated to addressing workplace bullying, harassment, and abuse with a mechanism for follow up that was discrete for those involved but transparent in outcomes enough that it signaled that there is accountability and consistency … The response has been inconsistent. When reports have been filed or informally when behavior has been observed, sometimes it has been addressed, other times, it has been ignored … I would have documented the incidents and made as many people aware of what was going on as possible. My silence enabled "them" to get away with what they were doing for a long period of time with not just me but probably others with little to no accountability.

Michelle: Organizations must make these issues priorities and find the resources to ensure the message is given the time and the opportunity to become engrained across the system.

Tang: I think it's important for schools (organizations) to be transparent and share with employees the channels for reporting this type of behavior.

Wilma: There are so many ways that some of my past organizations could have handled issues of injustice. The Human Resources department should have built stronger relationships with staff and been unbiased in the addressing of these issues. Policies and procedures could have been communicated more clearly to ensure that all staff knew their rights. Regular training could have been provided to staff as well. I should have been direct and straightforward … I should have used the resources at my disposal internally to advocate for myself and others … Because the bullying and harassment were coming from the management, there was no one to check that behavior and address it.

At a minimum, such strategies can include appointing neutral third parties to whom complaints are taken and by whom they'd be investigated, conducting regular training, and delivering onboarding that addresses these issues and how to handle and report them. Deeper efforts could include incorporating respectful treatment of others into performance evaluations including the leadership team, making public the aggregated evaluation evaluations, and avoiding appointments of singletons (or onlys) from a marginalized group to a team or department. Leaders can shut down disrespectful, silencing, and belittling behavior when it occurs. Additionally, organizations can positively reward those who demonstrate allyship and contribute to Diversity, Equity, and Inclusion (DEI) efforts. Zelda speaks to this issue.

> **Zelda**: Talk about racism and bullying and harassment can only happen authentically when there is a culture that has mutual trust and respect. Without trust and respect, any professional development or discussion remains at a surface level. Everyone must be willing to be introspective and vulnerable in order for difficult conversations to be heard. Too often organizations do not lay the groundwork for that to happen.

DEI and anti-racism (and/or anti-sexism) each connote different levels of action and moral courage on the part of organizational leaders. Diversity has to do with numerical objectives such as hiring more women or more people of color. Equity has to with conditions and treatments that are fair and result in similar access and outcomes across groups—whether racial, ethnic, or gender. Inclusion focuses on environments, which welcome, value, include, and encourage participation from people who represent all types of backgrounds. Anti-racism requires the greatest level of moral courage and action because it focuses on challenging and addressing—in real time—racist structures, practices, and cultures that perpetuate the notion that people of different races are not equal and inequities based on race. Similarly, being anti-sexist requires people who see gender bias in systems and interactions to speak up, intervene, and take action to change such biases. Allyship is critical to women's success in educational leadership roles.

Transformational Resilience

Sometimes colleagues and supervisors questioned my motives, decision-making, and place in the organization. I encountered identity microaggressions when my work cut across different parts of the organizations and into colleagues' areas of responsibility. In earlier chapters, I share some of the fraught cross-organizational and cross-partner projects with which my supervisors or boards charged me. Naively, I thought my roles, commitment to collaboration, pantsuits, and project scopes conveyed that I possessed authority to identify problems and generate solutions, regardless of which departments and leaders the recommendations affected.

On occasion, a supervisor questioned my approach because another leadership team member complained about me. Alternatively, a colleague could question whether I knew or understood what a project scope entailed. Once, a supervisor wanted to reduce my role from what a prior leader had sanctioned. Another supervisor interpreted my job description differently than he had described it. This same supervisor wanted to know about and authorize every decision I made, thus chipping away at my ability to perform my job. I knew colleagues who assumed I pursued various analyses because of a desire to possess power rather than to solve complex and matrixed problems.

Examples involving two different women supervisors, both women of color, follow. These women served initially as mentors before deciding I wasn't loyal enough to them because of something they perceived I did or didn't do. One of these women supervisors—who I call "Mariana" and who worked at the senior most organizational level, and to whom I reported—recruited and promoted me prior to a new leader taking the organizational helm. I had a prior working relationship with the new leader who quickly promoted me to the same level as Mariana. At multiple leadership team meetings, Mariana publicly called into question my new status as her professional peer. I was bewildered, because I thought I was just doing my job and could now do it with a broader impact and a different type of credibility. It took me awhile to realize—or accept—that Mariana's coded disparagement of me wasn't coded at all—she truly was speaking disrespectfully of me with relish and the intention of publicly discrediting me. I now know that referring to Mariana as a queen bee is apropos. This moniker is ascribed to women typically already at the top of an organization, who may possess token status (be the only one, or one of a few, of their ethnic, racial, or gender background), and who actively sabotage and target other women, because they often want to protect their own token status and thus see other women as competition.[43]

The other leader, who I call "Gabriela," accused me of undermining her because of a rumor she heard about something confidential I supposedly shared. Even after learning that the other person already possessed the information, which Gabriela accused me of divulging, she blamed me. This situation was more difficult because I truly valued our relationship. Gabriela provided me with actionable, on-point, and timely feedback and we worked effectively together. However, Gabriela made assumptions about my integrity. Neither Mariana nor Gabriela provided me with the opportunity to share my own perspective. They silenced me, which happens frequently to women. Although they were from their own oppressed groups, I wasn't considered as their professional peer. They still had the power to shame me. Ester E. Shapiro and Jennifer M. Leah (2007), say that:

> Institutional and interpersonal processes preserving an oppressive status quo count on our co-operation by calling forth deeply internalized messages and self-in-relation schemas in which we deserve reprimand, or preserve polite silence, or focus on our imperfections, or feel deeply shamed by mistakes.[44]

"Norm" was a supervisor whose microaggressions were also of the silencing and disregarding nature. If Norm walked into my office and my radio was playing softly, he told me to turn it off. Alternatively, when we were discussing an issue and Norm wanted me to stop contributing, he made a sound like hsszzt and a pinching motion with his fingers. Imagine a grown professional man treating a grown professional woman as I do my cat when I don't want him to scratch the couch. The following Chemaly (2018) quote comes to mind: "We learn to expect women to speak less, so when we talk, it always seems like we are talking too much."[45]

Other attempts at silencing and disregard—along with attempts to make me feel othered and as an imposter—were semi-veiled in questions like, "Why are *you* involved in the redesign of this process?" Or, "What can *you* possibly know about how to change the design of schools?" (Code for "*You've* never worked in a school building.") One colleague (Bud) challenged me when I made a statement about how to effectively work with community members and parents, because I'd not been awoken at 5:00 a.m. by a concerned or angry parent or I hadn't run a school and managed community partners within a building. Yet I've visited numerous schools and classrooms to learn and teach others about their practices, managed numerous community and parent groups, and calmed irate parents and community members, often because someone at a school failed to do so.

Another time a team's leader (Nancy) seemed to hire people for their names, prior positions, and their domain expertise but not necessarily for their understanding of, or ability to navigate, leadership or the sector in which we were employed. I informally coached and mentored several of these people. Nancy said I was too nice and that if these new people couldn't make the transition, they should leave. Nancy effectively silenced me for being too nice and silenced the others for being too slow to adapt to her expectations.

Once, I found myself in a meeting with someone who had a leadership role in special education, who I will call "Julie." Julie publicly responded to something I said or did as follows: "Oh that would be your ADHD [Attention Deficit Hyperactivity Disorder] talking Jana," which insinuated I was incapable of focusing, planning, organizing, and balancing a variety of tasks due to hyperactivity or inattention. Planning was in my title and was my core area of responsibility. I don't recall if Julie ever apologized but there were plenty of times when someone would attempt to discredit me in public and feign an apology in private. My father calls this a public humiliation and private apology. It doesn't count because the damage has been done.

One situation with a peer, who I will call "Sally," involved a different type of personal attack. We'd just returned from a national conference where I'd spent time networking. Sally attacked me for showing a side of myself that she didn't like. I suppose she perceived me as being self-promoting. Reflecting on that conversation, and during and immediately following the argument, I felt embarrassed, defensive, and angry that my motives seemed calculating. I knew networking to be a strategic approach. I unfortunately didn't handle the feedback or accusation well because I got vocally angry with Sally. I raised my voice. I see now that my overt networking (as well as the anger I showed her) ran against type—I was displaying agentic characteristics! Women are not supposed to show anger. Chemaly (2018) cautions that, "we learn as girls to read faces and other body indicators, and we develop tactics for lowering the temperature of encounters, a process known as de-escalation"[46] but also we learn to suppress our true emotions.

Notably I moved my family of five to a different part of the country for a role in a coveted organization for which there was a line around the block for each position (figuratively speaking). This organization paid relocation costs, provided temporary housing while my children finished the school year and my husband sold the house, assigned us a realtor, and provided airfare for my family to house hunt. The family car came to me on a flatbed truck. My five family pets came to me in a van. Prior to these steps, I'd interviewed for a particular position on a particular organizational team and received a job offer. On arrival, I discovered that the division leader was reconfiguring all teams, changing the entire strategy, and replacing division deputies (the people who brought me to the organization and with whom I'd previously partnered). I also didn't know that the average tenure of staff was, at that time, two years' long! I reported to six different supervisors during that period and assumed four distinctly different roles.

Because women are taught from a young age not to rock the boat, I didn't feel comfortable pressing the organization about a variety of details when accepting the role. I effectively engaged in self-silencing deferral, which "can include behaviors such as crying (seen as weakness), acquiescing, smiling, deflection, soothing, shrugging, laughing, giggling."[47] Yet my experience indicates that it is important to feel comfortable asking questions before you leap regardless of where you are going. I should've asked whether there were any major or consequential organizational changes that were planned or underway that may have affected my position or reporting relationship.

I made my second major move—alone and in the opposite direction this time because the kids were in college and my marriage was over—to a place I always thought I wanted to live. It was expensive. It was cold. I found out after starting work at this new organization that it was confronting a shortfall of one third to one half of its multimillion-dollar budget and had no clear plan for making up the shortfall. Its cash cow was cashing out. Still, I tried to help. I developed plausible structural and financial scenarios and sought out new funders and partners. Before I joined that organization, there were questions I should've asked. If I'd asked about its fiscal health, I could've avoided one major move or at least been better prepared for and informed about the challenges. Granted when one is under her own financial strain, relocating for a position, and is suddenly making decisions alone, one's decision-making can be muddled or opaque. Still, it's important to ask the right questions and seriously contemplate the answers even if the placement is expected to provide value.

During this period of fiscal peril, a headhunter approached me about an attractive opportunity, which appeared to resolve much of my own financial distress, provide me with an opportunity to return to urban education, and fulfill my desire to make a difference and live in a warmer, less costly locale. I thought the role was a great fit. In hindsight, I realize I didn't (again) undertake sufficient due diligence but this time it wasn't because of a reorganization or fiscal health. In this case, I didn't call around and ask about my future leader, colleagues, and board's leadership styles; their personal and professional ethics; and their communication and management approaches.

I also ignored a major red flag and pushed my feelings of misgiving aside given my excitement for the position. The red-flag situation occurred before I arrived on the job, but just after my supervisor announced my appointment. The red flag involved a vitriolic and narcissistic board member, a well-formed parent constituency, and their combined commitment to traditional public schools. They thought my sole focus was for every school to become a charter school because I'd worked with charters elsewhere. The departments involved in constructing a response to the outcry over my appointment were departments that would soon report to me and drew on expertise I possessed. My new boss (Bill) didn't want me to get involved in the resolution of the situation. I wasn't consulted about my own defense. This was the red flag. Once in my role, the ill will toward me dogged me regardless of what I did on the organization, the board, or its leader's behalf. In addition, this situation—cutting me out of a decision involving my areas of expertise—was repeated and foretold why I eventually left.

In each of these roles, I worked with and on behalf of great people, learned tremendous amounts about leadership and education, and believe I contributed to the organizations. I would've preferred to enter these roles with my eyes wide open. Those who serve as chiefs or deputy superintendents don't often receive a separation package, are typically at-will employees, serve in roles directly supporting CEOs and superintendents, are often required to relocate, and may take numerous professional risks. After my last high-visibility, highly political leadership role, I found myself with a canceled contract and thirty days of pay and benefits. I'd led projects for fifteen grueling months in the public spotlight. I was in a city to which I relocated for the leadership position, having expected to be there until retirement. During those fifteen months, I started my job a day after ending the prior one, relocated (again), spent several months in corporate housing with my cat who awoke when I returned, and purchased and moved into a condo. After my father returned my thirteen-year-old Labrador to me on move-in day, within months I had her put to sleep due to dementia. (It was undoubtedly one too many relocations for her!) I worked minimally ten-hour days, led several major projects, and tried not to get knocked off my center. I often ate dinner at 9:00 p.m. standing in my kitchen while drinking a glass of wine and reading the news. For breakfast, I ate a yogurt at my desk. I attended one or two meetup events.

When I was finally able to get out of bed and reflect on what I'd accomplished and the reasons for my devastation and trauma, I took stock. I realized that attempting to be a superwoman—who is "someone who tackles both professional and family life with perfection"[48]—was not sustainable. I told myself if I got out of bed and got going by 10:00 a.m., I was resilient and if I got out of bed and got going by 8:00 a.m., I was transformationally resilient. To me this meant I was willing to make lemonade out of lemons! One definition describes resilience "as the ability to adapt or bounce back, so-to-speak, subsequent to adversity and challenge. The term connotes inner strength, competence, optimism, flexibility, and the ability to cope effectively when faced with adversity,"[49] whereas another refers to social resilience as:

> The ability to maintain positive social relationships and effectively lead … [and] as the capacity to foster, engage in, and sustain positive relationships, and to endure and recover from life stressors[50] … Similar to personal resilience, this framework classifies itself among terminologies concerning adapting, transforming, and persistence despite adversity.[51]

I took up paper art. My oldest child refers to this as my art bender. I traveled to Tuscany with my then 84-year-old father, his wife, and five of their friends. I finished my taxes, Christmas shopping, and holiday cards early. I underwent back surgery. I acquired a new mouth guard. I gave away my pantsuits. I moved again. My family and friends provided me with enormous support as did the people who were my direct reports. I recovered. I had hope. I secured a long-term contract that carried me through. I wrote this book, which offers me the opportunity to reflect on and share leadership frameworks, lessons, and strategies. Stephanie Vanek-Smith (2021) recommends that women, women of color, and other marginalized group members wake up to your worth: "feeling the sting of discrimination is hard and painful. But not facing it is worse. Feel the pain, make a plan, and then go back" and start again.[52]

Two of the five categories included in the Center for Creative Leadership's Lessons of Experience (LOE) framework point to the ways in which hardships and personal life experiences can provide leadership lessons. The other three elements include challenging assignments, developmental relationships, and courses and programs.[53] Both hardships and personal experiences affected and informed my leadership approach and contributed to my leadership knowledge. Hardships involve "adverse situations [that] can teach resilience and integrity, compassion for others, and a more balanced approach to life."[54] Hardships include career setbacks, crises, ethical dilemmas, and mistakes. Personal experiences include those things or events, aspects of one's upbringing, and traumas that inform one's leadership approach.[55]

Hardships were part of my leadership schooling. The role changes and organizational environments—and related adjustments I made—didn't always turn out the way I'd hoped. The micro-aggressions and macro-aggressions threw me off and then made me doubt myself before I deduced the underhanded intent and learned to protect my personal mission, ensure I treated and managed others with respect, and safeguard my values. Early in my leadership career, it was only in hindsight—during those middle-of-the-night, cannot fall back-to-sleep, after-action reviews—that I realized these microaggressions were efforts to undermine and devalue my power and authority. These situations were frustrating and puzzling. The resistance I encountered felt—and likely was—personal. The hardships I experienced built my skillset, mettle, and adaptability as a leader. I learned that many people were not as authentic, kind, or self-aware as they purported themselves to be and that organizational leaders weren't as transparent as I would've liked. I learned to read a room and gather intelligence on why some people did or didn't support an initiative. I used humor precisely because this work is so hard and consequential. I built alliances and worked collaboratively between, across, and among internal and external players. I also told myself that there were little piles of shit around and I would inevitably step in them. When I did, I would reflect on what occurred, wipe off my shoe, assess how I ended up in that particular pile, recalibrate, and keep going.

With those whom I manage and lead, I share my reasoning and knowledge about a situation or organizational change because I practice transparency—it is possible, without sharing confidential information, to give people insight into organizational decisions and changes. This allows people to feel in control. They also are less distracted and anxious because of lack of knowledge. I seek to deliver timely and constructive feedback, conduct regular debriefings and postmortems, and engage in real-time reflection. I also keep an open door policy, encourage people to come to me to unpack an issue, and regularly discuss expectations—both my own of others and others of me. I ask at the end of each meeting, "Is there anything else I could do to support you?" (when I'm meeting one-on-one with a direct report) and conduct end-of-meeting evaluations (when I'm working with a group). I ask my employees to contribute to my performance reviews even if the organization doesn't conduct 360° feedback (and I've never worked for an organization that does use such a tool). I also seek to shield my employees from politics and support them publicly by clarifying which fights are for me to take on and to provide political cover to those reporting to me. If someone is going to step on a landmine (or in shit), it will be me.

I also create situational opportunities. One example involves a senior leader, with whom I served on a leadership team, who I will call "Betty." She bullied, belittled, and intimidated staff—including several leadership team members. I intentionally embedded my office and the department staff, who Betty antagonized, near Betty's office. Embedding the at-issue staff—who had as their charge to communicate about and raise funding for the organization's projects—meant this team could now informally talk to Betty's program staff and learn about what might be newsworthy or fundable without orchestrating meetings.

Prior to this, Betty perceived any time her program staff spent in meetings, which focused on public relations or funding, as efforts that detracted from the real work of the organization. It also enabled me to diffuse Betty's upset, discuss her concerns, and jointly arrive at solutions.

During challenging times, I expanded my use of imagery and metaphor to manage my own frustration with bureaucratic environments along with others' questioning, undermining, and devaluing of me. I describe the rope bridge, my Wonder Woman shirt, the pinball machine, and the piles of shit. Additionally, when someone tasked me with a new project and I uncovered calcified and problematic structures, practices, and cultures, I conjured the image of lifting a large rock only to discover tons of creepy crawly bugs. I often wanted to slam the rock back down and not look. I always looked. This tendency is undoubtedly why I received glass cliff assignments that I may have conquered but didn't always survive. The result of accepting and succeeding at glass cliff assignments was my acquisition of ever-increasing levels of responsibility focused on resolving numerous gnarly issues. I was perhaps more fearless than I should've been. Like a moth to flame, I flew toward the fire. I joked, when asked what I did, that I was the one in the yellow coat with the hose.

Conclusion

This chapter names a variety of challenges to women's leadership—which include legacy practices such as gatekeeping, fit, bias, blind spots, hepeating, and manels—that prevail and thwart women from advancing. Vignettes about respondents' and my own experiences with silencing, othering, disregarding, and ignoring depict the ways in which we experienced overt and veiled microaggressions—all experiences that furthered our resolve to navigate leadership to change experiences and outcomes for children, communities, and colleagues. Whereas I find it is unnecessary to wield power in hegemonic ways, to obtain credit, or accumulate power, I sometimes garnered or sought power to move people and practices. Yet overall, I choose to lead with and for people—through collaborative means and influence.

To combat hostile work environments—and inept or toxic supervisors and colleagues—that reinforce structural and systemic racial and gender bias, this chapter exemplifies the need for women and their allies to seek changes to workplace cultures, practices, and policies. Regardless of one's profile, to facilitate the transformation of an organization, its culture, and its people's associated behaviors, a leader will likely draw from a variety of approaches. Taking controversial and adversarial stances will put them at odds with dominant values, behaviors, norms, and cultures. Recall the Chapter 2 portrayals of leaders who draw on many models of leadership and do so simultaneously. They are nimble, adaptive, and reflective.

The following chapters discuss strategies for ensuring that one's access to leadership is transparent and fair. This isn't to say that the organizations that—and the leaders who—employ aspiring and sitting women educational leaders have a pass or that the women are to blame for experiencing or bringing forward incidences of bias and discrimination. This is to say that in addition to calling on organizations to ratify, clearly communicate, and enforce airtight and zero tolerance antibias structures, practices, and cultures, the women in leadership must still equip themselves to navigate tricky people and thorny terrains. Let's move now to Chapter 5's discussion about the use of metaphor to describe the routes women take to leadership and the different leadership frameworks that guide educational leadership roles.

Reflective Questions

1. Do you believe you've encountered or contributed to bias based on fit, gatekeeping, homosocial reproduction, or unconscious bias?
   a. What remedies did you or would you apply?
2. Do any of the terms—hepeating, bropropriating, silencing, disregard, double bind, double jeopardy, good woman, microaggression, imposter syndrome, glass cliff, other—reflect your own experience?
   a. Were you surprised by them?
3. What if any form(s) of discrimination have you encountered, or observed others experiencing, in the workplace?
4. How have you—or your supervisors or organizations—addressed bullying, racism, harassment, or abuse in the workplace?
   a. What, if anything, would you change? Why?
5. What type of environment do you work in?
   a. How does the culture affect how you lead?
6. How have you overcome, been informed by, or grown as a result of challenges?

5

Leadership Routes and Areas of Knowledge: Yellow Brick Road

Leadership Story

Upon realizing I would pursue a career inside of a public education institution— but not one that commenced with a teaching, classroom, or school-based role—I knew I needed legitimacy in the eyes of traditional educators.

I'd been employed as an education policy wonk (or specialist) proposing improvements, policies, and programs. I'd served in a variety of partner roles that had me implementing—alongside district, state, and national partners—different business-education programs. These interventions used exposure to employer standards and expectations as a core component of their theories of change for equipping students for future success in school and work—with theory of change comprised of the assumptions surrounding, the research supporting, the actions delineating, and the impact expected from a particular intervention.

I had no playbook for my career, little book that provided direction, and early insight into what I needed to know and be able to do. My awareness about what was necessary grew over time. Having been told that I wasn't management material, I left an early career role to take one that would give me budget, supervisory, and management experience. I asked to attend a weeklong leadership seminar, which included 360° feedback, personality and leadership testing, practical application with observation and feedback, and an action plan to take back to my job. I understood that I could be a better manager and even become a leader. I then— as a district insider—learned about schools, school systems, and educational improvement approaches.

I made my own playbook. I sought out challenging opportunities, to rebound and learn from mishaps, to practice self-reflection, and to identify my own skill set—or as one of my first managers said my "bag of tricks." This manager had advised me to move beyond having a bag of tricks to learning how, where, and when to apply these tricks, deepening my understanding and application, choosing a domain, and developing domain knowledge.

To be credible, further develop my understanding of public education, and truly make a difference, I required a different set of experiences and credentials. To embed myself within a school district, I sought district credentialing first by applying to an educational leadership doctoral program. The university didn't accept me because I lacked the requisite three years of prior teaching experience—a criterion required for the state's School District Administrator certification. Eventually the university relented but I ended up deferring (and then going elsewhere) because I secured a school district job classified under a unique worker category, which didn't require me to have taught. I continued to encounter a series of bureaucratic, certification, academic, and civil service barriers not just to entry but also to remain in the district due to state, civil service, and union leaders' resistance to the unique hiring category. I sought and finally received a waiver to the state's certification requirements.

By the time I received the waiver, I'd worked for an urban district for six years, supervised certificated department leaders, earned my doctorate, and led cross-district and school-level projects. I'd planned for this set of experiences, education, and credentials to demonstrate my qualifications for leadership roles within school districts.

Overview

This leadership story shows that, as is the case for many women, my route to leadership was not direct or easy. I encountered twists, turns, and barriers and benefitted from numerous lessons, mentors, roles, and opportunities opened for or pursued by me. While difficult and at times frustrating, I'm pleased I pushed myself and acquired new knowledge, skills, and allies.

I could've returned to school for a teaching credential and spent time as a classroom teacher to demonstrate skills in, understanding of, and experience delivering high-quality, equitable, student-centered teaching and learning. Teachers are gifted and committed. I know this not just because of those whose classrooms I studied, those with whom I collaborated and from whom I learned, or what I witnessed teachers managing during the pandemic. I know this also because of the elementary, secondary, and postsecondary educators in my family who have made such commitments. These individuals feel called to teach as others of us feel called to lead. Some have gone on to lead outside of the classroom. I didn't credential as a teacher, because I believe people who are called to teach are much better equipped and skilled than I would ever be. Instead, I rely on my systems-oriented skill set to contribute to education in a different way.

Along with the leadership model a leader espouses to follow and their motivation for leading, leaders' profiles paint a picture of their styles, traits, behaviors, skills, and experience. Such leaders and leadership portraits can translate into *leadership standards. Characteristics* link to standards. *Routes* guide progress. This chapter first highlights the *metaphors*, *routes*, and approaches that apply to women in leadership and isolate those my respondents and I find most salient. The labyrinth as a route women must traverse to leadership resonates strongly with me. I introduce national frameworks and share a draft group of standards I test with respondents. After presenting standards I drafted based on these national models, my own experience, and an earlier client project, I share which standards are extremely important to the respondents and me. Respondents assign the highest priority to Communication (thirty-one respondents), People and Relationships (thirty people), Culture as well as Vision (twenty-eight people), Resilience (twenty-five people), and Teamwork (twenty-four respondents).

Leadership Routes

I use the Yellow Brick Road in this chapter's subtitle—and the leadership story—to convey that I took an unfamiliar and untried path to leadership. My own career route was akin to Dorothy and friends traveling on the Yellow Brick Road (see Figure 5.1). There were twists, turns, stop offs, delays, challenges, dreams, misinformation, realizations, friendships, frenemies, saboteurs, guides, and accomplishments. As I indicate in earlier chapters, my education career began in graduate school. I interned as a policy wonk in a nonprofit education organization and then became employed there. A local president of an employer association then recruited me as director of its prekindergarten through twelfth grade (PreK-12) education partnership programs. In these roles, I partnered with districts and educators to facilitate practice changes from the outside in.

I next transitioned to the urban school district, first with responsibility for organizational development, then planning and strategy, and finally in the superintendent's office. I oversaw consequential projects, policies, and departments. When there, I earned my doctorate in educational leadership as

Figure 5.1 Yellow Brick Road.[1]

part of an accelerated cohort-based program. Next, I relocated my family to a different city for a foundation position. There I worked in evaluation, strategy, and impact planning. After the foundation, I returned to the nonprofit for which I originally worked as a policy wonk right out of graduate school. After that role, due to national travel and the need to be more place based because of my three adolescent children, I led a statewide education nonprofit linked to a different employer association. Next, I relocated to join a national nonprofit focused on preparing educational leaders. I relocated again for a cabinet role in an urban school district.

Many terms about routes to leadership have a tongue-in-cheek quality to them while others present a stark truth about women who are aspiring to, preparing for, or serving in leadership roles. Prior to conducting research for this book, several of these terms existed on the periphery of my awareness while others were either unknown to me or prominently centered in my sight line. Earlier I share many of these descriptions. They reflect sobering descriptions of discrimination, subterfuge, and arduousness. Workplace discrimination involves women experiencing "subtle and overt forms of bias that impede their success at work ... [and that] operate within groups and organizations."[2] The following frames and descriptions help facilitate my own understanding of my experience with educational leadership.

Concrete is a metaphor for women who simply cannot move from one role to another or change others' perception about the work women can and should perform. The point of using the word concrete in concrete ceiling and concrete wall is to convey that a woman finds herself stuck in hardened concrete and thus unable to move anywhere—forward, sideways, or up. Jo-Ann Tan (2016) indicates that concrete ceiling applies to women of color and conveys something that,

> Is practically impossible to break through by yourself. It's definitely impossible to see through. There is no visible destination, just what seems like a dead end. This is what women of color face in the workforce: an often impenetrable barrier, with no vision of how to get to the next level. This new term had to be created, simply because the experiences of white women and women of color are extremely different, but too often ignored.[3]

Concrete wall(s) applied when women couldn't participate in certain positions because of

> "explicit rule and clear cut norms" that were often backed up by legal, political, educational, military, and societal barriers ... The concrete wall rested on a division of labor dictating that men should be breadwinners and women should be homemakers. Women were denied entry to prestigious careers because of the assumption that their proper work was in the home ... [and was viewed typically] as part of the natural order.[4]

Glass is another group of metaphors and involves something one can see through but not reach because the glass is unbreakable or too thick. Glass metaphors include glass escalator, glass cliff, glass ceiling, and glass cushion. Glass cliff roles come into play as a discriminatory practice, when there are all-male decision-makers (manels) who assign riskier roles to women and others, favor their own group (in-group favoritism), seek to reduce threats to the status quo, or assign glass cushion jobs (those without risk) to other in-group members—men.[5] Ryan and Haslam (2007) propose that, "women are appointed to glass cliff positions because ... [they] may be regarded as more attractive candidates for such positions because they have greater potential as scapegoats who can be shouldered with blame should things go wrong."[6]

Women can perceive men—of color and white—who take a quick ride to the top of an organization (even in women-dominated professions such as health and education) as riding a glass escalator into leadership positions while women remain on the lower floors.[7] Glass walls refer to the situation where "women tend toward certain occupations, such as human resources or marketing, which are unlikely to position them for senior positions."[8] The most prominent of the glass metaphors is the glass ceiling, which has, for years, described women who cannot rise to the topmost leadership positions. Eagly and Carli (2007a) indicate that a glass ceiling represents:

> An absolute barrier—a solid roadblock that prevents access to high-level positions. At the same time, the image of a "glass" obstruction suggested that women were being misled about their opportunities because the impediment was not easy for them to see from a distance ... Central to these beliefs was the conviction that it would be risky to invest in women because they might well quit their jobs to raise a family. Such assumptions about a division of labor continued to disqualify women ... Even though women increasingly attained lower-level positions, they remained excluded from most positions at higher levels.[9]

The next group of metaphors regarding women's routes to leadership concentrate on pathways or *routes*, which are unclear, arduous, or tricky. Jungle Gym conveys women's need to ascertain how to climb, swing, or jump from one role to the next and implies that women can:

> Forge a unique path [to leadership] with occasional dips, detours, and even dead ends [and applies especially to] women who might be starting careers, switching careers, getting blocked by external barriers, or reentering the workforce after taking time off.[10]

Leadership web signals that there are layered elements in which women first become ensnared and then somehow extricate themselves. The leadership web describes:

> The personal and environmental factors that shape a woman's approach to leadership and her aspirations for leadership. The leadership web is shaped by: (1) work, or the often unconscious biases and gendered dynamics of work (that is, "male" jobs and "female" jobs) and other features within a workplace; (2) relationships with others in all aspects of life; and (3) place, or "the physical and geographical location in which the women leaders were brought up and in which they live" ... All three elements of the leadership web are shaped, modified, and informed by the social environment.[11]

Marathon implies a long road ahead and conveys that a woman's route to leadership requires "inner persistence, doggedness, and inner strength,"[12] and the route is long and arduous.

The labyrinth is reflective of idiosyncratic, often unpredictable, and not typically transparent, leadership paths. Labyrinth conveys the complications, innumerable lanes, and potential for success women encounter when pursuing leadership. Women can and do assume leadership roles even if they do not follow linear paths. They can and do ascend to leadership if they are persistent, reflective, skilled, lucky, informed, and supported.[13] Halloween corn mazes disorient and confine me, yet I gravitate to Eagly and Carli's (2007a) labyrinth metaphor to describe my own experience with becoming a leader. Eagly and Carli (2019) maintain that:

> For women who aspire to top leadership, routes exist but are full of twists and turns, both unexpected and expected. Because all labyrinths have a viable route to the center, it is understood that goals are attainable. The metaphor acknowledges obstacles but it is not ultimately discouraging … As a contemporary symbol, it conveys the idea of a complex journey toward a goal worth striving for. Passage through a labyrinth is not simple or direct, but requires persistence, awareness of one's progress, and analysis of the puzzles that lie ahead.[14]

Glass ceiling is still conjured as a metaphor even though Eagly and Carli (2007a) argued fifteen years ago that its use was inappropriate, because the notion of a glass ceiling connotes an absolute obstruction to women's leadership. At that time, Eagly and Carli (2007a) argued that:

1. It [glass ceiling] erroneously implies that women have equal access to entry-level positions.
2. It erroneously assumes the presence of an absolute barrier at a specific high level in organizations.
3. It erroneously suggests that all barriers to women are difficult to detect and therefore unforeseen.
4. It erroneously assumes that there exists a single, homogeneous barrier and thereby ignores the complexity and variety of obstacles that women leaders can face.
5. It fails to recognize the diverse strategies that women devise to become leaders.
6. It precludes the possibility that women can overcome barriers and become leaders.
7. It fails to suggest that thoughtful problem-solving can facilitate women's paths to leadership.[15]

The labyrinth characterizes women's leadership as possible and the barriers and challenges as surmountable though real. To apply the labyrinth metaphor, the authors suggest several essential elements.[16] First, working mothers must finesse a balance between their professional and family lives. Working women must also plan for, develop skills for, seek out support for, and be strategic about navigating through a variety of challenges and opportunities. Organizations should provide a variety of leadership development supports to women such as removing barriers associated with women's ability to balance work and family. Additionally, organizations can remove barriers associated with women's ability to access skill development, leadership positions, networks, stretch assignments, mentors, and promotions. Organizations can also create and communicate transparent and fair pathways to leadership roles, and non-gendered requirements. Chapter 7 discusses supports that facilitate women's leadership.

Respondents provide glimpses into their leadership roles and trajectories. Some speak to the ways in which they took charge of their careers and overcame any real or perceived shortcomings. Others discuss ways they navigated through opportunities and challenges and developed effective formulas for leadership. These respondents mention the complex nature of leadership for women and the importance of staying true to oneself.

> **Avril**: A significant decision that I made was to stay in the district that I was in, even though it would have been financially beneficial to seek employment elsewhere. I chose quality of life—meaning that I loved the educational staff and community, and it was a good fit—but I definitely would have commanded a higher salary had I left.
>
> **Jean**: I chose to leave my position in a large, diverse school system both to no longer have to deal with a bullying supervisor and also to complete my dissertation. I chose a part time leadership position in a nonprofit that allowed me to both work and write. Although I deeply missed a system that I had worked in for more than 20 years, the decision to leave was positive. It allowed me to become a leader in educational nonprofits and to complete my doctoral studies.
>
> **Michelle**: I decided to leave my district leadership position for a new job at our state education agency. The risk was that this was a completely new role in a new location with all new colleagues, several hours from my home. I had limited familiarity and history with the agency, but I was disappointed with the direction of the leadership in the district and was eager to depart. I was strongly encouraged by another woman education leader who told me I should 'grow' my repertoire of education leadership abilities by working in

a different environment, i.e., state level versus district or school level. It was a wonderful learning experience, and very rewarding, although probably one of the most demanding jobs I have ever done.

Nola: Each move up the ladder proved to have inherent risk involved. Leaving tenure, security, success in order to move to a new organization where culture and climate were unknowns. Being able to work through challenges and adapt to new climate while remaining true to my educational values allowed me to have mostly success. During an especially difficult time of intense turmoil, relying on my personal support system was the only thing that got me through this time. Eventually, the situation became too toxic for me personally and required a move to a different position. The lack of support from close colleagues, who were, in fact, working to hold on to their own positions, proved detrimental to my continued work in the district.

Zelda: I made the decision to step out of a school leadership role because I felt that the job had become too difficult to maintain with a family. The frustrations and expectations were not conducive to a healthy work life balance with three young children. Moving into other sectors in educational leadership provided me with more flexibility and ability to focus on the aspects education that I am most passionate about …. Having worked at traditional public, charter public, private, higher Ed, and nonprofit settings has given me unique perspectives on education and leadership. Within my current role as an educational leadership professor, I also have the opportunity to interact with educational leaders in a variety of settings also broadening my perspectives. In addition, I've had the privilege to be in settings that have prioritized research and inquiry specifically in leadership.

Consistent with the labyrinth metaphor, the respondents and I share the ways in which the twists and turns we took allowed us to become leaders on our own terms. We managed our own careers, recognized the need for balance, garnered support from personal and professional arenas, and discovered our own leadership sweet spots.

Knowing and Doing

When considering how to overcome challenges and develop skills, women may study frameworks describing what leaders should know and be able to do. The first component is knowing, or areas of knowledge. The Corporate Leadership Council (CLC) defines knowledge as, "A familiarity with information or facts that can be learned through experiences or education."[17] Jerome Murphy (2013) describes three types of knowledge—that extend beyond educational leaders' possession of foundational knowledge—which focus on schools and organizational change to include situations, organizations, and people:

> Effective administrators bring to their jobs a store of relevant knowledge, such as an understanding of schools and a firm grasp of theories of organizational change. But much of what happens—or *should* happen—in organizations is highly dependent on information that administrators frequently do not possess. This includes "local" knowledge (the organization); "situational" knowledge (the who, what, where, when, and how of a given issue); and "people" knowledge (staff members' thoughts and feelings, their perceptions of reality, and the meanings they attach to these perceptions).[18]

Competence (or competency) describes what educational leaders should be able to do. This is one's ability to put all the pieces of one's knowledge and experience together in an effective manner and includes their style and behavior. Kramer and Nyack (2013) cite the CLC as indicating, "Competencies are made up of groups of behaviors—the specific actions a leader needs to demonstrate her competence."[19] Also important is one's prior experience, which includes things like education, training, and prior responsibilities performed.

Examining knowledge and competence is consistent with both a style and a skills approach. A Skills Approach "identifies the essential competencies of good and effective leadership, and focuses on the measurement and development of those competencies."[20] Kramer and Nyack (2013) cite CLC as declaring that, "skills are learned capacities that enable a person to perform a task."[21] Leadership style is "characteristic of ways of behaving that have a consistent meaning or function."[22] Jean Lau Chin (2007b) describes the Style Approach as focusing "exclusively on what leaders do (behaviors) and how they act (process), where style is understood as relatively stable patterns of behavior."[23] This approach encompasses both behaviors and dispositions (also known as "traits" but not the definition of traits comprising things like maleness, whiteness, or tallness). I link dispositions such as integrity, trustworthiness, and adaptability to a style approach. Using the dispositions' definition of traits, Kramer and Nyack (2013) indicate that dispositions are "the feelings, attitudes, perceptions, and beliefs that a person displays,"[24] and represent the third element of a development framework: knowledge, competence, and dispositions.

There are multiple national frameworks, which articulate what educational leaders should know and be able to do—such as those for independent school leaders, principals, principal supervisors, and equity-focused leaders. Standards can serve as a foundation for continuous growth. I share national frameworks as a foundation for the draft standards framework I test with respondents and then, in Chapter 6, customize for women educational leaders. Although some authors have written entire books on a singular leadership competency or disposition, which these authors believe women should employ—for example, confidence, growth mindset, grit, emotional intelligence, resonance, or leaning in—the educational leadership framework and standards' landscape is as varied as it is similar. Potential leaders may find the multiple frameworks, when shared together, overwhelming. Such variations highlight the importance for women to isolate and develop their own specific leadership muscles—whether to resolve a particular leadership issue, overcome a gnarly leadership challenge, or realize an exciting leadership opportunity.

The Leadership Academy (2020) developed its Culturally Responsive Leadership framework, supporting documents, and trainings in response to widespread disparities in school quality, experiences, and outcomes for children from marginalized (or, what they call minoritized) communities:

> It is well-documented that students in the United States live and learn in racially segregated spaces, a result of generations of racialized oppression, both codified and cultural ... Within and across segregated spaces, inequity is constantly reproduced through both action and inaction—and will continue to be reproduced and further entrenched without strong leadership to disrupt systems of inequity and oppression.[25]

The Leadership Academy aligns its culturally responsive framework of actions—which identify areas of practice, skills, knowledge, and dispositions—with national frameworks. Rather than referring to their framework's elements as standards, they use the term "actions" and then nest subcomponents (called dimensions and characteristics/qualities) within each action statement and its dimensions. To be consistent with their training services, which they tailor to school and school system (or network) leaders, the actions align with specific school- and district-level positions. The categories are aspiring principal, principals, principal supervisors, and superintendents.

The Leadership Academy (2020) also defines eight, high-level actions customized to each one of the four position levels. The eight actions are: (1) Lead for Equity and Access; (2) Align Mission, Vision, and Core Values; (3) Focus on Instruction; (4) Facilitate Adult Learning and Development; (5) Manage Operations and Resources; (6) Engage in Personal Learning and Development; (7) Strategize Change and Continuous Improvement; and (8) Cultivate Community Care and Engagement.[26] The Leadership Academy (2021) also shares a definition of Culturally Responsive Practice, which cuts across the aforementioned actions and requires educators to:

> Understand and simultaneously attend to: a strong foundation of cultural understanding[,] … the academic success of all students[,] … cultivating and deepening the cultural competence of themselves and the adults they lead[, and] … the cultivation of sociopolitical consciousness … [with sociopolitical consciousness being defined as the] ability to question and critique social norms, values, practices, and systems and facilitate conversations that generate inquiry about inequity and change in the context of their schools.[27]

The National Association of Independent Schools (NAIS) is the primary organization for recruiting, selecting, and training people who work in independent schools and are members of NAIS. This includes school heads, division heads, and board of trustee members. Independent schools are typically stand-alone unless they have a lower school and an upper school on the same or adjacent campuses. Many independent schools have a PreK-12 grade configuration. These schools are tuition-based schools, admissions-based schools, board of trustee governed, and dependent on robust fundraising arms. Thus, the role of a head of school includes aspects of governance, student recruitment and selection, fundraising, and overall budgeting that aren't the typical purview of public school principals or principal supervisors. Many elite independent schools also recruit international students who may board onsite, which constitutes another major difference from traditional public school leaders. Some of these responsibilities may be present in stand-alone, nonnetworked charter schools whose leaders must run the school, raise funds, manage funds, market their school, and work with a board.

With an emphasis on ethics, professionalism, and sound operational practices, NAIS established what it calls Principles of Good Practice for its member schools. The practice categories are: (1) admissions, (2) athletics, (3) board of trustees, (4) business officers, (5) early childhood education, (6) education of international students in independent schools, (7) elementary school educators, (8) environmental sustainability, (9) equity and justice, (10) financial aid administration, (11) fundraising, (12) educating for global citizenship and international mindedness, (13) head searches, (14) heads of schools, (15) hiring process, (16) independent school trustees, (17) middle school educators, (18) parents (working with schools and schools working with parents), (19) secondary school educators, (20) teachers and supervisors of teachers, and (21) teaching and learning in the digital age.[28]

In 2015, the National Policy Board for Educational Administration (NPBEA), a member organization of nine national councils and associations, released *Professional Standards for Educational Leaders 2015*. Tens of educational experts, scholars, funders, and practitioners contributed to the document, which delineates ten separate standard domains that NPBEA views as foundational for multiple leadership roles. NPBEA organized the ten standards around three clusters—excluding the standards associated with school improvement because it affects the other standards. The standards are: (1) curriculum, instruction, and assessment and community of care and support for students; (2) professional capacity of school personnel, professional community for teachers and staff, meaningful engagement of families and community, and operations and management; and (3) mission, vision, and core values, ethics and professional norms, and equity and cultural responsiveness. Each domain includes a standard statement and elements aligned to the statement (see Table 5.1 for the standards and clusters only).[29]

NPBEA cited its purpose for developing the standards as to "define the nature and the quality of work of persons who practice that profession, in this case educational leaders[,] … guide professional practice and how practitioners are prepared, hired, developed, supervised and evaluated [and] … inform government policies and regulations that oversee the profession."[31] This document doesn't differentiate the standards by position but rather sees these as "cast more toward school-level leadership than district-level leadership [given that] district-level leaders have additional responsibilities associated with their particular roles (e.g., working with school boards and labor relations), and those responsibilities extend beyond these Standards."[32]

For postsecondary graduate accreditation purposes, NPBEA also developed program standards for National Educational Leadership Preparation (NELP) programs which prepare masters and doctoral educational candidates. NELP standards "specify what novice leaders and preparation program graduates should know and be able to do after completing a high-quality educational leadership preparation program … and will be used to review educational leadership programs" for accreditation purposes.[33]

Table 5.1 National Policy Board for Educational Administration Professional Standards for Educational Leaders 2015[30]

Cluster	Domain	Standards
3	Standard 1: Mission, vision, and core values	Effective educational leaders develop, advocate, and enact a shared mission, vision, and core values of high-quality education and academic success and well-being of *each* student.
	Standard 2: Ethics and professional norms	Effective educational leaders act ethically and according to professional norms to promote *each* student's academic success and well-being.
	Standard 3: Equity and cultural responsiveness	Effective educational leaders strive for equity of educational opportunity and culturally responsive practices to promote *each* student's academic success and well-being.
1	Standard 4: Curriculum, instruction, and assessment	Effective educational leaders develop and support intellectually rigorous and coherent systems of curriculum, instruction, and assessment to promote *each* student's academic success and well-being.
	Standard 5: Community of care and support for students	Effective educational leaders cultivate an inclusive, caring, and supportive school community that promotes the academic success and well-being of *each* student.
2	Standard 6: Professional capacity of school personnel	Effective educational leaders develop the professional capacity and practice of school personnel to promote *each* student's academic success and well-being.
	Standard 7. Professional community for teachers and staff	Effective educational leaders foster a professional community of teachers and other professional staff to promote *each* student's academic success and well-being.
	Standard 8: Meaningful engagement of families and community	Effective educational leaders engage families and the community in meaningful, reciprocal, and mutually beneficial ways to promote *each* student's academic success and well-being.
	Standard 9: Operations and management	Effective educational leaders manage school operations and resources to promote *each* student's academic success and well-being.
Over-riding	Standard 10: School improvement	Effective educational leaders act as agents of continuous improvement to promote *each* student's academic success and well-being.

The Council of Chief State School Officers' (CCSSO) shares its national standards' framework in its *Model Principal Supervisor Professional Standards 2015*, a document the Wallace Foundation funded. Like the NPBEA standards for educational leaders, CCSSO clustered its eight standards for principal supervisors into three groups. The first focuses on supporting and improving principals' capacity for instructional leadership, the second on ensuring the smooth and effective functioning of the district, and the third on the improving the capacity and effectiveness of the principal supervisor as a district leader (see Table 5.2).[34]

Table 5.2 Council of Chief State School Officers' Model Principal Supervisor Standards 2015

Category	Standard	Standards
Support and improve principals' capacity for instructional leadership	1	Principal supervisors dedicate their time to helping principals grow as instructional leaders
	2	Principal supervisors coach and support individual principals and engage in effective professional learning strategies to help principals grow as instructional leaders.
	3	Principal supervisors use evidence of principals' effectiveness to determine necessary improvements in principals' practice to foster a positive educational environment that supports the diverse cultural and learning needs of students.
	4	Principal supervisors engage principals in the formal district principal evaluation process in ways that help them grow as instructional leaders.
Ensure the smooth and effective functioning of the district	5	Principal supervisors advocate for and inform the coherence of organizational vision, policies, and strategies to support schools and student learning.
	6	Principal supervisors assist the district in ensuring the community of schools with which they engage are culturally/socially responsive and have equitable access to resources necessary for the success of each student.
Improve the capacity and effectiveness of the principal supervisor as a district leader	7	Principal supervisors engage in their own development and continuous improvement to help principals grow as instructional leaders.
	8	Principal supervisors lead strategic change that continuously elevates the performance of schools and sustains high-quality educational programs and opportunities across the district.

Instructional Leaders must:

- Model learning for others—reflection, personal growth, ethical practice, and a focus on improvement
- Willingly confront issues of equity that impede student learning
- Recognize and respond to the diverse cultural and learning needs of students
- Develop staff to increase their capacities for improving student learning
- Make decisions based on how they will affect student success
- Understand how all systems affect student success
- Share and distribute responsibilities for student learning

Transformational Educational Leaders must be:

- **Growth-oriented**: Transformational education leaders believe that students, education professionals, educational organizations, and the community can continuously grow and improve to realize a shared vision for student success through dedication and hard work.
- **Collaborative**: Transformational education leaders share the responsibility and the work for realizing a shared vision of student success.
- **Innovative**: Transformational education leaders break from established ways of doing things to pursue fundamentally new and more effective approaches when needed.
- **Analytical**: Transformational education leaders gather evidence and engage in rigorous data analysis to develop, manage, refine, and evaluate new and more effective approaches.
- **Ethical**: Transformational education leaders explicitly and consciously follow laws, policies, and principles of right and wrong in everything they do.
- **Perseverant**: Transformational education leaders are courageous and persevere in doing what is best for students even when challenged by fear, risk, and doubt.
- **Reflective**: Transformational education leaders reexamine their practices and dispositions habitually in order to develop the "wisdom of practice" needed to succeed in pursuing new and more effective approaches.
- **Equity-minded**: Transformational education leaders ensure that all students are treated fairly, equitably, and have access to excellent teachers and necessary resources.
- **Systems-focused**: Transformational education leaders are committed to developing systems and solutions that are sustainable and effective district-wide and that generate equitable outcomes for all schools and stakeholders.

Figure 5.2 Instructional Leader and Transformational Educational Leader Practices.

This CCSSO principal supervisor document—in addition to sharing eight standards and their associated elements—identifies seven activities as essential to modeling instructional leadership and nine dispositions as essential for transformational leadership—both sets of which the CCSSO extracted from the aforementioned NPBEA *Professional Standards for Educational Leaders 2015* (see Figure 5.2).[35]

There is consistency across the national practices, actions, standards, and dispositions' frameworks, which highlight what educational leaders should know and be able to do—from operations to teaching to curriculum to assessment to student learning to professional development to culture to operations. Moreover, there are numerous ways for educational leaders to show up, to behave, to act—from being perseverant to reflective to equity minded to growth oriented. The national actions, practices, standards, and disposition themes hold up in most ways, but I conclude that there is a need to bolster and explicate additional areas that address women educational leaders' unique needs and approaches.

Reflections on Leadership Standards

When I commenced this 2020–2 book study, I read deeply about women educational leaders and became interested in testing an enhanced list of draft standards. This draft list of standards drew on my own experience; trends in the literature; the abovementioned sets of national standards, actions, and dispositions; and other standards I've developed. I test the following standards with the thirty-seven respondents: (1) Teaching and Learning, (2) Vision, (3) Performance Management, (4) Communication, (5) Culture, (6) People and Relationships, (7) Teamwork, (8) Innovation, (9) Continuous Learning, (10) Development, (11) Administration and Operations, (12) Resilience, (13) Confidence, and (14) Competence (see Figure 5.3).

Scholars and authors articulate the need for women to be confident, lean in, be tireless, be visionary, navigate, network, mentor, and be resilient. Furthermore, women need to bounce back, balance, and adjust while simultaneously drawing on their culturally and societally derived collaborative, collectivist, and social justice dispositions. To determine my list's resonance, I asked the respondents to indicate the fourteen standards' importance to their leadership practice based on ratings of not important, important, very important, and extremely important. The top six reasons the thirty-seven women identified as extremely important were: (1) Communication (thirty-one respondents), (2) People and Relationships (thirty people), (3) Culture and Vision (each at twenty-eight respondents), (4) Resilience (twenty-five people), and (5) Teamwork (twenty-four people) (see Table 5.3).

STANDARD	DESCRIPTION	STANDARD	DESCRIPTION
Teaching and Learning	Facilitate and support stakeholders' understanding and implementation of instructional, curricular, technology, and assessment goals, objectives, and/or strategies	Teamwork	Facilitate, build, and engage collaborative and capable teams and individuals
		Innovation	Generate and apply new, agile, and relevant solutions
Vision	Espouse, model, and enact a vision, a mission, values, goals, and program/agenda (academic, advocacy, philanthropic, etc.)	Continuous Learning	Expand—on an ongoing basis—your own knowledge to gain new skills and expertise
Performance Management	Establish, build consensus around, and monitor goals, objectives, and performance to ensure quality, consistency, and accountability	Development	Establish and support opportunities for others' ongoing professional learning and growth
		Administration and Operations	Create and manage systems, processes, services, and structures to enable cohesive implementation of the mission and achievement of goals
Communication	Communicate with ease, clarity, respect, and professionalism with a variety of stakeholders in a variety of settings and via a variety of mediums	Resilience	Respond to pressures, disappointments, and/or tragedies quickly, adaptively, and effectively
Culture	Forward diverse environments that cultivate and build respect for each person's unique potential, contribution, background, and culture	Confidence	Possess and project, through calculated risk-taking, mastery, and self-assurance about one's own abilities
People and Relationships	Work constructively and build relationships with a variety of stakeholders	Competence	Apply acquired managerial, technical, and leadership knowledge with consistency and appropriateness

Figure 5.3 Dr. Carlisle's Fourteen Draft Standards.

Table 5.3 Respondents' Very Important and Extremely Important Ratings of Draft Standards

Reasons	Respondents Very Important	Respondents Extremely Important	Dr. Carlisle Very Imp	Dr. Carlisle Extremely Imp
Teaching and Learning	7	21	1	
Vision	7	28		1
Performance Management	15	17	1	
Communication	6	31		1
Culture	8	28		1
People and Relationships	7	30	1	
Teamwork	13	24	1	
Innovation	23	11		
Continuous Learning (self)	13	21		1
Development (of others)	13	20		1
Administration and Operations	11	20	1	
Resilience	10	25		1
Confidence	18	17	1	
Competence	21	15	1	

My own draft standards' ratings aren't included among respondents' extremely important aggregated responses in Table 5.3 though I include mine in a far-right columns. My own extremely important rated standards overlapped, for the most part, with the participants' aggregated responses. I also rated as extremely important the following: Vision, Communication, Culture, and Resilience. Unlike the respondents, I rated Development and Continuous Learning as extremely important and didn't rate Teamwork and People and Relationships as extremely important (I ranked these as very important consistent with my collectivist approach).

Notably, when combining the very important and extremely important ratings, thirty-two or more respondents assign almost every draft standard—except for Teaching and Learning as well as and Administration and Operations—a very important or an extremely important rating. When combining the ratings of very important and extremely important, my own responses track with the majority of respondents. The exception is that I included Teaching and Learning along with Administration and Operations among my highest two ratings. Additionally, I didn't include Innovation among my highest ratings—I rated innovation as important even though I employ creativity when solving complex problems. Respondents' highest ratings of the draft standards are associated with communal and tone-setting approaches to leadership such as collaboration, teamwork, people, vision, culture, and communication. Respondents, when I combine very important and extremely important ratings, also strongly indicate the need for a focus on resilience and confidence. Some would argue these are softer skills (which in the following chapter I capture as dispositions) whereas categories like Teaching and Learning, Administration and Operations, and Performance Management are more technical in nature.

The two areas on which schools of education have traditionally focused—Teaching and Learning, and Administration and Operations—are the two categories that respondents rate the lowest: seven people rated Teaching and Learning as very important and twenty-one did so for extremely important whereas eleven people rated Administration and Operations as very important and twenty respondents did so as extremely important. Even with my own nontraditional career path into a district setting, I rate Teaching and Learning, and Administration and Operations as very important. This is due to PreK-12 education's focus on educating students and making sure all systems are poised and resources allocated to support instruction and learning.

Based on the draft standards participants identify as most important, respondents provide descriptions about the strategies that facilitated their ability to exercise sound educational leadership practices. Participants' remarks focus on strategies that reinforced the standards and indicate that the standards reinforce one another. For communication, respondents emphasize listening and ensuring people are, and feel they are, heard; being transparent; speaking openly, respectfully, intentionally, clearly, regularly, authentically, thoughtfully, and honestly; attending to how one delivers messages; and asking questions to understand. Participants also note that employing such standards requires that leaders employ executive functioning skills such as decision-making and implementation. Regarding collaboration and teamwork—which revolve around trust, diversity of thought, and diversity of contributors—respondents' comments reinforce relationship development, skill development of themselves and others, and constructive, safe, and accountable work environments. Some additional concepts focus on the need for a growth mindset and resilience.

Conclusion

This chapter highlights many metaphors, routes, and approaches that can apply to women in leadership and isolates those respondents and I find most salient. The labyrinth as a route, which women traverse to leadership, resonates strongly with me. I use the Yellow Brick Road in this chapter's subtitle to convey that I took an unclear path to leadership and provide examples from respondents' own careers.

This examination of frameworks, which describe what educational leaders should know and able to do, illustrates synergy among the nationally developed standards, practices, actions, and dispositions' frameworks. The results I capture in Tables 5.3 and 5.4—and other summaries of respondents' comments—suggest that my fourteen draft standards are appropriate and resonate with the thirty-seven respondents albeit with multiple tweaks and some additions, which follow in Chapter 6. The draft standards also track with the transformational leader dispositions shown in Figure 5.2.

As I share, there are standards and areas of expertise required for skilled roles, including teaching and leading. I suggest in the following chapter that the current approaches that require women to demonstrate their competence, navigate bias, balance their agentic and communal traits, and work themselves harder than anyone believes is possible do not sufficiently prepare women for educational leadership. Thus, I next introduce a proposed group of standards for women educational leaders. My aim is to facilitate some ease for women leaders such that they learn about what they should know and be able to do. Particularly when coupled with the leadership development strategies Chapter 7 outlines, application of these standards and dispositions can help women become good if not great leaders.

Reflective Questions

1. What route to leadership have you taken?
   a. Is there anything you would've preferred was different?
   b. Is there anything you would change for current aspiring and sitting leaders?
2. What about the various frameworks resonates with you?
   a. Do you see anything missing from them?
3. What is your reaction to the notion of standards, competencies, dispositions?
   a. Do you believe they are helpful or harmful?
   b. Why?
4. How would you have rated Dr. Carlisle's list of standards?
   a. Why?

6

Standards and Dispositions for Women Educational Leaders: The Dance

Leadership Story

Wouldn't it be great if women had a playbook outlining the knowledge, competencies, and dispositions they need to master so they can become successful leaders? Wouldn't it be beneficial to apply knowledge with ongoing constructive feedback? Wouldn't it be practical to demonstrate and attain different levels of mastery? Medical students and residents practice their skills in hospitals and offices—in practicums. In any technical field, there are foundational facts and concepts to master. It's also true in the arts—dance fundamentals are the technique. Can a person Plié with her knees, feet, and hips in the correct position? Does the dancer know the first, second, third, fourth, and fifth positions of the knees, feet, hips, and arms? Does she understand that Port de bras translates into moving one's arms from one position to another?

One doesn't become a competent physician simply by accomplishing items on a checklist. Physicians must know when and how to apply their learning to real-life situations and gain experience that supports their ability to diagnose and treat patients with increasing levels of sophistication. They keep learning. In dance, one's knowledge of the fundamental technique and vocabulary positions (sic) the dancer to follow ever more complex patterns which comprise a dance. Eventually a dancer learns to follow a choreographer's sequences to perform a dance onstage. None of these fundamentals indicates that the person is a good or great dancer, but the person possesses basic competence and demonstrates appropriate behaviors— smiling during an upbeat dance, breathing silently, and incorporating guidance from a dance master. Multiple steps are joined to make a sequence, the sequences a pattern, and the patterns a dance.

Along the route to becoming a good dancer, there is frequent instruction and feedback. I for one would make faces when concentrating and hold tension in my hands. I learned to send my earnestness into holding an arabesque Allongé and launching myself into a Grand jeté, as well as to hold a pencil weaved through my fingers to avoid scarecrow hands. While I'm a dance enthusiast, becoming a great dancer eluded me. I didn't want to sacrifice everything to become a short-term professional dancer, my body couldn't take the demands of the brutal technique, and, when I was deciding between and Master of Fine Arts (MFA) and a Public Policy Master of Science (MS), I followed my sensible self instead of my creative self. I chose to apply my creativity to analysis, framework development, and innovative approaches to decalcify bureaucratized systems.

Overview

The leadership story illustrates the ways in which competence, knowledge, and behaviors become fit together as a dance. I use the dance to convey that like a well-executed dance—based on choreography, skill, and verve—women educational leaders need to follow a roadmap and acquire competencies to become great leaders. I build on the *standards* and *characteristics* from Chapter 5 and propose that women educational leaders should have their own set of leadership standards and dispositions.

While it is efficacious for women who aspire to educational leadership to be adept at applying skills, behaviors, and areas of knowledge, standards can serve as a starting point and a guide rather than a checklist for hiring and promotion. I propose that it is possible to establish common, non-innate standards—which are learnable and teachable—for educational leaders, as well as to craft dispositions that can set women educational leaders up for success. I also suggest that the current sets of standards are insufficient to address the needs of women educational leaders. It is important for a panel of women scholars and experts to assemble and establish and test a framework for women educational leaders—whether the list is specific to a position or as an addendum to existing standards' documents such as the way in which Leadership Academy presents its culturally responsive leadership actions. I also want scholars and experts to use these standards and dispositions as a launching off point, and for leadership development programs and graduate schools of education to incorporate their importance into their courses.

This chapter commences the conversation about, highlights the need for, and shares recommendations for broad categories that explicate and can help women educational leaders prepare for and carry out their roles.

Where Do We Go Now?

Even after I asked the thirty-seven respondents to react to my draft list of standards, I continued to read resources focused on women in leadership. I culled through and coded respondents' answers and concluded I should modify my draft list. My intention is to help women become better equipped at navigating educational leadership and for their allies to support them more effectively in a collective pursuit to improve workplaces for everyone.

To establish standards and dispositions for women educational leaders worthy of further investigation, explication, and validation, these revised standards combine several of Chapter 5's draft fourteen, assign some to become dispositions, add new dispositions, and edit many definitions and titles. The governing statement in Figure 6.1 conveys that the purpose of the standards and dispositions is to enable women educational leaders to, "forward equitable teaching and learning outcomes for all children." The seven standards' categories are now: (S-1) Administration and Operations, (S-2) Competence, (S-3) Development and Support, (S-4) Equitable Culture, (S-5) Performance Management, (S-6) Teaching and Learning; and (S-7) Vision (see Figure 6.1).

Consistent with the Council of Chief State School Officers (CCSSO)'s cross-cutting transformational educational leaders' dispositions (see Table 5.2),

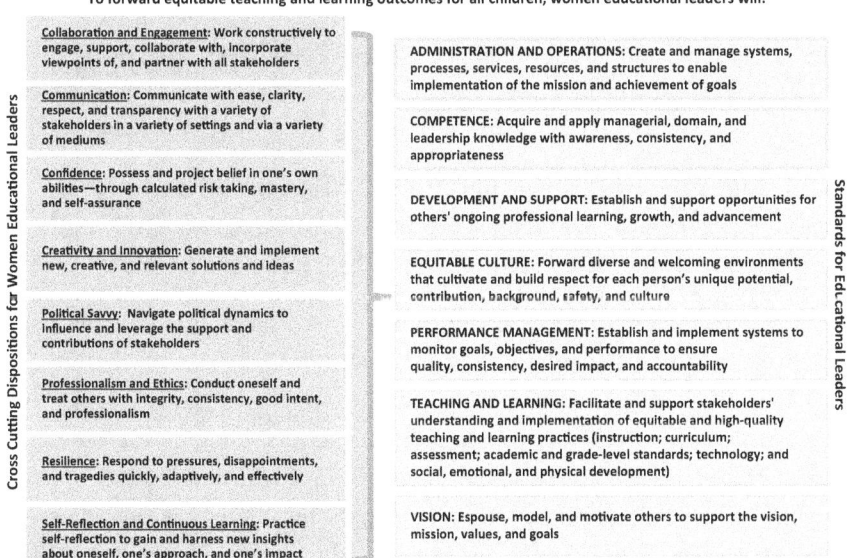

Figure 6.1 Proposed Dispositions and Standards for Women Educational Leaders.

Figure 6.1 provides a set of dispositions customized to women educational leaders. The eight crosscutting dispositions are: (D-1) Collaboration and Engagement, (D-2) Communication, (D-3) Confidence, (D-4) Creativity and Innovation, (D-5) Political Savvy, (D-6) Professionalism and Ethics, (D-7) Resilience, and (D-8) Self-reflection and Continuous Learning.

The changes to Chapter 5 standards include:

1. Collaboration and Engagement is a newly named and combined category derived from the original draft People and Relationships and Teamwork.
2. Communication and Competence have slightly revised statements.
3. Confidence and Resilience include new wording.
4. Creativity and Innovation is a new title that replaces Innovation.
5. Political Savvy as well as Professionalism and Ethics are new categories.
6. Self-reflection and Continuous Learning replaces Continuous Learning.

Revised Standards' Statements

As the National Policy Board for Educational Leaders established, "Professional standards define the nature and the quality of work of persons who practice that profession, in this case educational leaders. They are created for and by the profession to guide professional practice and how practitioners are prepared, hired, developed, supervised and evaluated."[1] What follows are descriptions of, practical application examples of, and respondent examples relating to the seven standards for women educational leaders.

(S-1) Administration and Operations: Create and Manage Systems, Processes, Services, Resources, and Structures to Enable Implementation of the Mission and Achievement of Goals

Leaders spend the most time on and convey a need for additional training on practices associated with administration. Superintendents indicate that the top two areas they find the most time consuming are "school finance (45%) and personnel management (41%)."[2] Keeping the trains running—or providing stewardship of the organizational entity—is time consuming and vital to teaching and learning. Other related practices include operations, program implementation, resource allocation, and organizational management. Activities and requisite skills range from budgeting and financial analysis to selecting, hiring, assigning, and managing people to selecting, understanding, and using technology for operational and communication purposes.

When well executed, the vital role of Administration and Operations, while managerial in nature, requires a systems orientation—where "a system consists of interrelated parts that work together or in some fashion and impact each other."[3] Consider how administration and operations' capacity and capability negatively affected teaching and learning during the initial phases of the coronavirus pandemic: schools and educators weren't prepared to deliver, the Internet accounts weren't in place to enable, and students' homes weren't prepared to receive, remote instruction.

Additional expertise for Administration and Operations can include:

1. carrying out services with fidelity
2. ensuring safety and security of students, staff, and buildings
3. staying abreast of, interpreting, and implementing local, state, and federal laws and policies
4. managing change
5. operation and oversight of services and systems (such as placing students, maintaining physical plants, and scheduling staff and buses, etc.)
6. resource allocation
7. understanding and implementing local rules and procedures

One of my first in-district assignments was to support the development of a hundreds-of-million-dollars budget, which I thought of as a house of cards. One major component drove the entire budget. This fundamental decision involved moving sixth-grade students from middle schools to elementary schools so the grade configurations would become PreK-6, K-6, PreK-8, K-8, and 7-8. School grade configuration influences many expenditures and decisions—from teacher and assistant principal staffing to student assignment to teacher certification requirements to classroom location. Also affected is bussing, food service, and school capacity. Grade configuration drives acquisition of instructional materials, alignment of lessons and curricula, and state accountability reporting. The board of education did not approve the change in grade configuration, which required the superintendent (and staff) to redevelop and resubmit the entire budget. Instead of going back and rejigging a handful of budget components, the budget came apart when the board of education insisted we pull out one card—grade reconfiguration.

Another time a leader asked me to ensure compliance with a particular grantmaker's terms. Because the grant required that the organization transform two large high schools into multiple small high schools, attaining compliance affected many operational and academic aspects. The process included determining the academic program and themes for each new small school, the employer and college partners, the new schools' state identification numbers, and the state accountability parameters. We identified how to organize the physical plants. We resolved whether there would be lab space dedicated to, built for, or shared among each high school. That decision affected student transitions and scheduling. We determined student entrance and egress, which was especially important because one of the new colocated schools was an elementary Montessori. We negotiated with the teachers' union about both teacher reassignment and rehiring, and how the Montessori accreditation and staff training requirements meshed with existing union agreements and state certification requirements. Finally, we added the schools to the elementary and secondary parental choice and student placement processes.

Respondents also reflect on some ways in which administrative issues can define, thwart, and support educational leadership.

> **Avril**: Over my tenure as an administrator, the factors that have most interfered with sound leadership practices probably fall under the category of Administration & Operations—fiscal constraints and competing priorities.
>
> **Crystal**: The ability to manage and optimize the operational realities of school system management … The traditional silo'd approach of large district also undermines effective and efficient operations.
>
> **Reese**: In education, leaders need to prove themselves capable of managing high-level, complex strategic projects but at the same time they must be willing to be of service in the smallest ways that make a difference for schools … I will say that my early roles in education non-profits, at the associate and coordinator levels, definitely facilitated my strengths as a project manager and systems builder. When you're at the lower levels of an organization, you often are tasked with organizational systems, project trackers, and other tools that facilitate strong project management. Working my way up the non-profit ladder has been invaluable in that regard.
>
> **Sharon**: The word leadership implies that one's work is to … remove barriers that interfere with their success, and build the capacity of the organization to methodically bring the vision to fruition.
>
> **Sonja**: Track record of follow-through and high-quality.

(S-2) Competence: Acquire and Apply Managerial, Domain, and Leadership Knowledge with Awareness, Consistency, and Appropriateness

Competence reflects the need for leaders to regularly learn new teachable skills; solve problems; and make quick, informed decisions based on data, information, and managerial, domain, and leadership knowledge. Furthermore, competence addresses the ongoing need to acquire and apply new knowledge—that which is necessary to carry out operational and instructional objectives.[4] This definition of competence doesn't extend to developing self-awareness about one's positionality, impact, and approach, which is a crosscutting disposition called Self-reflection and Continuous Learning. Here, competence is a response to, and navigational strategy to address, the expectation that women demonstrate high levels of skill and knowledge.

My own journey includes participation in teamwork, communication, presentation, facilitation, and management workshops and in weeklong leadership sessions. I earned baccalaureate, master's, and doctoral degrees. I recently met a Black woman who earned three master's degrees along with a doctorate. Over the course of my career, I attended conferences on numerous subjects ranging from youth apprenticeship to improvement science. It seems like every day it was necessary for me to learn something new. If my boss charged me with reconfiguring large high schools into small ones, I read broadly about small schools and interviewed people working in, funding, and researching them. I conducted site visits with teams who used observation protocols I developed. Often, a supervisor, board member, community member, or new policy relied on me to develop my understanding of, to implement, or to communicate about an issue I hadn't yet encountered. On the job I studied various topics to teach others, manage associated changes, or create implementation plans. This included:

1. accountability frameworks
2. charter schools
3. collective impact models
4. evaluation protocols
5. grant writing and monitoring
6. impact metrics and monitoring
7. instructional and information technology systems
8. legislation

9. marketing, public relations, and communication mediums, vehicles, tactics, and plans
10. procurement protocols
11. remote learning strategies
12. school redesign approaches
13. strategic and annual planning processes
14. survey design

Similarly, several of the respondents reflect on the need to gain new knowledge.

> **Catrina**: Read extensively and build your professional knowledge. Build relationships with others—it is hard to get things accomplished without the knowledge and persistence of others.
>
> **Dedee**: While I recognize that nothing is more certain than change, attention to the change process (research and practices) can guide an organization to adapt. However, when a process for change is not considered, structures, systems, and individuals begin to deteriorate and the organization can fail.
>
> **Diedre**: Stretch[ing] yourself to take on experiences that prepare you for the job you want and to apply for that job as soon as it is available. Do not wait for the "right time" to have more experience, more knowledge, more anything.
>
> **Michelle**: The first strategy is to select a position with a boss or mentor who is wise, encouraging, supportive and can help me grow in my own abilities. The second strategy is to gain as much field experience as possible as most learning in education occurs by being hands-on. The third strategy is to be a continuous learner and keep up with all research and be active and involved in professional organizations that can also act as a support network. The fourth strategy is to have trusted colleagues who will be there to provide feedback on ideas and actions. The fifth strategy is to not be afraid of new ideas or taking risks.

(S-3) Development and Support: Establish and Support Opportunities for Others' Ongoing Professional Learning, Growth, and Advancement

Educational leaders—who practice collectivist, cultural, social justice, feminist, or teaching and learning approaches—invest in relationships and others' growth, development, and contributions. Such leaders commit to supporting—through coaching, mentoring, modeling, encouraging, training, providing feedback to, and evaluating—individuals and teams. Leaders may facilitate others' personal and professional goal development and attainment so that each person can reach their potential and develop skills and expertise necessary to realize individual and collective missions. Leaders practicing this standard strive for transparency in sharing information about expectations, progress, and organizational objectives.

Bierema and Madsen (2017) share the following insight:

> We often think of organized, formal training classes as a way to facilitate leadership development but most of the learning that leaders engage in to learn their craft is experiential; informal knowledge acquisition through observation, conversation, mistakes, reflection, and experimentation. Experiential learning of this this type is the hallmark of effective adult learning and human resource development.[5]

My management style involves coaching staff through assignment completion, supporting staff members on an ongoing basis, and ensuring staff feel valued, informed, and sufficiently resourced. I provide regular and unscheduled access to me and assess staff members' individual strengths, areas of growth, and professional development priorities. I facilitate their realization of their individual development goals. Once I oversaw a six-person team, whose office assistant was a skilled copy editor. During our annual goal-setting meeting, we discussed her interest in becoming a senior-level executive assistant. During the six-month period following our meeting, I connected her with CEOs' assistants for informational interviews and observation. She concluded that she wasn't interested in such a career track and we jointly identified technical editing as a possibility. I assigned her as the primary copy editor for our program materials and allocated resources for her to attend a technical editor certificate program. This situation was a win-win because she—although on a small team in a small organization with limited advancement—could grow and extend her learning within the confines of her existing situation while concurrently pursuing a long-term goal. Our team benefited from her editing and positive attitude—the latter due in part to the investment we made in her future.

Investment in others' development and growth goes hand-in-glove with my collectivist, cultural, social justice, and feminist approaches to leadership. I don't provide colleagues, team members, and other stakeholders with support and incentives to benefit me. However, it is likely that such investment can result in reciprocal support and loyalty and a common commitment to work for meaningful change. Seeking to draw on this standard helps me cultivate my knowledge of the people with whom I'm working. I commit to their growth so they can develop their own skills and abilities, make adjustments, and pursue their aspirations. They grow. I grow. The work thrives as well as the individuals. Chapter 7 delves more fully into effective leadership development strategies.

Respondents also support the importance of this standard.

> **Crystal**: Adapt and adopt processes that will empower school leaders, district leaders and teachers to ensure academic achievement for ALL students.
>
> **Georgette**: Creating opportunities for others to lead initiatives, committees, programs and projects … [and a] professional development based on annual needs assessment … Developing, implementing and monitoring professional development based on an annual needs assessment informed by faculty and staff.
>
> **Lydia**: Very early in my career, ["Julia"], who at that time was my principal, identified me as a leader and encouraged me to take risks. I was teaching severely and profoundly retarded students and one of the students in the class was a plaintiff in a class-action lawsuit that eventually led to the development of ESY [the program]. Rather than worrying about the outcome of the lawsuit, [Julia] encouraged me to take the opportunity to hone my skills and that led to my leadership role as a special education supervisor … I was absolutely committed to ongoing professional development for issues of equity and understanding.
>
> **Mathilda**: Education systems are about developing people. One strategy that I have used often is to invest in developing the people who work for me not only professionally but personally. Once we establish the action plan for the department, I have 1-1 meetings asking each team member to identify at least 2 professional goals and 1 personal goal. In our conversation, we develop a strategy for how I might support them in reaching all of their goals. When people know you care about developing them, it has been my experience that they exceed your expectations for the work they accomplish.

(S-4) Equitable Culture: Forward Diverse and Welcoming Environments That Cultivate and Build Respect for Each Person's Unique Potential, Contribution, Background, Safety, and Culture

Equitable Culture incorporates the creation, reinforcement, and maintenance of a social justice-oriented teaching, learning, and workplace environment.

Equitable culture encompasses two different perspectives. First, it focuses on one's awareness of, understanding of, and respect different vantage points—due to privilege, positionality, roles, rituals, cultural backgrounds, and opportunities. The second component of equitable culture incorporates the working conditions, professional communities, and stakeholder interactions associated with teaching, learning, working, and leading diverse systems and groups of people. Equitable culture signals that the educational environment—in the corridors, conference rooms, offices, and convening spaces of schools, central offices, and third-party education organizations—is positive, safe, and welcoming for all stakeholders.

My calling, experience, and leadership approaches drive me to prioritize the people I'm entrusted with educating and serving. This includes treating others considerately and fairly; creating work and learning environments that are welcoming and safe for students, parents, educators, staff, community members, and partners; and valuing the involvement, backgrounds, and perspectives of stakeholders. It means monitoring the extent to which my employers—and their employees, systems, and structures—meet these objectives.

Once, an organization's leader charged me with representing their office on an equity initiative. Several factors led up to our organization's shift in focus and deliberate choice to emphasize racial equity as core to carrying out our organizational mission, which focused on preparing educational leaders. There were plentiful data about the disproportionate negative educational outcomes among students of color—including reading levels, algebra enrollment by ninth grade, and standardized test scores. Also concerning were students of color's suspension rates, dropout rates, high-school progression rates, and college-going and retention rates. Other drivers influencing our focus were such students' inadequate access to challenging courses, high-quality teaching and educational materials, and equitable per pupil funding. Lastly, CCSSO's *Model Principal Supervisor Professional Standards 2015* and the NPBEA's *Professional Standards for Educational Leaders 2015* included equity standards in their frameworks. We sought to respond proactively to those frameworks.

Our organization—through a cross-department approach—established racial equity priorities and launched efforts to change our culture. We modified our program standards, curriculum and pedagogy, program facilitator training, and coach support. We trained our entire staff alongside the leadership team. We changed our value statements, funding priorities, and communication documents. We asked employees to focus on racial equity for at least one of their annual professional goals—even if it was to explore how the prioritization of racial equity affected that employee. We created virtual simulations to allow program participants to practice responses to thorny racial equity situations. We launched a mini-grant process for program graduates to address disproportionate outcomes among boys of color. We established strategies, budgets, and objectives associated with each of these racial equity priorities.

The last piece was the most difficult—the leadership team needed to practice what we preached. We had to model values of openness, transparency, continuous learning, allyship, and commitment to a modified mission. This meant I, a white woman on the organization's leadership team and with the ear of the organization's leader, had to model a level of comfort with my own discomfort. Employees challenged my contributions to and participation in racial equity committee meetings, named my privilege, questioned my understanding of and commitment to racial equity, and wondered aloud about my appointment to colead this effort. It was frustrating, difficult, stressful, and rewarding. We made systemwide changes in our stances, our culture, and our programs.

Respondents also commented on the importance of culture and equity.

> **Diane**: I think the organizational environment is what helps me live out important leadership strategies. If the environment is not one that embraces these strategies the same way I do it hinders my leadership.
> **Diedre**: I think about leading to create a culture that empowers others to bring a high degree of performance to the work and to sustaining environments that get positive academic and emotional outcomes for children, that is often NOT from the positional focused leader, but rather from the relational focused leader.
> **Jaimie**: They should have promoted a culture of inclusion, created goals and follow-through around the issues, have courageous conversations, had a culture of no-tolerance for such [bullying] behaviors and projected that everyone mattered and needed to treat each other like human beings each other for the success of the district.
> **Jean**: Creating a culture of inclusion and respect.
> **Joan**: Culture—this is the hardest one to work with and to change. We can only influence change in culture by being active role models and leading with the values we want the culture to embrace. It can take a lot of time and a lot of patience to influence people and large organizations to improve their culture.

Kelly: As I've gotten more leadership roles, It can feel risky to raise issues of inequality or racism because of possible repercussions (not being considered for a role, raise, asked to speak).

Mathilda: Culture—I love that the definition you used talked about fostering diverse environments. I see many educational leaders surround themselves with "yes" people, which often led to the leader being blindsided. For me, I want as many diverse perspectives at the table as possible, so that when a decision is made it accounts for more issues that might arise during implementation. Diverse perspectives also foster healthy, productive conversations, which is vital for the success of an organization as it fosters psychological safety.

Wilma: I have taken the risk of directly and openly discussing issues of racism and white supremacy within the context of team meetings in an organization that has historically shied away from openly addressing such issues among the staff. I decided to be open and transparent with my team at the time because it is important to look at our work through an antiracist lens. We have to be able to address big conversations to know what areas we need to focus on to move our work towards being more equitable and just.

(S-5) Performance Management: Establish and Implement Systems to Monitor Goals, Objectives, and Performance to Ensure Quality, Consistency, Desired Impact, and Accountability

Determining how well a team, program, department, school, district, network, or organization enacts their vision, mission, goals, and values is as important as is developing such statements. Many aspirations don't come to full fruition, break down, or may be improved upon during implementation. Performance Management is about realizing an espoused vision through defining and implementing systems and processes that facilitate the realization of the aligned goals and objectives. Such systems and processes then focus on ensuring implementation progress on various elements of the standards.

Organizational performance should concentrate on system coherence—aligning all resources with the core mission and strategic priorities. The point is to collaboratively identify, assign, and monitor how a project, team, initiative, school, or classroom is fairing against its performance targets. Performance management's scope includes the development, implementation, and examination of coherent ways to monitor the implementation and effectiveness of a range of undertakings from accountability to measurement to resource allocation to evaluation. Here are some examples:

1. grant reporting
2. impact analysis
3. performance target and evaluation objective establishment
4. practice and program adjustments and improvements
5. progress monitoring (feedback loops, after action reviews, and regular reporting)
6. strategic abandonment

Often people interpret a strategic plan or a school improvement plan—and the associated budget and assignment of responsibility—as delivering coherence. A plan is merely espoused—it must be resourced, assigned, implemented, and monitored. Then and only then can you know if it was enacted with fidelity. The adage, what gets measured, gets done, is central to the function of performance management. It's important to know if something has happened and to know how well it occurred, whether the time and resources were assigned and expended appropriately, and about which barriers and enablers impeded or facilitated implementation. If something didn't happen as planned, performance management allows leaders to understand what prevented its on-time, on-budget, high-quality implementation, and to identify improvements or areas to abandon.

Many of my roles focused on the performance management function. One example includes an early-career executive director role when I assumed leadership of a program that had been receiving five- and ten-year funding commitments with little to no required grant reporting. The year I arrived, the corporate funders switched from five-year allocations to annual grant awards tied to specific grant objectives. It was my job to teach program staff about measurable grant objectives, project plans, and grant reporting. The program design espoused support for students of color's access to post-secondary Science, Technology, Engineering, and Mathematics (STEM) programs. Many participating junior and senior high-school students weren't on grade level and hadn't taken grade-level science and math courses. Some students earned grade point averages of 1.0 or lower. The program's coaches—even though they were responsible for selecting, supporting, and coaching students for eventual acceptance to demanding STEM college programs—were earning a regular weekly paycheck regardless of how many students participated on a weekly basis, how many GPAs were increased, or how many students enrolled and passed grade-level STEM courses.

Later, I assumed responsibility for an urban district's research, evaluation, and testing division at the height of the No Child Left Behind (NCLB) era. NCLB required districts to define graduation cohorts consistently across the country and report the percent of students—disaggregated by demographic and socioeconomic background—who graduated on time from a four-year high-school cohort—that is, within four years. We monitored academic performance, suspensions, enrollment, and attendance by school and grade level. Data breakdowns provided districts and schools (and states) with vital information about inequities. I worked closely with a consulting group that isolated when middle-school students started to fail. Failure commenced in two places—at second grade, students' gains from pre-kindergarten (PreK) participation began to decline, and at fourth grade, students' command of (or lack thereof) reading and math followed them into middle school.

Additional examples demonstrate the ways in which performance management techniques apply to decision-making, course correction, and communication. In yet another district, we conducted an enrollment and facility analysis to identify which elementary and middle schools were at less than 75 percent of enrollment capacity. This led to recommendations to change some elementary-to-middle and middle-to-high school feeder patterns and to consolidate some schools into one site. When I worked for a major funder, I co-led a cross-organizational team of scholars conducting a large-scale evaluation of the funder's investment in a city's redesigned high schools. Based on the espoused purpose of the investment—to improve low-income and minority high-school students' academic performance, graduation rates, and postsecondary retention—the evaluation team collaboratively identified the research questions, the qualitative and quantitative data sets, and evaluation methodology of each evaluation organization.

Respondents' comments also address the importance of this standard.

Crystal: [The ability] to use a comprehensive data set to evaluate current academic needs and academic initiatives.

Ester: I noticed that our African American population historically never improved at our school. I was able to use subgroup data to help others see it has been a problem for years and helped to push teachers to be aware of all students in the classroom.

Georgette: Setting and monitoring performance standards and publicly reporting progress or lack thereof.

Joan: Performance Management—systems, performance management processes, mid-year and annual reviews, etc. All forms of accountability in place enable work to be measured and highlights areas of improvement. Intentional conversations about where we are and how we will measure our progress.

Mathilda: Performance Mgt.—This area is a weakness for most educational leaders. However, I have used this strategy often when leading others and find it so helpful in prioritizing the work to measure & communicate our impact.

(S-6) Teaching and Learning: Facilitate and Support Stakeholders' Understanding and Implementation of Equitable and High-Quality Teaching and Learning Practices and Systems (Instruction; Curriculum; Assessment; Academic and Grade-Level Standards; Technology; and Social, Emotional, and Physical Development)

As the core function of a school system, Teaching and Learning's scope is broad and encompasses instruction, curriculum, assessment, technology, grade level and academic standards, and social, emotional, and physical development. This standard focuses on fulfilling the promises, which I share in Chapter 3, and is the core mission of the prekindergarten through twelfth grade (PreK-12) educational enterprise. It incorporates the design and implementation of the major components of teaching and learning, each of which has myriad sub-elements and aligned areas of knowledge. Assessment alone involves creating and aligning classroom, unit, district, and state formative and summative assessments with domain standards and best practices. Assessment incorporates analyzing and using student data and interpreting and implementing local, state, national, and partner assessment protocols. Assessment also involves one's ability to monitor and intervene to support student progress (which is also part of instruction); manipulate database and software programs for assessment development and analysis; and execute numerous additional daily, weekly, reporting period, and annual evaluations.

Increasingly, district leaders believe their boards hire them to be instructional leaders. According to *The American Superintendent Decennial Study* (2021),

> Almost 58% of all superintendents reported that the school board hired them to be an instructional leader in 2020, compared to a mere 20% of all superintendents in 2010. Seventy-two percent of the women in this [AASA decennial] survey believed this to be one of the three primary reasons for their hire compared to only 33% of women in 2010. Only about 52% of male superintendents believed they were hired to be instructional leaders.[6]

Furthermore, instructional and academic roles have traditionally been more accessible to women as "women are twice as likely as men to have prior service as curricular specialists (31.3% of women and 16% of men)."[7]

Although I haven't overseen the academic components of schools, districts, or third-party education support organizations, it was integral to my career to develop and expand my knowledge of the teaching and learning process. Much of what I learned about teaching and learning was on-the-job—including from colleagues, reading, and observation. My roles put me in the position of leading various teams of educators to learn about or affect some change relating to instruction, assessment, or curricula. Recall my research on different school models, structures, practices, and cultures. My analyses examined the organization of students in K-8 grade configurations; how K-8s fare in comparison to 6–8 middle schools; how Montessori programs teach students, train teachers, set up their classrooms, and receive accreditation; and effective small school practices. Such research facilitated the way in which I led teams of principals and teachers to implement new or different school models. One boss tasked me with studying the practices of two high-performing elementary schools to identify their teaching, learning, cultural, and structural practices; and then cowriting a best practices case study. I also sat with a team of school principals to design and articulate their instructional models for a successful magnet school grant.

As a partner to a district, I convened school staff and employer partners to develop youth apprenticeship programs, which also involved identifying program standards and delivery techniques for which the employer and the school program were each responsible. There, I immersed myself in manufacturing, community college program, Associate of Occupational Studies (AOS), and health standards. I developed career ladders based on the standards and aligned them with the corresponding postsecondary coursework and technical roles. In another partner role, I worked with groups of superintendents, principals, teachers, and third-party education model partners–including vendors for International Baccalaureate (IB), Cambridge Assessment International Education (AICE), Advanced Placement (AP), and American College Testing (ACT)—to reconfigure high school programs in two southwestern states. At one point, I learned about teaching the scientific method to support multiple aspects of a district's science team in its professional development of teachers and related communication efforts. The coleads gave me my own white coat with my name on it!

Possessing a working knowledge of teaching and learning—and remaining open to my own learning and lack of PreK-12 teaching experience—enabled me to facilitate various teams. Such knowledge and experience influenced my insertion of the word, facilitate, in the draft "Teaching and Learning" standard to indicate that educational leaders might lead from a variety of vantage points and to recognize they may or may not directly oversee teaching and learning in classroom or school settings. This was the case with my own educational leadership roles. Keeping one's focus on the fundamental purpose of educational organizations allows for purpose-driven leadership. Respondents speak to the centrality of teaching and learning.

> **Bonnie**: All aspects of leadership must unite around instructional outcomes for students. Once those outcomes are clearly identified, leaders must adapt their practices to maximize those outcomes … [It is] important to stay focused on students and what is educationally best for them.
>
> **Jackie**: No matter what, make your decisions based on what is in the best interest of students and families. Let your staff or co-workers know up front that this will guide your decision-making. Ask others what their values are—what are they willing to lose their jobs for? If values are in conflict, discuss them, align them as best you can. But never lose focus on the students.
>
> **Lottie**: Teaching and Learning has been the strategy that has enabled me to exercise sound leadership practices.
>
> **Mathilda**: Being in the business of education, this is the heart of the organization.
>
> **Patty**: I have always been motivated by the public-school ethos that dictates equitable education for all students.
>
> **Zelda**: Within educational settings a leader maintains a focus on teaching and learning for all students.

(S-7) Vision: Espouse, Model, and Motivate Others to Support the Vision, Mission, Values, and Goals

Articulating and influencing others to follow a compelling Vision—which is a desired future state and typically includes articulating corresponding missions, values, goals, and strategies—is a regularly cited requirement for effective leadership. Vision is what separates leadership from management. Russ Marion and Leslie Gonzales (2014) see that "management involves seeing to the routine, standardized operations of a system … [whereas] leadership involves activities that influence change in a system."[8] In addition to articulating and realizing the need for change, Ibarra et al. (2019) propose that, "vision has been found to be the central component in charismatic leadership and the essence of the oft-noted distinction between management and leadership."⁹

Leaders must look into the future, translate a vision into compelling messages and strategies, possess a systems orientation, and use evocative imagery to influence uptake. Vision is also about the ways in which a leader employs communication and political skills, creates a compelling rationale for the vision, and establishes a purpose and meaning for individuals' work. One can develop a vision at a myriad of levels—program, department, team, school, district, network, organization, and community. However, if the vision is at the team, department, program, or school level and a district vision exists, then leaders must align the departmental visions with the district vision to ensure coherence. If there is no such systemwide vision, the focus then becomes an attempt to clarify that group's vision, mission, goals, and responsibilities nested within their interpretation of the systemwide direction, which guides them.

Additional elements of vision can include:

1. engaging in long-term strategic thinking
2. envisioning change
3. espousing goals
4. establishing organizational coherence
5. facilitating consensus
6. identifying opportunities and threats
7. influencing, inspiring, and motivating others to buy in to and implement the vision
8. seeing the big picture its component parts
9. understanding and conveying planning terms

I've possessed responsibility for shepherding, on many a boss's or client's behalf, strategic plan development and also led such processes for my own team or organization. Such planning involves facilitating teams, committees, and community, school, organization, network, or district stakeholders to develop a compelling vision and elucidate the steps necessary to enact a vision. Fortunately, several leaders to whom I reported were strategic thinkers and visionaries. Sometimes they used a theory of change diagram to demonstrate what undergirds their vision. One leader employed a diagram of a house, which placed the mission and crosscutting components as the foundation and the columns as the major goals and capabilities needed.

Leaders bring many different strengths—and areas for growth—to the table. A leader may be a compelling visionary as well as a competent implementer. A leader may be a great visionary but not a great implementer. Sometimes leaders are unrealistic visionaries whose visions come across as rhetoric perhaps because the leader doesn't walk the talk or has not assigned adequate support or clarity to realizing the vision. Sometimes leaders are charismatic visionaries who people want to follow and who also understand how to assign capable staff to the aspects of implementation that the leader either couldn't, or didn't have the capacity to, implement themself.

If a leader with whom I'm working is too lofty, I think of myself as a person wearing a yellow hat holding onto a runaway monkey's legs as he floats skywards holding too many helium balloons (see Figure 6.2). I once reported to a leader whose espoused vision was a 100 percent cohort graduation rate when existing

Figure 6.2 Yellow Hat.[10]

rates were 80 percent. When we disaggregated the data, they reflected much lower graduation rates and significant gaps based on race, ethnicity, gender, and disability. A different leader wanted me to complete a comprehensive organization-wide strategic plan—with internal and external stakeholder involvement—within a four-month period. This would have been difficult even without organization- and community-wide planning fatigue and without me having just started my job in a new city.

Respondents also have things to say about vision(ing).

Catrina: Creating a vision, identifying values, and placing students at the center of all decision making is crucial to the success of the organization and to the success of our future.

Diedre: Building relationships and getting to know the strengths of others around me has allowed me to focus on vision and culture building of the organization and to allow myself to trust teams to attend to the management and accountability aspects of leading their divisions … Know what you value (I would say this to any leader) and stand up for what you value.

Joan: It would be nearly impossible to lead and mobilize people without a common goal, or a shared vision. My belief is that we are as a nation are able, capable and well-resourced to close equity and achievement gaps is one of the grounding principles. This belief enables me to reimagine all of the possibilities we have that can enable our system to remove barriers of access to a high-quality education for all students. Vision enables innovation. New ideas are better accepted when they are seen as part of a larger vision.

Mathilda: Leadership is defined as influence. As a leader, you must engage others at all different levels to establish a vision for the work … I see this step get left out often in educational settings; however, it is vital for the strength of the organization that everyone knows the vision, mission, and values. Furthermore, it has been my experience that if they have a voice in developing them, the work gets aligned much better and people go above and beyond your expectations.

Michelle: Leaders share a passionate vision for success combined with an action-oriented plan that focuses on the whole child.

Nola: Leadership is the ability to move a group of stakeholders, likely extremely diverse, to a common goal for the betterment of the students and families.

Reese: Much of my work has to happen in collaboration with other staff, so it's critical that I inspire and lead with vision.

Zelda: A leader provides guidance and direction for the mission and vision of the organization.

Dispositions for Women Educational Leaders

Recall that dispositions include characteristics and behaviors—how and from what stance someone carries out her work. What follows in this section are the eight crosscutting dispositions outlined in Figure 6.1.

(D-1) Collaboration and Engagement: Work Constructively to Engage, Support, Collaborate with, Incorporate Viewpoints of, and Partner with All Stakeholders

Internal and external stakeholders are vital partners and contributors to the delivery of teaching and learning and realization of student and family support. Collaboration and Engagement—previously People and Relationships and Teamwork—highlights the need for leaders to involve stakeholders, seek their individual and collective perspectives, and synthesize and make sense out of their ideas. Collaboration and engagement also speak to the contexts and situations in which, and the spirit with which, leaders bring people together. Further, collectivist (feminist, social justice, and cultural) leaders may mobilize different groups—whether parents, the community, staff, or colleagues—by building trust. Earlier chapters convey that working with and through others can be key strategies aligned with women's approaches to leading for social justice and from a collectivist standpoint.

My own roles placed me in the thick of leadership that drew on collaboration and engagement. Earlier, I introduced the large-scale community planning process during which period I designed—with teams, technical support, participation incentives, and trusted colleagues—a community plan. This plan reflected the community members, community leaders, and school district's priorities to change outcomes for children and families in a designated area of the city. Earlier in this chapter, I describe a grant process to convert two high schools to small schools during which time I convened—and arrived at consensus with—stakeholders including teachers, unions, principals, board members, employers, and a major funder.

Here is a sample of the functions for which I was responsible:

1. Communicator
2. Evaluator
3. Facilitator
4. Framework designer
5. Grant manager and writer
6. Partner
7. Planner
8. Problem-solver
9. Relationship manager
10. Researcher
11. School board liaison
12. Thought leader
13. Writer

When I convened—with a colead—a large community committee, members contributed to the district's understanding and decision-making about student enrollment, student placement, and school feeder patterns. This committee's work relied on an internal cross-divisional team comprised of placement, facilities, research, parent engagement, communications, and school leadership. It included representatives from the board of education, city government, principals, parents, and unions, among others. We held large community meetings—which involved real-time voting from community members—to help guide decision-making and recommendations. In Chapter 2, I describe the ways in which my work with stakeholders influenced my collectivist approach to leadership which showed me that empowering stakeholders to contribute and make collaborative decisions had a positive impact on projects and on those involved.

Many respondents note the importance of teamwork, collaboration, and people and relationships.

> **Avril**: Strong people skills—People & Relationships and Teamwork—facilitated my ability to practice sound educational leadership.
> **Bonnie**: Leadership in educational settings is the act of bringing together multiple and varying stakeholders to focus on what is best for students.
> **Crystal**: It was vital for me to develop relationships with my colleagues in Academics, School Leadership, Principals, as well as other central office team members to create a collaborative culture, to solicit feedback and

reflection, to access student and school needs and to learn and develop new ways to align resources to meet school needs.

Diedre: The relationship aspect is critical to allowing the people to raise their hand and ask for help when they need or want it, to identify what supports they need to meet the expectation/outcome and also to be daring in trying something that may be novel.

Ester: Build[ing] and maintaining relationships with all stakeholders is the main pillar to all of the work we do.

Joan: Strong relationships with academics and teaching and learning leaders have enabled my ability to design operational processes that capture the needs of our school based staff. Getting their input and feedback and leveraging their networks with school based leaders has been essential in the success of new operational process development and implementation.

Kelly: The ability to listen to the needs and concerns of your school community. Be intentional about building a community and partnership among your colleagues, families, and community at large. Embrace accountability and acknowledge the history & knowledge of your school community.

Nola: By working collaboratively, I have been able to identify priorities and engage in problem solving with diverse groups.

Sharon: Allow a diverse group of stakeholders to participate in the planning and implementation process.

(D-2) Communication: Communicate with Ease, Clarity, Respect, and Transparency with a Variety of Stakeholders in a Variety of Settings and via a Variety of Mediums

Communication is critically important to a leader's success as highlighted by respondents' high ratings of it in the Chapter 5 discussion. It is a requirement for every component of leadership and especially for women—whose voices are silenced, policed, usurped, and strategically softened, and whose communication must be impeccable and mediated. Hourly, daily, weekly, and monthly a leader must draw on a vast repertoire of speaking, listening, and writing skills and methods to motivate, cajole, instruct, inform, collaborate, facilitate, contribute, and navigate. From a personal standpoint, I believe that if I hadn't felt comfortable, confident, and capable as communicator, I wouldn't have risen to the level of nonprofit or district leadership that I did. As a graduate student, I wouldn't have made it through an accelerated program if I hadn't been able to quickly frame and write papers, listen, contribute to class discussions and team projects, and synthesize ideas and information.

In one early career role, I rewrote everything the vice president there penned—she gave me handwritten notebook pages with no punctuation in them. Her writing lacked paragraph breaks, verb-subject agreement, sentence clarity, and accurate spelling. As the young policy wonk, I researched, analyzed, synthesized differing viewpoints, and built positions on a broad array of education topics—from employability standards to curriculum standards to school choice to governance to resource allocation. Such projects commenced with initial research, which followed with stakeholder and expert meetings, and then with listening to varied perspectives. I took detailed notes and developed written analyses based on the notes. I read broadly, organized information, and presented to groups large and small—including advisory, nonprofit organization, and school boards as well as corporate, government, and funding leaders. As a partner, I identified areas where agendas could intersect and consensus be realized. I listened to understand. When facilitating small and large groups, I synthesized ideas and tested to make sure stakeholders were on the same page.

As a special assistant and chief of staff, I was a ghostwriter, message preparer, board liaison, public spokesperson, and agenda developer. As an evaluator or evaluated entity, I presented written and cogent strategy elements including visions, missions, goals, objectives, strategies, actions, and impact measures. As an organization leader, I met with and presented to a cross section of community, state, and national leaders, and the media. Such situations required me to articulate my message clearly, transparently, and diplomatically. Simultaneously I sought to modulate my body language, dress, and nonverbal cues.

Once I was a new leadership team member working in the office of a new superintendent who was receiving questions from board members, the press, and parents about a policy I helped research, develop, and finalize. He called me into his office and said, "Tell me about this policy and where we are with implementation. One of the TV channels is out there and is awaiting an interview." I explained the policy and provided him with key contextual points all while he was sitting in front of his computer writing something else. He turned to me and said, "You go talk to them!" That was my first press interview. Following that first interview, I ended up in front of various rooms of parents—as well as the board of education—to discuss the policy's key elements and then, ultimately, to recommend and secure approval for an implementation delay. Eventually the policy's implementation became my responsibility.

After that, I kept a suit coat in my office, and participated in media, communication, and public speaking training. College and graduate school forced me to write thirty-page and five-page papers, a thesis, and a dissertation. I participated in a Language for Women Who Lead seminar and learned about the ways in which one's language and physical mannerisms can diminish what is intended. Women often pepper their statements and writings with weak or hedging words such as just, I think, I'm sorry, I feel, could I, would you, I'm only, I'd like to, I hope, I guess, kind of, I want, I need, maybe, like, just, really, and so on. Women may twirl their hair, touch their jewelry, not look people in the eye, or hold their arms around themselves. Having gifted, to many a young woman colleague, Phyllis Mindell's 2001 book, *How to Say it for Women: Communicating with Confidence and Power Using the Language of Success*, I made sure to eliminate such words and actions from my own repertoire and coach other women accordingly.[11] Overall, I wrote and edited descriptions—and presented to key stakeholders about the content—of a variety of issues and programs using numerous document types, most of which I've outlined below:

1. Applications
2. AP shorts
3. Book (writing and editing)
4. Brochure copy
5. Case studies
6. Dissertation
7. Elevator speeches
8. Evaluations
9. Frequently asked questions (FAQs)
10. Frameworks
11. Graduate thesis
12. Grant proposals and reports
13. Handbooks
14. Job descriptions
15. Legal contracts
16. Letters
17. Memorandum of understanding (MOU)
18. Memos
19. Message triangles
20. Plans

21. Position and white papers
22. Presentations
23. Press releases
24. Program, course, and performance standards
25. Proposals
26. Protocols
27. Reports
28. Requests for proposals (RFPs)
29. Talking points
30. Website copy

Multiple respondents speak about the importance of communication whether it be for information sharing; listening and learning; or conveying honesty, transparency, and respect. Respondents also discuss the role of inquiring, delivery quality, and collaborating as well.

> **Angela**: I believe the foundation for all areas is communication. Not just speaking with each other, but honest/open/respectful communication. Everything else will fall in its place should this type of communication be the core.
>
> **Joan**: Being intentional about how information gets delivered, perceived and potential ways in which it can be misinterpreted is key. Taking the time to craft communication that is concise, balanced and clear is critical in not only getting the point across but in building relationships as well.
>
> **Julie**: Listening to others is critical. Making sure people feel like they are being heard.
>
> **Kelly**: An important strategy overall is focusing on LISTENING. It's simple in concept but the art and science of listening to understand, for me is a focal point of how effective leaders strategize.
>
> **Lottie**: [Sound educational leadership] strategies would fail if a leader did not communicate at all levels. I have always been a listener and a teacher—whether it be in a classroom or across the desk from a staff person—whether it be my CEO or a teaching assistant. My most recent Executive Director would call on me to communicate with staff because she felt that I could be direct without causing harm, that they were better able to accept a communication from me rather than her on some occasions. I am a respectful communicator, no matter who I'm speaking to.

Mathilda: As a leader, you can never communicate enough and have to always be looking for different methods of communication. This area also helps you be transparent with the team you are leading.

Natalie: Communication is important and keeping in mind when we think something is clear, it will be interpreted based on relationships and whether the information disrupts processes or thinking.

(D-3) Confidence: Possess and Project Belief in One's Own Abilities—through Calculated Risk-Taking, Mastery, and Self-Assurance

There is synergism among the Competence, Resilience, and Confidence dispositions, which informs my rationale for retaining this category. The circular thinking goes like this: build knowledge; take action; face trials, tribulations, and successes; overcome trials and tribulations; feel good about overcoming and learning from them; feel good about your successes and learn from them; and build confidence. Key elements of confidence range from belief in oneself and one's successes; confrontation of challenges; positive expectations; and self-compassion, self-efficacy, and self-worth. Below are additional elements:

1. Achievement
2. Action orientation
3. Assertiveness (sometimes quiet assertiveness)
4. Belief in oneself and one's successes
5. Bias navigation
6. Competence
7. Knowing and being driven by one's calling
8. Overcoming doubts
9. Persistence
10. Positive expectations
11. Risk-taking
12. Willingness to take on new things

I recognize that calling on women to demonstrate confidence is controversial because it may appear to place the onus on the women to show up differently rather than placing the onus on ensuring that their workplaces change to better accommodate and support all their employees. I am not saying women should be the only ones to adjust. However, I do wish to emphasize the importance for women and others to avoid presenting as if they don't believe what they are saying, don't believe in themselves, or don't believe in their ability to speak up about or build a case for something. According to the literature, the antithesis of confidence constitutes dead ends, imposter syndrome, inaction, overthinking, people pleasing, poor sense of self, self-doubt, and not letting go when things don't go well—all of which can erode a woman's confidence.[12]

Returning to the scrappy youngest-child and birth-order references, demonstrating confidence is a consistently identified characteristic of the youngest child. Even without such awareness of my birth order's influence, I learned early how to balance and channel my persistence, action orientation, willingness to take calculated risks, and proclivity for trying new things. Some early life situations come to mind. After ninth grade, I attended a summer dance academy at North Carolina School of the Arts and decided to attend for the school year too. Right after my high-school graduation, I participated in a European Cultural History tour where I studied history in and visited seven countries earning college liberal arts credits. Then on my return, I delayed starting college and moved to a different state to establish residency. After completing college, I moved without a job to New York City and found one. Then I went on to pursue an econometric public policy degree, which required me to learn the algebra, calculus, statistics, and multivariate calculus I'd avoided over the course of entire my K-16 education.

When pursuing my masters, I approached a new education think tank's CEO, after having read about the think tank's arrival in town, to secure an internship there. This then determined the rest of my career route as, after graduating and interning for a full year, I went to work there. While I clearly had Chutzpah, I didn't make these decisions or find myself in situations without deliberation and a healthy dose of reality. The point is I took calculated risks that were both scary and required confidence.

Several respondents remark on the importance of confidence. They often link confidence to possessing sufficient competence to implement strategies thus reinforcing Katty Kay and Claire Shipman's (2014) remarks about the links between confidence and action. They say, "Confidence is linked to doing … one of the essential ingredients in confidence is action, that belief that we can succeed at things, or make them happen … If confidence is a belief in your success, which then stimulates action, you will create more confidence when you take that action."[13]

> **Crystal**: Relationships enabled a feeling of Confidence and Competence with my peers that I was intentionally focusing on the needs of schools and school leaders in developing resource allocation strategies that aligned to academic goals and district initiatives.

Joan: Confidence/Competence: these two go hand in hand. I have met leaders with a lot of confidence that are not very competent and leaders who are competent that have no confidence and none of these two go well without the other. A strategy for me has been that I build my confidence through preparation, excellence in the work I do and this is possible because I have the professional training and experience that allows me to prepare and do my best. Competence builds confidence in my experience.

Lottie: I believe that my confidence and competence has been a value to those I have reported to (primarily Presidents and CEO's).

Mathilda: Confidence and Competence: People do not want to follow a weak and incompetent person. It is ok to be transparent, authentic, and vulnerable but you must walk the walk and model to others excellence … My current boss has been an influence for me. She exudes confidence and integrity. She is solution oriented.

Michelle: I was blessed to have most of my beginning career take place in a district that embraced and supported strong and diverse women leaders. Therefore I never felt uncomfortable or intimidated in settings which were more male dominated. However, I have a fairly strong personality and high level of confidence, so I may not be a typical example.

Reese: I did battle with confidence as a woman in the space. I think we are more self-aware, more reflective, and oftentimes (unfortunately) way more critical of ourselves than others are. This has the effect of making me feel less confident in a space that I really belong in, and I have a lot to contribute to. So in lots of ways I know my own distorted perceptions of my knowledge, skills, and value can lead me to hold back, or not share or lead in instances when I totally should have confidence to do so.

Tanya: My mentors before me and members of my sorority push me to keep pursuing my goals and to remain confident in myself, causing me to strive for higher positions than were previously suggested to me.

(D-4) Creativity and Innovation: Generate and Implement New, Creative, and Relevant Solutions and Ideas

Building the Creativity and Innovation (previously just innovation) muscle can help women navigate their outsider status. Through entrepreneurship, navigational techniques, workarounds, and agility, women can introduce ideas to combat the dominant culture in bureaucracies and systemic and structural challenges. Innovation can help women leaders implement social justice and feminist leadership models.

There are several different lenses to consider when explicating Creativity and Innovation. In "Tempered Radicals as Institutional Change Agents," Debra Meyerson and Megan Tompkins (2007) discuss the ways in which people can view entrepreneurship as an outsider role—a status my own and respondents' stories describe as common for women leaders. Entrepreneurship is "most likely to emerge from the margins of organizations because actors are less aligned with and are disadvantaged by dominant interests, have less at stake when they challenge prevailing arrangements or experiment with new ones, and, importantly, are more likely to be exposed to institutional contradictions."[14] Tempered radicals are "'under the radar rebels' [who] by pushing back on conventions, they create opportunities for change within their organizations."[15] Entrepreneurship and creativity are components of the personality trait, openness to experience. One of five personality traits, openness to experience, is about "exhibiting creativity, nonconformity, autonomy, and unconventional qualities"[16] and found to be an important predictor to one's emergence as a leader—"Excellent leaders are creative and put forward new ideas."[17] A change agent is a characteristic of those who are "inspirational, risk taker[s], energetic, decisive, persuasive."[18] Next, is the concept of workaround, which Russel Bishop (2011) defines as a:

> Method for accomplishing a task or goal when the normal process or method isn't producing the desired results. Workarounds can range from the simple to the complex, from the temporary to the permanent ... There are two basic categories of choice: what you can do directly that doesn't require permission or approval from anyone else, and what you could do with approval, cooperation, or permission from someone else. We will call the first area a choice of control, and the second a choice of influence.[19]

In my last role, I created workarounds, acted as a change agent, and inhabited the thinking of a tempered radical although 1 was in a leadership position. Before starting that job, I had access to my new leader's 100-day workplan. This document incorporated the leader's own priorities, data gleaned from community and district sessions, the school board's expectations, and a community education plan developed prior to this leader's selection and placement. The action item that stood out for me in the workplan was the leader's commitment to complete a strategic plan by a due date, which was approximately four months hence. I was already behind. This local community—and organization—had planning fatigue. In addition to the community plan and the community and district sessions, the organization's leader had also formed a task force to recommend broad organization-wide strategies. The Chamber of Commerce had previously convened committees to prepare its annual state of education report.

Transparency, timing, and broad participation are critical aspects of strategic planning processes so that the public, staff, and board don't perceive leaders as making uniformed and unilateral decisions. I didn't have the time for, the staff for, or others' interest in participating in such a process. I had to devise an entrepreneurial solution. My approach synthesized already-gathered but current data and orchestrated strategically timed opportunities for stakeholder feedback and communication. I reviewed other districts' plans for benchmarking purposes. My small team and I studied existing reports, data sources, minutes from various learning sessions, and the transition team's draft report. I synthesized key themes and then presented the themes to the leadership team, the board of education, and internal and external stakeholders. We communicated publicly—about where and how stakeholders could contribute—via social media, the automated phone message system, the website, meetings, and district newsletters. We analyzed the feedback, edited various strategic plan components based on the feedback, and told the story of the edits. The point I sought to convey is, we asked you for input, analyzed that input, drew conclusions from it, tested our conclusions, asked you again for your input, incorporated that thinking, and finalized the strategic plan elements accordingly.

We couldn't develop, within the short time period, the actual measures that would tell our stakeholders at what rate, by what amount, and by when a particular objective would be achieved. We instead articulated why, what, how, and sometimes by what means we would measure our plan. We couldn't include the level of improvement we were seeking for every category as we simply did not yet have measures and thus had no baseline numbers. I called this Phase III, Annual and Baseline Measures, with the formalized planning process being Phase II, and all that came before it as Phase I, Gather Input and Information. It was a workaround. It required agility. I tell this story not to recommend anyone follow the process I concocted or to cause shivers among other planning professionals, but rather to illustrate the application of out-of-the-box thinking, leveraging limited resources in creative ways, and changing dominant patterns of thinking.

Respondents also comment on the role of innovation.

> **Diedre**: I have worked in both traditional public and public charter schools, with universities and philanthropic entities … There were a

lot of aspects of the charter world that allowed for the creativity and innovation and responsive changes to address needs that led to quick success. Traditional public schools can operate with the same focus, but internal systems seem to beat that innovative and creative problem solving out of the leaders and thus the teachers in these schools.

Dionne: Innovation and pushing my department forward in the research and effective instructional practices and doing what is best for students always drove my department head leadership.

Jackie: Working in organizations that allow flexibility, autonomy, and encourage creativity and implementation of novel ideas, such as charter schools and non-profit organizations, has allowed me to exercise all of the leadership standards I labeled as important or very important.

Kelly: I feel in education that innovation is still an area of untapped potential. Leaders in education have a moral imperative to be wary of quick wins, results or programs of that nature. We inherently understand that risk taking doesn't always yield positive results for our students and they pay the costs when we don't succeed/or our risks don't pay off. It's a delicate balance of being innovative/moving quickly and sticking to what we know/has worked/does something.

Mathilda: Innovation: Another reason why I love having diverse perspectives at the table when leading is to spark innovation. By facilitating a conversation with diverse perspectives at the table, each person can build upon the previous idea, think about things in a different way, and generate innovative solutions to problems.

Tanya: Others' unwillingness to be open to innovation and culture has been a huge barrier for myself and other leaders who come from marginalised communities. People do not always want to see change that requires them to allow others to have the same resources and experiences as them.

(D-5) Political Savvy: Navigate Political Dynamics to Influence and Leverage the Support and Contributions of Stakeholders

The national education culture wars reflect the political nature of public education. Political Savvy is one of the areas I neglected to include in my initial draft list of fourteen standards. While my personal experience demonstrates the need for political navigation, deeper review of the literature and analysis of respondents' answers indicate that understanding politics and being politically savvy are critical for leaders in education. Superintendents indicate they spend up to 37 percent of their time on conflict management.[20] Political savviness includes negative and positive connotations—from amassing power to scheming to jockeying to managing conflict to using power shrewdly for improvement purposes.

In educational leadership, the ability to navigate difficult situations, processes, people, and organizations is an essential muscle particularly for women whose upbringing focuses on being nice, complacent, and conciliatory. Navigation suggests that women are adept at "finding their way from one point to another, determining how to navigate lives, careers, relationships, conflicts, and a variety of other issues (i.e., gender bias, racism, ageism, societal structure, religious structure, cultural issues, etc.)."[21] This ongoing navigation can include knowledge of micro-politics, which encompasses "a range of ways to influence behavior and the usage of social skills and interpersonal assets for reaching change through daily, often informal, activities."[22] When a micro-political issue (such as teacher pay, professional development days, or school safety) is influenced by, or nested within, a broader community, district, state, federal, or partner policy (such as teacher certification or state laws that ban unionization), then macro-politics are influencing the micro-political issue.

As an educational leader, one must dissect and traverse varied political dynamics and contexts—to employ power and influence to achieve desired goals. Depending on the type and level of leadership role one assumes, on any given day, one may manage board of education, collegial, community, teacher, parent, employer, local government, funder, state, and federal relations. This requires leaders to assess political dynamics and implications in a nimble and strategic fashion. To anticipate where I might encounter buried landmines, challenges, and culprits, I developed real-time questions, discernment abilities, and facilitation and navigation techniques. I learned how to read a room and whom to trust. I also planted allies—into discussions, project teams, and meetings—who could help with redirection, de-escalation, co-facilitation, and observations, which people may have dismissed had I made them. One former colleague coined the term "facipulation," because political savvy involves both manipulation and facilitation. More positively, it involves anticipation, calculation, and facilitation.

I recall a graduate school discussion about ways in which one can examine, accrue, and wield power. Is it through the building and facilitation of relationships, control of resources, influencing of key players, or awareness of rules and the effective employment of them? The course clarified that my political power was a result of the way in which I collaborated with stakeholders, influenced them, and leveraged their support, knowledge, trust, and contributions. I sought to work through and with others to accomplish organizational goals. I did my best to treat all stakeholders with respect, advocate for those whose voices wouldn't otherwise be heard, and remain focused on purpose. Nonetheless, there were cases where I swore or raised my voice at a colleague, walked out of a meeting in tears, misstepped, or wanted to ask an aggressive community member who was threatening me if he was going to break my knees. I cannot say that I was always thrilled with or liked myself, because jockeying and scheming often made me uncomfortable (it ran against type). Yet I sought to adeptly read people's intent; build internal and external alliances and allegiances; and anticipate, dodge, and feign disinterest in the personal and professional attacks. I also gathered insights and intelligence and managed through conflict.

Recall when a superintendent asked me to fix a funder's concerns. It required me to understand what was and wasn't working. This analysis involved visiting school sites, meeting with principals and faculty, observing the academic programs, and determining the principals' and faculties' understanding of the grant and funding uses. I identified internal challenges to implementation and found that the principals did not understand what they were supposed to do. They hadn't received sufficient support to move forward. Then I worked with other colleagues to convene teams from each of the affected schools, negotiated staff changes with the union, established implementation plans and steps, and developed facility and programmatic plans with the teams and union.

Grant relations and compliance included macro-political negotiations and actions such as conducting regular virtual check-ins and site visits with the funder, renaming schools and campuses (and securing board and state approval on the name changes), and unpacking legacy accountability issues with the state. Actual implementation included micro-political maneuvering, which ranged from communicating with the district's leadership team and board of education to building staff's understanding about grant requirements. Micro-politics were also at play when determining how to relocate students and programs, rehire faculty members, reallocate resources, and relaunch former schools as new schools. At each step, it was necessary to negotiate with a variety of parties and adjust my interactions based on the stakeholders, the issue's contentiousness, or a person's stance toward the grant's purpose.

Several respondents also noted the role and impact of politics on their work and environment.

> **Billie**: Having served as a superintendent in three school districts, all of which improved student outcomes, there is little doubt that the

governance structure and relationships at the top play a significant role in the capacity to move systems in a positive direction. While state and federal policy interpretation and implementation are influential, the BOE can facilitate or hinder the speed of progress.

Bonnie: Politics and competition can often be deterrents to that goal [of women leading in an education setting] and it is easy to be absorbed in negative behavior on a leadership team.

Diedre: Operating in systems that are more bureaucratic than supportive or that are led by people who believe everyone should "stay in their own lane" seems to be the antithesis of the kind of work we need to do in education, especially as we take on new challenges. I am working to figure out how to get better at "managing up."

Jaimie: Educational leadership is more focused on politics than on educating all students.

Kelly: Navigating the ed space as a Latinx woman requires juggling different hats. There are still stereotypes of how social engagement is viewed, how tone is policed and overall respectability politics is the bread butter in Ed Spaces still. There are very few places that I can feel myself 100% and I acknowledge the role I have in trying to build a better space for other educators that want to bring all of themselves to work.

Lara: My role is to advocate collectively on behalf of school educators who support children and youth. It is often hard to do this when fighting enemies both internal - our own members; and external, political foes, at the same time.

Mathilda: There can be too much back-biting, dirty politics in educational organizations when the wrong people get into leadership roles, which wastes lots of taxpayer dollars and does harm to students.

Zelda: Sometimes in educational leadership we find ourselves as middle-management and there are directives from above and pressures from below that prevent us from being the best leader that we want to be.

(D-6) Professionalism and Ethics: Conduct Oneself and Treat Others with Integrity, Consistency, Good Intent, and Professionalism

Professionalism and Ethics constitutes an area I neglected to prioritize among my draft standards. This additional crosscutting category is complementary to the *Model Principal Supervisor Professional Standards 2015* discussion about the ethical disposition, which states that, "transformational education leaders explicitly and consciously follow laws, policies, and principles of right and wrong in everything they do."[23] However, professionalism and ethics focuses on ethical behaviors that extend beyond being right and wrong. Natalie Porter and Jessica Henderson Daniel (2007) indicate that "values make up the heart of feminist leadership … [and that part of feminist leadership include] ethical practices that promote inclusiveness, integrity, and responsibility."[24] Additional behaviors range from acting honestly and with good intent to employing a moral compass to keeping one's word to holding oneself accountable.

Professionalism and ethics includes additional elements:

1. Building trust
2. Following professional norms
3. Modeling the organization's values
4. Possessing integrity
5. Presenting oneself professionally

My own experience with professionalism and ethics includes me taking deliberate actions based on awareness and reflection. When I was an eighteen-year-old hostess at a busy restaurant, the manager told me that one should present as serenely as a swan above the water while paddling like mad below the surface. In terms of professional presentation, I chose to wear pant or skirt suits, stand up straight, look people in the eye, shake hands firmly, and speak articulately. When I was younger, I also eliminated jewelry that made noise and avoided clothes with lots of color or patterns. When there was a dress-down day, I did not dress down. Someone once asked me if I owned jeans! My own task orientation, work ethic, and mission-driven focus, while often misread, caused me to prioritize the work and mission over self-aggrandizement. Colleagues and partners could rely on me to be honest, direct, and fair. I sought to be professional and calm in the face of most storms or assaults. They also knew me to walk the talk, to chip in, and to take hits on their behalf. I was available and accessible to share insights, feedback, timely information, and explanations.

Because of regular participation in meetings with or presenting to CEOs of nonprofits, businesses, universities, and government, I sought to represent my different organizations, their leaders, the missions, and work products with integrity, consistency, and aplomb. I couldn't become unhinged in the face of adversity. Unfortunately, I knew men who could. It would never and I mean never be okay for a woman leader to shout, stamp her feet, or let go, lose it, and demonstrate frustration and anger. This could result in me (or someone else) being identified as an angry woman, which would "cast me as overemotional, irrational, 'passionate,' maybe hysterical, and certainly a 'not-objective' and fuzzy thinker."[25] Colleagues would not view me as professional.

One supervisor and one colleague were what I call Ragers. This is someone who freely, consciously, and seemingly with the organization's tacit consent, publicly—such as in the center of shared workspace, in a cross-team and cross-functional meeting, or loudly enough for people across an office floor to hear—melts down, yells, and complains about or blocks another's position or decision. I watched, mouth agape, as a different senior colleague yelled that I wasn't permitted to ask him to do something (even though the organization's leader had asked me to do so). He yelled so loudly that that leader's office staff heard the diatribe from 100 yards away.

It is astonishing to watch a grown man in a position of authority willfully transform into a difficult child and then to pick up as if nothing was awry. Ragers demand that others do something their way, threaten others, and belittle others. This isn't the middle-school bully whose characteristics can morph into those of a narcissistic sociopath or psychopath but rather this person's characteristics are befitting of a frustrated three-year-old child throwing a temper tantrum. The result is that their teammates and direct reports end up avoiding them, tip toeing around them, and anxiously recalibrating so as not to set them off. Some might call this managing up and yet the behavior is so clearly outrageous that it makes me wonder why everyone other than the Rager must modify their behavior?

A different leader was what I refer to as a Coverer—he lost his center by lying, deflecting blame, excusing missteps, denying an alternative path exists, and carrying on in an overbearing manner (i.e., this condescending and overly explanatory, uninterruptable type of lecture, delivered to someone who is quite knowledgeable about the topic, is called "mansplaining."[26]) This type of covering is not the same as when one may seek to hide an identity potentially considered by others to be unfavorable.[27] Here covering is in reference to someone who clearly doesn't walk the talk but espouses leadership rhetoric based on favorable models. This leader loses sight of what is real and what is not. Because this type of person is insecure, they lash out in a personal manner at others who are seemingly confident and competent. They change their mind frequently and are dismissive of others' perspectives and input. They have little or no trust in others and lie to cover up something seemingly trivial, but which can morph into something not so trivial. They come up with excuses for negative feedback, will throw anyone under the bus, and probably possess narcissistic motivations. One Black male supervisor asked one of my direct reports if he wanted my job and lied to the person when he said he'd talked to me. Unsurprisingly my direct report checked with me to see if what Bill had told him was true. We had a good, but painful, laugh about the fact that this leader didn't think we would triangulate our data (i.e., check multiple sources for consistency).

Respondents' reflections reinforce inclusion of Professionalism and Ethics as a disposition.

> **Diedre**: The biggest risk I have taken is leaving a job without another job lined up because I could not philosophically condone what I saw as a manipulation of students and families who would not feel like they could confront the system. I felt staying made me complicit in the decisions being made and I would be working counter to the direction my supervisor wanted to go. Leaving a lot of money on the table and not being certain where I would end up was terrifying, but I know it was the right thing to do. I ended up writing my own job description and working on things I enjoy doing.
>
> **Jaimie**: On multiple occasions, I have reported unethical practices by senior-leaders … [and] my ethical stance has prevented me from getting promoted as I refuse to do something that is unethical. [Examples cited included:] My immediate Supervisors: Told me that I needed to hire unqualified candidates because they had personal relationships with them such: Best friend's husband [and] Family members … There was an instance where my supervisor wanted me to lie about a non-bid contract. When I chose not to lie, I was then formally reprimanded with a letter. Had I stayed, I know I was going to get fired/moved out of the position … I reported these practices because they were wasting tax payer money and were not the best decisions for students. In one instance that I reported, nothing was done. I ended up leaving as the senior-leader began bullying me. When I sought help from HR, I got none, so I left the organization. The second instance I reported, there was a third party investigation and finally the senior-leader was made to leave the organization … We need ethical leaders who will do what is best for students.
>
> **Lara**: When you play on a national or international stage, the spotlight is small and intensely bright. It requires someone who has to trust their work will stand under the glare of that type of pressure, that light, and often be okay with not getting credit for its success and most of the blame for its failure. Balancing this with the knowledge that those successes and failures equate to actual lives of people—teachers,

students, parents, families. The egos, politics, and time that is often outsized and wasted often loses sight of this. As a leader, I have felt frustrated or hamstrung by doing what is right under the weight of these constraints.

Leslie: THEY WILL NEVER TREAT YOUR FAIRLY, YOU WILL NEVER BE SEEN AS EQUAL, BUT STAY PROFESSIONAL!

Patty: Whether or not someone is perceived as a "good" or "effective" leader ultimately rests on the level of trust they engender.

Sonja: Building trust with folks at all levels … Never asking someone to do something you would not do yourself.

Tang: Connecting with trustworthy and ethical leaders is a must for women and women of color.

(D-7) Resilience: Respond to Pressures, Disappointments, and Tragedies Quickly, Adaptively, and Effectively

Respondents and scholars alike define resilience with words such as grit, inner strength, courage, adaptability, and confidence. Resilience is tied to adaptively solving and responding to problems, adjusting to change as needed, and countering pressure. Resilient people overcome adversity—they learn from, bounce back from, and cope with difficult situations and perceived failures. Furthermore, resilient people maintain positive relationships, support structures, and work–life balance during difficult times.

It is an odd thing resilience. Those who grow up navigating bias, crime, catastrophes such as floods and fires, and income inequality tend to possess resilience because they've overcome and persevered through so many hardships, whereas those who've grown up in privilege or without such challenges may be less resilient. These are not universal truths; they are stereotypes. Resilience is also not an innate characteristic. One can become more resilient just as one can learn to change her self-talk and acknowledge her achievements thus gaining confidence, learn more about her identity and privilege through reflection, or learn a new skill or deepen her knowledge through practice and study. In thinking about my own resilience, I return to my work ethic and task orientation. Other contributors include birth order, upbringing, and even possibly my astrology sign (Capricorn). I am stubborn and a fighter.

When I took ballet lessons, I was perpetually behind my friends because they had studied ballet longer. Although the teacher allowed me into the more advanced classes, I also studied in lower-level classes to improve my technique.

I became better. I did this same thing when facing a quantitative public policy degree. My then husband taught me algebra with a simple maxim, if you don't know the answer it is because you don't know a rule. This helped me to reframe the way in which I looked at myself—not as a stupid person who was bad at math but rather as someone who needed to ask questions and work until I succeeded. The teaching assistant was my best friend! When confronted with the possibility I would be unable to work in a leadership position within a district, I fought to secure a non-civil-service, special-category position. I was hired! When I initially applied for a doctorate, I kept trying even when confronted with the three years of prior teaching entrance criteria. I twice applied to an educational leadership program for people from outside of education. They did not accept me. However, I went on to earn a doctorate in educational leadership and alternative certification as a school district administrator.

On the job, I came up with hacks and humor as part of my resilience toolkit. I wore that Wonder Woman T-shirt under my blouses. I developed euphemisms for the rough situations I came across from developing the monikers Rager and Coverer, creating passwords with bully variants in them, and envisioning a rope bridge when having to confront a bully. I learned problem-solving and solution generation through my master's degree. I studied leadership in other ways by applying to and participating in the city's yearlong leadership program, attending that leadership a weeklong seminar, and participating in a formalized women's network. I eventually served on its board and on others.

I thought learning algebra, calculus, and multivariate statistics were the hardest things I undertook. Then, I married and went through infertility, miscarriages, and three children's births. I sought childrearing information and provided enrichment opportunities for my children. Then I earned a mid-career doctorate while working full time, commuting monthly to do so, and raising three young kids. When finishing my dissertation, I moved my family of five cross-country to start a new job. Eventually I divorced, moved for other positions, and found myself in a new city with a canceled contract. It turns out that life is hard and many of the things I sought to do or become made my life that much harder including my chosen profession.

Having observed my mother, I concluded that leadership in a PreK-12 education setting was all consuming and political. Leadership roles drew me in anyway. My eyes were open though I must say that the work environment in educational settings was more political and patriarchal than I anticipated. Shocks came when I realized the glass ceiling was not broken and women could not truly have it all. I was flummoxed to learn that the legal system and human resource departments did not actually protect others and me from day-to-day harassment, bullying, sexism, and discrimination. I was also not pleased about the educational bureaucracy and persistent educational inequities found among students from marginalized groups.

Yet, I did not slam the rock down each time I uncovered creepy crawling bugs because the work—supporting all children so they could enjoy the kind of education my own children have experienced—was too important. I reframed issues and problems such that I could work around or through challenges. I learned to work smarter and to acquire more knowledge. While picking myself up when someone or something succeeded in knocking me down, the employment of workarounds helped me navigate intransigent systems and people. It was essential to take care of myself as well as those around me. My support system included friends, extended family, direct reports, mentors, my then spouse, my kids, and network colleagues. Whereas I often joke that in a different era I would have been a chain-smoker and cocktail drinker, I made sure to decompress in yoga, jazzercize, biking, walking, and swimming. Still another renewal strategy focused on protecting my Saturdays to be offline, brain-rest days. I read (and still read) romance novels, which follow a formula where protagonists have a confusion of tensions between them, but they end up getting together anyway, only to be driven apart because of some challenge, and then they find their way back to each other. Problem solved! I read British mysteries, which are about the process of unpacking a crime to solve it. When I was in doubt, my purpose propelled me. I only now realize these were necessary coping strategies. Chapter 7 further discusses navigation, renewal, and survival strategies.

Respondents have much to say about the difficulty of their work, and the mettle they developed to overcome challenges.

> **Avril**: [A group of women peers] was always extremely helpful. Also, stepping away for a brief moment and breathing/running/yoga helped me to refocus and return to face the challenge.
> **Billie**: Know yourself, your values and principles. These are what will guide your leadership choices and decisions and serve as your north star in the darkest moments of being alone. It is not a job, but rather a life mission and allows you to shape a pathway for others to do the same. It's hard, but an incredibly rewarding way to use your life.
> **Dedee**: Time and space to think—stepping out of the challenge and reflecting and thinking rather than becoming burdened with the challenge.

Georgette: I think we have to be able to encourage ourselves when leadership becomes especially challenging.

Joan: Resilience—my favorite one of all. Without resilience we cannot survive in this work. Education is scrappy and complex. One strategy to be resilient is to use your WHY you are in this work to lead you beyond the barriers you will find in doing the work. Having a growth mindset, detaching from perfectionism, learning to be disappointed and to get back to being inspired for this work, navigating politics and allowing your WHY to be the leading force to show up every day and give your all. This work takes dedication, patience and a lot of commitment.

Karin: When I'm feeling most challenged as an educational leader, it helps me to spend some time in a school. The energy from the students is contagious.

Mathilda: Resilience: As a leader, you will always be criticized by others for whatever reason. You must be able to keep on keeping on.

Michelle: Those who aspire to lead understand the demands that can come emotionally, physically, and spiritually, and learn how to organize and prioritize, self-nurture, and become resilient.

Nola: During an especially difficult time of intense turmoil, relying on my personal support system was the only thing that got me through this time. Eventually, the situation became too toxic for me personally and required a move to a different position. The lack of support from close colleagues, who were, in fact, working to hold on to their own positions, proved detrimental to my continued work in the district … Higher levels of leadership can be more and more isolating as the supports are fewer and the risks larger.

Rachel: Stay the course. The work is hard and long but the payoff is great. We touch eternity with each student impacted.

Sonja: This work is hard! You have to be mentally, emotionally, and sometimes physically ready to take it on. Just because the sector is dominated by women does not mean that you won't confront patriarchy.

(D-8) Self-Reflection and Continuous Learning: Practice Self-Reflection to Gain and Harness New Insights about Oneself, One's Approach, and One's Impact

Continuing to learn, being aware of one's knowledge and learnings, and adjusting one's practice based on that learning is at the heart of a reflective practice. Reflection can separate out the resonant leaders from the nonresonant ones.

Leaders who are continuous learners "think in terms of renewal. The routine manager tends to accept organizational structure and process as it exists. The leader or leader/manager seeks the revisions of process and structure required by ever-changing reality."[28] Such people are leader learners.[29] Self-Reflection and Continuous Learning draws on practices[30] ranging from exercising emotional intelligence, humility, and intentionality to being conscious of others and all they offer, to reframing issues and challenges. A practice of self-reflection revolves around a leader's consideration of their strengths, areas of growth, and privilege—this includes engagement in self-care and self-empathy; a willingness to embrace areas of vulnerability and the unknown; and ultimately attending to their own improvement, personal mastery, and inquiry. Leaders must also employ learning and reflection to analyze and interpret contexts, develop new insights, and stay abreast of new information. Possessing a growth mindset and reflective practice enables women leaders to practice a level of critical consciousness and self-knowledge that allows them to look at themselves and navigate power, privileges, differences, and societal, historical, and political influences.

I haven't only learned about things, I had to learn about myself. That early-career leadership development program included analysis, observation, and evaluation of my strengths and weaknesses and 360° feedback that informed my improvement plan. Inward and outward mindset training taught me how to examine my view of others and the ways in which mindsets affected my ability to collaborate and lead. Courses in my doctoral program involved action research and a reflective practice, which caused me to ponder my positionality when leading projects and writing this book. A StrengthFinders' assessment told me I'm an achiever among other things and Myers Briggs told me I possess a high task orientation—both areas that I often must mediate! On-the-job feedback—even if an upset colleague, board member, or community leader delivered it—was invaluable. Being an effective leader involves trial and error, learning about oneself, being adaptable, and practicing reflexivity—that is, that "researchers [and leaders] reflect about their biases, values, and personal background, such as gender, history, culture, and socioeconomic status, and how this background shapes their interpretations formed during a study [or situation]."[31]

Respondents share a variety of perspectives on learning and growth including the link to students and one's own well-being.

> **Billie**: Developing self … to positively impact students and communities and leverage skills to improve life outcomes.

Crystal: I have pursued a Master's in Education, my teaching certificate (including a semester of student teaching), my Admin 1 and 2 certificates, and now a Doctorate in Organizational Development & education Leadership ... I had a female team leader my first two years in [my organization]. She took me on learning walk, allowed me to find myself, to locate myself in the work, and ultimately to pursue additional education in order to give my skills the context needed to transfer them successfully to the education sector. I made sure I spent as much time in schools as possible, learned from principals, observed teachers and office staff, and it really grounded me in the work. Unfortunately I think too many people in central office are disconnected from the work and as such aren't as committed to reconsidering their practice, to implementing new initiatives, etc .... because they don't understand that they work for schools and not the other way around.

Georgette: The challenge presented provides an opportunity to learn and grow and re-imagine.

Jackie: I was a teacher and a principal in schools that were primarily composed of Hispanic students, in primarily Hispanic communities. I was a young white girl with very little credibility—and was not able to speak Spanish. I had to break this barrier—it was my responsibility—so I did my best to demonstrate how much I truly cared about students and families; their well-being, success, and growth.

Mathilda: Educating all children is complex work. If one person knew the answer, then no child would be left behind and everyone would be achieving at high levels. Because that is not the case and since the educational landscape, particularly in the US, is ever-changing, a leader must be continuously learning. It also must be ok for a leader to be authentic, transparent, and vulnerable to say that I don't have the answer here, but working together we will find an innovative solution for supporting student success.

Patty: There is always risk in trying something new. My career in both the nonprofit and educational sectors has always been about trying something new, pushing farther. I've never taken a job that I knew how to do.

Reese: I left my old job, which I really did like and which afforded me a lot of flexibility, for my current role at the [my organization] which is a far more demanding and more strategic workload. At the time, I was really torn up about it and afraid to take the leap into this new school. But now that I'm outside of the decision and over a year into my role at the [new school], I can't imagine having stayed in my old job. It would have stunted my growth and I wouldn't have been pushed to the level I'm at now.

Tang: In the past, being micromanaged by my direct supervisor has hindered my ability to grow and exercise sound practices. I have thrived most and learned most when I have had opportunities to stretch myself and "own" certain projects, therefore taking responsibility for my actions.

Tanya: Leadership is the ability to guide others while still being vulnerable to learning more oneself.

Zelda: I place a high importance on my own personal professional development both through formal and informal avenues. I believe it is important to have a strong network of mentors and colleagues who can encourage self-reflection along with practical advice and problem-solving skills and knowledge. Being around other leaders provides an opportunity to learn from and reflect on my own practice. In addition, being intentional about inquiry into my own practice is important.

Conclusion

In this chapter, I share standards and dispositions that I propose to fill women leaders' preparation gaps. My aim is to facilitate some ease for women leaders such that they learn about what they should know and be able to do. Particularly when coupled with the leadership development strategies Chapter 7 outlines, application of these standards and dispositions can help women become good if not great leaders.

These standards and dispositions are just a starting point. My intention is for scholars and experts to further investigate, explicate, and validate the seven proposed standards and eight proposed dispositions to crystalize a framework for women educational leaders—whether the list is specific to a position or as an addendum to existing standards' documents. Employers and schools of education can also incorporate them into their programming for all educational leaders. Rubrics—aligned with standards and disposition frameworks (whether actions, dimensions, capacities, or standards)—are invaluable for organizational leaders to use when observing and providing feedback on leadership practices.

Reflective Questions

1. What differences do you see between the standards and dispositions?
   a. What makes them different?
2. In what ways could standards and dispositions tied to women educational leaders be helpful or harmful to women, their supervisors, and allies?
3. Think about the ways in which you've applied or developed—or seen others apply or develop—the various standards (administrative and operational acumen, competence, equitable culture, development and support, performance management, teaching and learning, and vision).
   a. In what ways can understanding and applying these standards facilitate your leadership?
4. Consider the ways in which the various dispositions (collaboration and engagement, confidence, creativity and innovation, political savvy, professionalism, resilience, and self-reflection and continuous learning) facilitate your leadership.
   a. In what ways can these cross-cutting dispositions inform your leadership practice?

7

Strategies and Supports: Still Standing

Leadership Story

My own leadership journey hasn't been straightforward. Nor has it been reliant on any organization's leadership development program, diversity initiative, performance standards, or commitment to me as an employee. I never worked for an organization with a leadership development program or a clear path to leadership especially for nontraditional candidates like me. In developing my path, I established my goals, joined networks, and sought mentors' advice. I took what I thought were informed professional risks. I identified the skills and knowledge I needed, pursued ongoing training and education, and overcame setbacks. Throughout the preceding chapters, I share my commitment to educating all students; seeking solutions to racist and sexist structures, practices, and cultures; and ascribing to collective approaches to leadership.

My journey wouldn't have been possible without mentors and sponsors who provided timely and applicable feedback and support along with access to high-visibility stretch assignments and roles. Like many women, I felt crushed even when the lack of perfection was a typo and embarrassed and humiliated when I blundered publicly, was misunderstood, or lost my composure. True, power stress was a burden as were overt and subtle forms of sexism. I also struggled to balance work and family. My commitment to continuous learning and reflection helped me bounce back. Reciprocal relationships supported me.

Monikers and euphemisms mitigated and deflected the impact of toxic cultures, people, and situations. Humor bolstered me. The opinions, feedback, and encouragement from professional networks and colleagues—and family members and friends—allowed me to persevere. Volunteering facilitated my acquisition of experience otherwise not available. I left organizations because a great opportunity presented itself, of organizational cultures or leaders, of unfulfilled employer promises, or of unsatisfactory upward mobility and career support.

Wouldn't it be great if every woman leader's journey were less fraught, more straightforward, and better informed? Wouldn't it also be valuable for their organizations, colleagues, and leaders to step up in knowledgeable and useful ways? To be true allies?

Overview

The work of educating all children is demanding and rewarding. So too is leading teams, projects, departments, and organizations dedicated to educating all children. Women educational leaders encounter and navigate numerous barriers to lead and rewards for leading. Prior chapters address why women pursue educational leadership and who influences their decisions and careers. I identify which areas of knowledge and skills are indispensable and how certain behaviors facilitate navigation.

The leadership story elucidates my own role in my development, support I received from mentors and sponsors, and the role, organization, and education changes I pursued in the absence of a formalized organizational program. For implementation at the individual and organization levels, this chapter covers success *strategies* and *supports'* themes—both for women themselves to employ and those for organizations, colleagues, and leaders. I provide insight into expert leadership and talent development approaches and individualized navigational tactics. Leaders don't materialize like a genie from a lamp. Before becoming formal leaders, leader apprentices engage in preparatory activities. Such activities allow aspirants to develop experience and expertise. They apply and refine skills, plan and manage their leadership trajectories, network with leaders, and learn from feedback. They lead projects, and inhabit roles, with ever-increasing levels of visibility and responsibility. While individuals aren't born as leaders, some may argue that societal privileges birth dynasties of leaders. If one is born into a family with the right pedigree, connections, and wealth, then it comes as no surprise that the American Dream is more accessible to some and more elusive to others. Societal expectations, individual aspirations, and family investments in educational, enrichment, and extracurricular activities matter. Ascending to the leadership of organizations—whether public, private, or political—isn't an egalitarian endeavor—especially for women and others.

Consistent with the communal and collectivist approaches women educational leaders may follow, the responsibility for delivering strategies and supports requires a village. Sarah Leberman and Jane Hurst (2017) suggest that:

The responsibility for developing meaningful and productive careers rests with both individuals and organizations. While career decisions are inherently personal, the organizational culture and structures of work are key influencers in those decisions and must no longer remain hidden behind a misleading discourse of personal choice.[1]

The organizational support and leadership development strategies, which I share in this chapter, encompass choice, customization, and coherence. Other supports include commitments to candidate diversity, coupled with the willingness and resources to disrupt biased structures, practices, and cultures. Individual strategies address the way women can traverse their own careers given the organizational reality and their personal and professional values, pressures, and priorities.

A Commitment to Leadership Development

Development connotes the provision of support and learning opportunities for people once they are in their roles. Management implies that one implements practices consistently, in an aligned manner, and according to timelines, laws, and regulations. Eva Gallardo-Gallardo and Marian Thunnissen (2016) define talent management as "both a philosophy and a practice. It is both an espoused and enacted commitment—shared at the highest levels and throughout the organization by all those in managerial and supervisory positions—to implementing an integrated, strategic and technology enabled approach to human resources management (HRM)."[2] The focus on talent sends the message that an organization's people are, and should be treated as, valued assets.

Kirk Kramer and Preeta Nyack (2013) define leadership development as the "identification and development of those individuals who will lead the critical functions of your organization and who, in partnership with other leaders, will be responsible for its overall health and impact."[3] The authors say, "In organizations that make such an investment, leadership development becomes part of the culture, a strong thread running through the organization's roster of activities. Building the leaders of tomorrow becomes an integral part of its identity."[4] Leadership development includes a variety of supports for people already employed in an organization. Presumably, the organization spent significant up-front resources to recruit, select, and place high-value leaders and to imbue existing employees with valuable institutional knowledge and experience. It follows that these leaders would be rewarded, retained, and supported in their growth and development—treated like talent!

There are many strategies to consider incorporating into leadership development. They include challenging, high-visibility stretch assignments; formalized leadership planning; and job-embedded training. Others emphasize work–life balance, self-care, and self-study. Courses, mentoring, coaching, and sponsorship are important to continuous learning and development. Aligning strategies with individual and organizational needs can create coherence and transparency. Networking opportunities can support women and provide access to well-placed people. Such best practices haven't been adopted to the extent that they could or should be. If they had been, we wouldn't have ineffective leaders in roles and effective women leaders shut out of or shut down in such roles. Still worse is that we have leaders in roles who are not merely ineffective but also who can cause harm to those whom they are entrusted with educating, collaborating, and serving. Effective leadership development and talent management playbooks and the intent of the laws, regulations, and policies require bolstering and monitoring.

Strategies for Organizations to Employ

To establish a village of support, I recommend that employers step up in deliberate, transparent, and sometimes uncomfortable ways. This section presents three key elements upon which organizations can draw as they strive

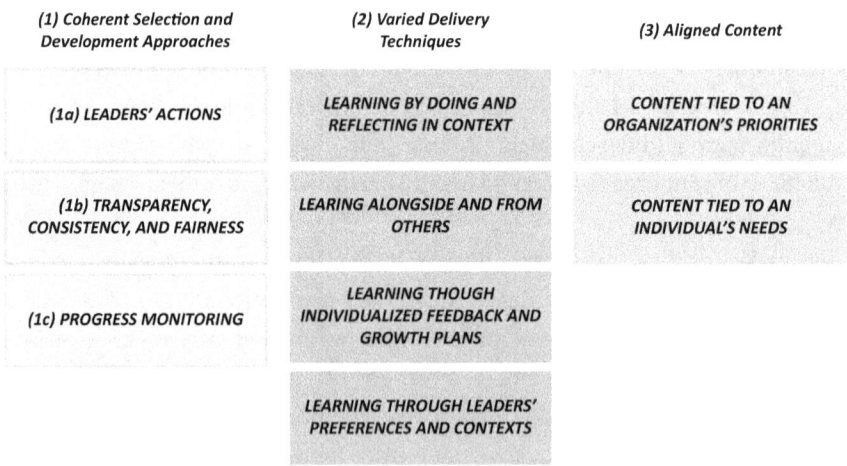

Figure 7.1 Strategies for Organizations to Employ.

to disrupt biased structures, practices, and cultures through talent development, leadership development, selection, and promotion.

The three elements I suggest employers adopt to facilitate women's ascension to and success in educational leadership are: (1) Coherent Selection and Development, (2) Varied Delivery Techniques, and (3) Aligned Content (see Figure 7.1). This section provides strategies, which organizational leaders can implement for women and others to advance to and succeed in educational leadership roles. Behind each strategy, there is a wealth of design and implementation nuance, which organizations can tailor to their unique settings, priorities, and readiness.

(1) Coherent Selection and Development

Coherence of leadership development and selection is the first of three elements I propose for cultivating, supporting, and promoting women educational leaders. Related sub-strategies focus on the leadership team and organizational leader's roles in ensuring success of the leadership development program. Sub-strategies encompass (a) Leaders' Actions, (b) Transparency, Consistency, and Fairness, and (c) Progress Monitoring.

These three sub-strategies provide a coherent framework for organizations committed to equitable leadership development, support, and advancement regardless of employees' gender, race, or ethnicity. Just as one isn't born a leader, an organization isn't suddenly reborn as an equitable learning organization that supports leadership development for those persistently underrepresented in leadership roles. The related organizational practices, structures, and cultures—and an organization's leaders' commitment and adherence to them—cannot be subjective, haphazard, or secretive. Nor can they be tainted by ego, identity, or fear. To implement an equitable leadership development and selection program—with the aim of eradicating leadership gaps within the context of effective teaching and learning for all students—there should be deliberate strategies, communications, resource allocations, and progress monitoring. Organizational leaders should demonstrate in words and deeds the extent to and ways in which the organization and its leaders commit to advance and support those who are persistently underrepresented in leadership roles.

(1a) Leaders' Actions

Leadership teams and heads of organizations are essential players in articulating and demonstrating the value of women and other underrepresented educational leaders. To do so, they can (1a-i) seek to establish fair organizational structures, practices, and cultures that are neither overtly discriminatory nor subtly biased. These organizational leaders can also (1a-ii) model and reward equitable leadership selection and development practices that are inclusive of and tailored to women and women with intersectional identities. Eagly and Carli (2007a) indicate that, "by conveying respect for and confidence in women as leaders, organizations can lessen the resistance to female leadership… [for example by conveying] that she was selected on the basis of her demonstrated ability."[5] Kramer and Nyack (2013) speak to the messaging and participation of the CEO and senior leadership team:

> The key player in forming and fostering that culture is the CEO, whose words and actions, passions and priorities, are a powerful signal to the rest of the organization. Simply put, the organization comes to value what the CEO values. CEOs who visibly invest time, energy, and attention to leadership development … send a powerful message that leadership development isn't just the buzz phrase du jour: It's fundamental to the organization's work.[6]

To dismantle biased leadership structures, practices, and cultures organizational leaders can also (1a-iii) conduct audits of existing leadership development and selection methods, talent management approaches, and organizational culture. Leadership teams can ask themselves the following questions:

1. Are we leaning into leadership parity, or are we merely saying we are leaning in and thus are requiring the underrepresented candidates to lean in by themselves?
2. Are we recruiting and promoting underrepresented people at every level (i.e., building the pipeline)?
3. Have we set objectives for women's leadership development and selection?
4. Are we identifying, and providing comprehensive leadership development to, prospective women leaders, creating succession plans, and addressing pay equity?
5. In what ways are we identifying, training, assigning, and rewarding high-quality mentors, coaches, sponsors, and supervisors to work with underrepresented leaders?
6. Are our leadership development programs tailored to meet the needs of women and others?
7. Are the programs based on a variety of delivery models?

Bierema and Madsen (2017) express the sentiment that should guide such monitoring:

> Developers of women leaders and their organizations should be willing and able to assess organization perspectives, policies, and practices that prevent women from advancing[7] ... [and taking critical action which] is the process of taking mindful steps to correct the self or group when slipping back into implicit bias or behaviors that marginalize women and other underrepresented groups.[8]

There are numerous subcomponents to incorporate into audits and improvement plans. A step organizational leaders can take is to (1a-iv) determine if they possess the internal capacity to establish their own formalized leadership development and selection program or if they can create a plan for framing such a program. Minimally, organizational leaders can (1a-v) assign resources to establish their priorities, create objective development and evaluation criteria, diversify selection committees, and identify and provide support to employees so they may access outside providers. They should also (1a-vi) train those involved in hiring and promotion.

An example of an actionable practice involves consideration of the ways in which managers support their direct reports and leader aspirants. Contemplate the following:

1. Do managers provide ongoing constructive feedback, employ clearly defined objective and transparent performance criteria, and volunteer to be mentors?
2. Do they model respectful relationships and inclusive practices when mentoring, coaching, leading, evaluating, managing, and delivering feedback?
3. Has the organizational leadership team embedded the responsibility for and commitment to employee goal setting, observation, feedback, evaluation, and ongoing support into their managers' own annual goals?

Leaders may model their own learning, which can signal a culture committed to organizational learning, transparency, vulnerability, and development. Respondents elucidate this need for organizations and their leaders to provide opportunities and encouragement to women leaders and leader apprentices. They also discuss rationales for dismantling overt and subtle sexist structures, practices, and cultures.

Diedre: I have worked for supervisors who were very hands off—not wanting to micromanage—but that leads to not understanding or knowing what the work is or why it is happening. This is often coupled with the supervisor who also wants all 'glory' for themselves and so cannot ask a question in front of their supervisors and has to appear as though they fully understand.

Leslie: I am encouraged by the fact that I am able to do this job because someone once BELIEVED in me.

Lottie: When I started working at a certain non-for-profit agency as a vice president, there were certain board members who questioned my ability to perform in my position as VP of Finance. When I met with the board treasurer, he would question my ability, when I attended meetings, I would need to state that "I'm a CPA," [and] I constantly had to defend my decisions with certain board members. It took some time, but with patience and expertise, I was able to convince them that regardless of being a black female, I could do the job. As an instructor, students who were non-performing, would get grades they did not accept, would complain and I recall one occasion I was asked to retest them. My supervisor came in and observed the class and took me to lunch to explain why I needed to let them take another test … Not being supported by your direct report [supervisor] is very frustrating.

Mathilda: She [my boss] empowers her people to make decisions that are best for students and if you are stuck, she comes along side you to support you. She encourages you to pursue excellence.

Reese: Positive feedback and affirmations from colleagues. It makes a huge difference to hear from senior leaders and peers when something goes well so that when you face challenges, you aren't as critical of yourself and can treat it as a bump in the road rather than the end of the world. Positive feedback helps to insulate you from too much self-criticism and makes you more resilient to take on challenges the next time around.

Tang: I decided that it was time for me to move on from my school (as Assistant Head of School) and I notified my head of school (a heterosexual white male) that I would apply for a senior administrative position at a larger, nationally ranked independent school that also happened to be a competitor. I made this decision because I felt I had outgrown my school. Instead of supporting me along my professional journey, the head of school consulted with some board members and ultimately posted a portion of my job a week later … I think it's important for women and women of color to be cautious with white male supervisors, especially those who have the potential to be threatened by their success.

Wilma: In a past role, I was brought on to build a program from scratch. I was able to be successful in that role over 4 years because of the following: 1) my direct boss believed in the work and trusted me …; 2) as a budget was needed to do the work, approval was easy to get given our ability to demonstrate purpose, goal, and the relationship of the project to the larger initiative; 3) openness across creativity and trying new methods of service delivery; and 4) access to professional development to continue to learn what we needed to as we moved forward with the work.

Zelda: As an Asian American woman there have been a number of opportunities where I feel my ability to take on leadership positions has been either affirmed or questioned. In some instances being Asian was seen as a plus of "oh she's smart in that area" … In other cases being Asian has been a negative such as when I was asked in an interview, "how can a little Asian woman like you deal with discipline if you're in a high school with seniors who are bigger than you." Or when it is assumed that I do not understand the realities of urban education.

My experience with the large community project led me to reflect in an ongoing manner about my positionality when engaging with community members and designing the planning process. I altered my leadership approach and proposed a collaborative process, because I knew that my identity was of concern and that engagement was of value, necessary for building trust, and essential to program effectiveness. The team and I discussed the elephant in the room—which included the trauma many community members felt due to their prior experience with the school district. By sharing my own challenges, I demonstrated my own Learning through Teaching, which Jeff DeSmet, Louise Axon, and John Alsbury (2016) identify as one of their six design principles and one that facilitates the engagement of senior leaders in developing others. Leaders (supervisors, project leads):

> Take on responsibility for leadership development and building a learning culture … The act of teaching or coaching requires leaders to demonstrate expertise. And the process of developing others reinforces their [own] previous learning, while providing ongoing opportunities to develop new insights.[9]

(1b) Transparency, Consistency, and Fairness

Organizational leaders can willingly, or unknowingly, perpetuate practices, structures, and cultures that shut women out of leadership. Such practices may include roundabout, covert, and undocumented information transmission. Also problematic is an overreliance on protocols, rubrics, and leadership frameworks based on male models. Homogeneous hiring teams (called manels when comprised only of men[10]) can develop recruiting pools that underrepresent women and use subjective or veiled selection criteria.

To address structural and systemic bias that may be embedded in organizations and their practices, structures, and cultures, organizational leaders can (1b-i) share transparent information about internal leadership openings, leadership recruitment and selection processes, and the leadership development options available. Organizational leaders can also (1b-ii) highlight and communicate the skills and experiences necessary to qualify for roles and development opportunities. Allyship and anti-sexism, like anti-racism, require recognition of the issue(s) and deliberate action. Organizational leaders can (1b-iii) build their key communicators' understanding of common messages and materials that outline recruiting, selection, and hiring processes and expectations. They can (1b-iv) disseminate the information to anyone who expresses interest and to targeted individuals and groups. They can also (1b-v) ensure that all related communication is shared across all members of the organization—not at a golf course, in a hallway, or in a bar after work.

Below, Mathilda speaks about the impact on organizations and aspiring women leaders when there is not transparency, consistency, and clarity:

> **Mathilda**: From my experience, an issue that has thwarted my ability to lead is culture. I find that in many educational organizations, many people get promoted based on their relationship with another person and that they are a "yes" person NOT on their job performance. Often times, these leaders lack the skills to lead others effectively. However, with no real checks and balances in education, this practice continues across the country.

In contrast to Mathilda's experience, if organizational leaders follow objective, clear, and open practices for leader recruitment, selection, evaluation, promotion, and pay, then the organization could reduce implicit bias, in-group favoritism, the effects of unequal standards, and excessive scrutiny of and prejudice against women. Furthermore, if organizational leaders reduce subjectivity in structures, practices, and culture, then the likelihood of homosocial reproduction ("the tendency of incumbents to reproduce their demographic composition in new hires or recruits ... [or in] top positions"[11]) will ideally decline, thus making it possible for women to inhabit leadership roles.

(1c) Progress Monitoring

Evaluation of professional or leadership development programs may be interpreted as merely assessing the way a particular session was delivered and the content covered—did people at the end of the session believe the provider met the goals of the session? The progress monitoring to which this strategy refers is aligned with the Performance Management standard (S-6). To be able to monitor systemic progress in dismantling biased talent management practices, the leadership team of organizations can (1c-i) develop a multiyear plan with goals for redressing the underrepresentation of women and others underrepresented in leadership. An empaneled diverse team of stakeholders and contributors could then (1c-ii) reinforce the goals with a willingness to track progress against the plan. They could do so when the plan explicates annual, measurable, time-specific objectives; key strategies; responsible parties; and measurement targets. Leaders could (1c-iii) publicly share the plan, the annual priorities, and the progress—thus demonstrating their pledge to deconstruct heretofore biased leader selection structures, practices, and cultures and to walk the talk.

One cannot monitor progress without explicit targets and designated methods for monitoring and reporting. Monitoring tools can include surveys, hiring and promotion logs for each role, and 360° evaluation systems, among others. Based on this information, leadership teams can (1c-iv) make course corrections when desired results aren't realized or mete out consequences if specific individuals are blocking or not carrying out implementation— Deborah Rhodes (2017) suggests that "monitoring can be important not only in identifying challenges and responses, but also in making people aware that their actions are being assessed."[12] Likewise those involved in providing, and those guiding, leader development can (1c-v) share the responsibility for measuring and monitoring the success of leadership development.

(2) Access to and Use of Varied Delivery Techniques

Organizations can draw from a variety of delivery techniques to deliver leadership development. The Center for Creative Leadership recommends that organizations deliver learning via on-the-job experiences and coaching more so than on formal training sessions—70 percent should focus on on-the-job training, 20 percent on coaching which can supplement the embedded job training, and 10 percent on formal training.[13] Together I recommend that the delivery methods for leadership development include: (2a) Learning by Doing and Reflecting in Context, (2b) Learning Alongside and from Others, (2c) Learning through Individualized Feedback and Growth Plans, and (2-d) Learning through Leaders' Preferences and Contexts.

When organizations use these four methods, deliverers are likely to employ them concurrently. For example, more than one person is apt to be involved in a stretch assignment—via some form of a collaborative process—so both learning alongside and from others may be combined with learning by doing and reflecting in context. Individualized feedback and growth plans may guide growth experiences—from stretch assignments to team leadership to budget development to project collaboration—and thus the ongoing feedback from a coach, peer, or project leader may contribute to one's success in meeting annual performance objectives. The following descriptions can guide leadership development delivery.

(2a) Learning by Doing and Reflecting in Context

DeSmet, Axon, and Alsbury (2016) separate learning in context from learning by doing. These two delivery strategies are among the authors' six leadership development design principles. In their model, they define Learning by Doing and Reflecting as, a "learn-practice-reflect" cycle, through which facilitators move people and "teach participants how to learn consistently from experience through multiple cycles of practice and reflection—enabling them to continue this practice back at work."[14] And they identify Learning in Context as occurring within:

> The context of the organization's strategy, culture, and values, and when it's highly relevant to the learner's real work ... Learning in context also means that skills are explored in relation to how the skill will be used, and in conjunction with other related leadership skills. This kind of understanding requires that development brings the goals, systems, and values of the organization into the development experience.[15]

When combined—as I suggest—these concepts reflect the reality that most of learning occurs on the job. Learning by Doing and Reflecting in Context can incorporate experiential, situational, and job-embedded delivery techniques.

It can also involve setting clear objectives, creating opportunities for frequent feedback and adjustment, pausing for deliberate reflection, and making course corrections. Such learning can include stretch assignments.[16] Such assignments may include a designated project leader who possesses responsibility for identifying potential learning projects and related objectives and incorporate clear goals and objectives for both the individual and project. Like regular teacher observations followed by feedback sessions with the observer and teacher, a project leader could observe the leader apprentice and provide ongoing constructive feedback, over time, on the apprentice's practice. I recommend that such sessions align with relevant and timely problems of practice unique to the organizational context and the leader apprentice's site, or their skill- and behavioral-development needs. The leader apprentice may also suggest or volunteer for projects aligned with their own goals and needs.

Effective leaders make ongoing decisions about the leadership approach needed, given their day-to-day strategic calculus and reflection. This means leader apprentices not only need to be politically savvy but also able to gauge the dynamics of different contexts and switch approaches based on contexts. Ideally, they do so as part of a deliberate application of a reflective practice. As Chapter 6 suggests, a leader's reflective practice involves "read[ing] and respond[ing] to changing and complex realities … understand[ing] diverse cultural realities … [and recognizing] various frames of reference operating in particular situations."[17] Reflection is also "a vital component of leaders' daily life, not a detached or disconnected action but primal, promoted by the culture and structures of an organization, which affects choices, policies and decisions together with the emotions and politics related to them…to be reflective should [be considered as] … an inherent component of what to manage or lead means."[18] Lydia concurs that learning by doing and reflecting in context is invaluable.

> **Lydia**: Experience is the best teacher. Learning comes from what works and what doesn't work. The key is to analyze each episode and adopt the strategies that work, remain flexible and not dwell on failures.

(2b) Learning Alongside and from Others

Another delivery strategy amalgam, Learning Alongside and from Others, involves learning through teamwork, professional learning communities, and affinity groups. Such learning can also include cohort learning during coursework, study groups, and networks. Developmental relationships, such as those with varied role models (coaches, mentors, supervisors, and sponsors) can also provide key opportunities for learning. Some areas may require individualization, such as when an individual leads a team as part of a stretch assignment, conducts and documents regular check-ins, and gleans feedback from team members about their role as team lead. They may also conduct an after-action review to learn alongside the entire team about how each member experienced the project and what they each could improve going forward. Did they meet the goals and objectives laid out? Did the team leader meet their learning and growth objectives? What was the nature of the team culture? Problems of practice, which a group of professional peers in similar or different positions or locations, could also constitute learning alongside each other. A coach could train a team of school leaders on how to coach others so the school leadership team would be learning alongside each other about coaching their protégés. Or an individual could learn directly from their coach, mentor, or sponsor about a particular skill or practice.

DeSmet, Axon, and Alsbury (2016) suggest that Learning with Others, one of six leadership development design principles, is predicated on the notion that:

> Learning is a social activity, and it requires space and time with others to exchange ideas and make meaning from individual and collective experiences … Learners construct knowledge through interactions with those who know more than they do or those who have different experience and perspectives—whether a peer, coach, boss, expert, or facilitator.[19]

A few descriptions, which pertain to the delivery method of Learning Alongside and from Others, could include mentoring, coaching, networking, and sponsorship. According to coaching expert Elena Aguilar (2017), "A mentor is an insider in a system, an expert in a field, who supports a novice … shows a novice the ropes, the tricks of the trade, … passes on knowledge, experience, and helps a mentee make connections to others."[20] Mentors help the leader apprentice in a variety of ways. Strategies range from navigating systems to acquainting a mentee with norms and practices to supporting and encouraging a mentee. Mentors may serve as role models, share knowledge, parse power dynamics, and provide recognition. Mentors can also demonstrate their own learning. And, when the mentor is well-placed and well-respected, mentors are critical to women's advancement as leaders.[21] Organizations could tap men for mentoring and coaching women, and women could seek them out, given the preponderance of leadership positions men hold and their dominance in and knowledge about securing such positions.[22]

Aguilar defines coaching as being "far more formal than mentoring"[23] and requiring a deeper professional development focus. The coach serves as "a teacher, a facilitator of someone else's learning" and provides a specific structure and learning objectives.[24] Coaches deliver professional development by creating safe situations, sharing an area of expertise, and guiding the leader apprentice to take risks, improve their approach, and learn new approaches.[25] Sponsors "are successful people who understand how to develop effective relationships and networks with other successful people. They understand politics within their professional area and have a degree of power in influencing others."[26] Sponsors provide access to, and advocate on behalf of their protégés for, specific roles.

Recall that networks can be local, regional, and national in nature. Networks may affiliate with areas of interest (such as sororities, synagogues, and churches), professional groups or associations, graduate schools, and alumni groups. Networks (and their members) can provide invaluable support to women and serve as allies. Women can join different networks for different purposes such as for emotional support from like-minded women and professional support from well-placed individuals.

Networks may

1. develop members
2. design common learning goals
3. meet the needs of people based on gender or demographic background
4. exclude—intentionally or not—women and women with intersectional identities
5. facilitate information sharing
6. encourage goal accomplishment
7. provide access to job and mentor leads
8. foster influential connections with decision-makers and diverse role models (providing the network isn't comprised of homogeneous members)
9. develop social and political capital
10. encourage or thwart the distribution of power
11. offer critical advice, support, insights, and visibility

I never employed a coach, though at one point in my last position, I sought one out. I'd barely commenced the relationship when my world blew up, which I suppose demonstrates my prescience. Primarily, my mentors and sponsors were self-assigned though they and I never called them sponsors. My leader-mentors and leader-sponsors supported me in many ways. One high-powered external partner, "John," delivered on-the-spot feedback, when he made the comment, "If you walk out of a meeting after that person publicly attacks and humiliates you, then you are giving him your voice and power." Matt, who I introduce in Chapter 2, once wondered if I was okay because I did not seem like myself due to my lagging processing speed. It turned out I was on a new sinus medication that made me groggy!

Critical support has also included situations when mentors contacted me about a potential job opportunity, wrote letters of support for job applications, and provided advice about securing a particular position. Another mentor, whom I call "Harry," and who was affiliated with my doctoral program, called me with a suggestion for a role and recommended me for that role and others. (I now recognize that this person acted more as a sponsor.) Another mentor-leader/supervisor approved vacation and personal days so I could participate in ongoing education. A different mentor-leader and supervisor, who I call "Ralph," supported my participation in the Center for Creative Leadership's Leadership Development Program and for the involvement of our organization's senior leadership team members in my 360° assessment. Two different mentor-leaders and supervisors assigned me to high-profile stretch assignments that both supported their agendas and helped me grow (whether or not they realized the assignments put me on a glass cliff).

(2c) Learning through Individualized Feedback and Growth Plans

This method of delivery can reinforce and guide a leader's learning. If carried out strategically—and when designers clearly define, and fairly assess, objective expectations and standards with transparent rubrics—then performance evaluations can support stretch assignments, promotions, and pay raises. Such growth plans and the performance evaluation and feedback practices accompanying the plans can support an individual's own leadership development plan as well as their annual goals. This way individuals continue to grow in the organization or department, encounter challenges, test out possible future roles, and participate in long-term career planning that retains them within the organization (or, if in a small organization, allows the individual to grow until they outgrow the organization).

Organizations can strive to create coherence between and among the following elements:

1. Supervisors' and organizational leaders' commitment to developing and evaluating each employee's annual goals
2. Meetings between a supervisor and direct report to scope annual goals
3. Goal revision and approval

4. Regular observation of the individual in context
5. Frequent check-ins—over the course of the year between the supervisor and direct report—to discuss job performance and goal progress
6. Formal evaluations at one or more junctures during the year

Because annual growth and performance systems typically occur over the course of the year and with supervisors contributing to ongoing feedback, this delivery method satisfies what DeSmet, Axon, and Alsbury (2016) refer to as another of their leadership development design principles: Learning Over Time. Development

> requires a continuous process that unfolds over time through a wide variety of experiences, relationships, observations, and reflections. These processes cannot be experienced via a series of formal learning events alone. They require a series of moments that "force a person to take stock, reevaluate, revise, resee, and rejudge" [and help participants to] achieve a deeper level of learning, personal change, and growth.[27]

(2d) Learning through Leaders' Preferences and Contexts

This fourth organizational delivery method reinforces the need for customized learning and organizational support aligned with one's developmental needs. When selecting a university or college for which an organization provides tuition reimbursement or signs off on coursework, an organization—along with the individual—will assess the offerings, a host of related costs, and delivery intensity and method—for example, part-time, at night, or in the summer. The program may be accelerated, require time away from home and work, be full time, or require a leave from employment. Learning may be virtual, place-based, or hybrid. This delivery method conveys that the primary drivers for leadership development are the organization's investment in talent, the individual's learning needs, the way that individual learns best, and the individual them self. This learning is not based on delivering lessons in a one-size-fits-all manner. One former colleague referred to the large-group one-size-fits-all type of professional development as spraying (the information at attendees) and praying (that individuals take it in).

The 2018 State of Leadership Development: Meeting the Transformation Imperative (2018) Harvard Business School report suggests individualization places:

> Learners front and center in their program design and delivery ... making learning experiences relevant, and providing trusted content that learners can access easily from anywhere, on any device ... offer[ing] omnipresent learning in the form

of experiences, while providing employees anytime, anywhere with frictionless access to content and shift[ing] from courses to resources to experiences.[28]

Recall my participation in a partner organization's facilitation, teamwork, and presentation training sessions as well as in a third-party organization's communication training. There were other individuals involved in those sessions yet we or our supervisors determined that the type of multiday training session, during which time we learned about and practiced our new skills in a safe cross-functional team environment, was an appropriate way for each of us to learn. Organizations can factor such individual flexibility into their leadership development program offerings and support. For example delivery options might include:

1. Cohort learning during coursework
2. Developmental relationships such as those with coaches, mentors, supervisors, and sponsors
3. Networks
4. Professional learning communities, affinity/critical friends' groups
5. Study groups
6. Teaming
7. Training sessions offered at one's department, school, district, organization, or union
8. Training sessions preceding or following a conference, which may involve professional development days and employer reimbursement
9. Stretch assignments

I selected learning opportunities that corresponded with my learning goals, outsider status, checkbook, and family life. This was like choosing a restaurant that offered the right menu selections based on my dietary needs and preferences. Such a restaurant would also be open at the right time of day, offer the type of dining that would satisfy my schedule and preferences (in-person dining, drive-thru, delivery, or takeout), and provide walk-in or reservation options that worked for me. It would also be at a price point I could afford and offer a turnaround time consistent with the time I had to eat, travel, or await delivery. The restaurant would also be located on my Yellow Brick Road!

(3) Aligned Content

This last component of Figure 7.1 links content tied to an individual and organization's needs. Using the restaurant analogy, and specifically the selection of what to eat at a restaurant, this step would entail me identifying—on my own, with a nutritionist, with a family member, or with a doctor—what I needed or wanted to eat for a healthy, filling, and satisfying diet and then matching restaurant offerings to those criteria. I would select the menu item based on what I needed or wanted at that point in time. Similarly, an organization could assemble—based on its own leadership standards, organizational goals, and individuals' needs—a menu of offerings. Organizations could calibrate such offerings to objective criteria and rubrics to guide and evaluate the leader apprentice's participation and development.

Establishing leadership development content priorities—and nesting the priorities in fair standards, dispositions, competencies, and rubrics—can provide individuals with a clear sense of what they need to know and be able to do, which behaviors they need to demonstrate, and what level of mastery they should attain to become an educational leader in a particular role. This could explicate the desired content priorities for the organization, its leaders, and its aspiring leaders, and target content for those underrepresented in educational leadership positions or those with token status.

(3a) Content Tied to Organizational Priorities

What might an organizational priority look like that would require new learning? We know what professional development targeting a new instructional endeavor can involve. Such sessions typically seek to provide teachers with the foundation and related strategies to support a new program (e.g., reading, math, social and emotional learning, etc.) There are similar such organizational content priorities for leaders when there is a systemic organizational change. The following examples demonstrate organizational (content) needs.

I once facilitated two schools' design teams charged with altering their schools' grade configurations from PreK-5 to PreK-8s. This collaborative analysis examined physical plants, instructional programs, teaching staff, and grade-level organizations. We learned collectively about the attributes of PreK-8s. Such features were social, cultural, structural, and academic. I conducted the research to identify relevant reading materials, assembled site-visit question guides, and organized PreK-8 site visits to observe practices, structures, and cultures. We debriefed upon returning and transferred learning into transition plans. The content, or organizational, priority was PreK-8 best practices.

A different priority focused on school improvement plan development. I facilitated a middle-school site-based planning team, whose school was in corrective action for not meeting adequate yearly progress (AYP) among non-white and low socioeconomic status (SES) students. I exposed the team to data-informed decision-making—together we examined student data on learning gaps, attendance differences, disproportionate discipline practices, and disproportionate placement of Black, brown, and poor students in special education classes. I familiarized the team with the school-based planning template, plan samples, and each planning term's meaning. Next, I shared draft plans, provided space for them to develop their own plan, and returned to provide constructive feedback. In either of these examples, my organization could've established leadership development content priorities—and aligned them with Chapter 6's standards and dispositions—so that both teams would've known where and why they were increasing capabilities.

(3b) Content Tied to Individual Needs

The next full section—strategies for individuals to employ—covers individual strategies. I include it under the organizational approaches because organizations need to ensure this approach is available to individual employees. When considered in the organizational context, such strategies support an individual's leadership development plan and annual performance priorities. Individual strategies also involve garnering experience and developing skills tied to standards and dispositions.

Strategies for Individuals to Employ

Throughout this book, I share efforts to bolster my career and physical and mental health whether through education, training, networks, or job changes. Other inputs include challenging assignments, attempts at work–life balance, and leaning on allies. Ironically, as a planner, I never developed a formal leadership development or learning plan. There was no clearly articulated path I set out to traverse, rather I pursued a series of roles and opportunities. Occasionally I felt as if I was in, or on my way to, Oz. I understood that I needed to learn more, could do more, and could become a leader. I set out to secure roles and opportunities that would build my skills and opportunities so I could do so.

As I indicate, I wish I'd established a formal roadmap with specific goals, strategies, areas for development, and timelines. It would've been helpful to discuss and share such plans with, and receive related strategic guidance from, a mentor, coach, sponsor, colleague, or supervisor. I likely would've been better

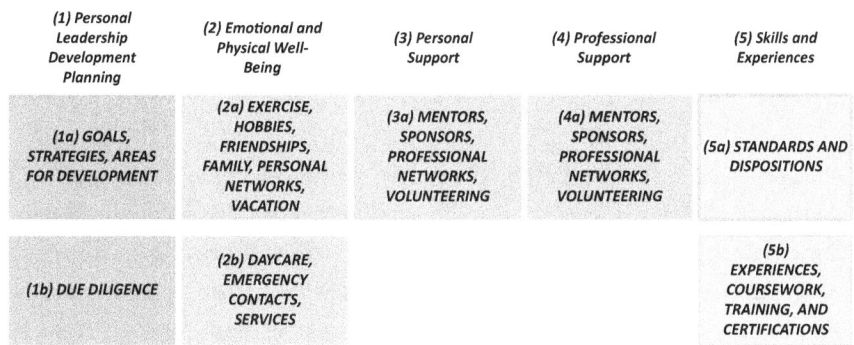

Figure 7.2 Strategies for Individuals to Employ.

prepared to anticipate and navigate around roadblocks, to arrange my pursuits, and to spend less time navigating or inhabiting glass cliff roles. No one sat me down and asked me where I wanted my career to go and helped me identify how to arrive prepared and in one piece—this is even true of my mentors, sponsors, colleagues, and supervisors.

If someone asked me about my career goals, it typically happened during interviews for positions in different organizations or as part of my applications to doctoral programs. My annual performance plans related to what I was to accomplish for a given year via an annual goal-setting exercise and included items like completing and securing approval for a strategic plan, developing an elementary schools-of-choice student assignment policy, passing a ballot initiative, or securing grant funding. Following my early career participation in the Center for Creative Leadership's Leadership Development Program, the plan I developed focused on how I would mitigate certain behaviors, refine others, and bolster skills. My comprehensive leadership development plan was a map in my head. For women aspiring to or serving in educational leadership roles, I suggest (1) planning your leadership development, (2) attending to emotional and physical well-being, (3) negotiating personal support, (4) identifying professional support, and (5) engaging in due diligence. Figure 7.2 outlines strategies individuals can employ to avoid, or better navigate, what I went through.

(1) Personal Leadership Development Planning

A leader's first step should be to take charge of their development and envision where they want to be and by when. For example, one can examine what to do for themself to progress in their career, make deliberate choices, and maintain positive relationships that develop social capital.[29] Another formal step is to envision how to get there. The "how" includes both personal and professional steps and can evolve over time based on professional and personal realities. A leader can identify where their support, experiences, training, and education will occur. Being deliberate about what is required for goal realization will help avert additional stress, misunderstandings, and missed opportunities. These elements—what, when, where, and how—are the core of a personalized leadership development or learning plan and where customization applies. Identify the education and training, skills and dispositions, and experiences that will help with goal attainment. What areas of strength and development are evident? A leader's path to leadership can and should be unique. In prior chapters, I share my rationale for moving into a school district role and pursuing a doctorate so I could truly understand and contribute to urban education. I also discuss the training I pursued, networks I joined, and board roles I secured.

Another step I suggest is to determine if this leadership plan—and one's development as a leader—requires support from one's supervisor or within one's own organization. A leader may schedule meetings to discuss their draft plan to solicit ideas and support from trusted people. If the current situation isn't a safe, constructive, or trustworthy one, a leader can take their plan to those outside of their organization where they are less likely viewed as a threat, defying type, or discontent. Based on my experience, I recommend that candidates for leadership roles find out as much as possible about the position, organization, and leader ahead of time—with whom will you be working, to whom will you be reporting, and what is the culture, climate, and governing body of the organization? Try to get a bead on the new organization's leader and colleagues' leadership styles, values, and track records. Verify the benefits and salary packages. Look into the organization's fiscal health, and its short- and long-term plans regarding reporting relationships and organizational structure. Lastly, even though the onus shouldn't be on the individual, my experience and that of respondents indicates that it's essential to take charge of your own career and look out for yourself and your interests.

Georgette, Jaimie, and Karin convey similar sentiments:

> **Georgette**: Apply to those organizations that have a mission and vision closely aligned to yours. Be mindful of your gender and racial perceptions operating. Be a good student of politics. Lead with confidence and do not compromise your values. Build a good

team. Establish an external network. If you love politics become a superintendent. If you love children become a teacher.

Jaimie: Before you take a position make sure as much as you can that it's a good fit and try and find a position with a seasoned school leader who believes in building leaders and not themselves. Ask questions and look at the make-up of the organization, are there any women in leadership roles? Also, if there is no diversity or minority women in leadership position, find out as much as you can before taking the position.

Karin: Keep going. It can sometimes get frustrating and is tempting to switch into a new, less demanding career path, but the future of our world depends on all students getting a high quality education, and it starts with strong leadership. Education needs to retain its passionate, compassionate, female leaders to set an example.

Last, one should refine their plan based on feedback and start implementing it! Regularly revisit it to incorporate updates based on life's twists and turns.

(2) Emotional and Physical Well-Being

In earlier chapters, I provide anecdotes about the ways in which I sustained my mental and physical health.[30] Leaders should consider what they require—from a physical, emotional, and relationship level—to stay sane, healthy, and content, and for their family to do so as well. It is not just important to attain one's leadership goals. I took yoga, early morning aerobics, and Pilates. I swam, rode my bike, walked, danced in the kitchen, and read romance and mystery novels. I went to see chiropractors and masseuses. I used humor. I also relied on graduate school cohort members as my professional sounding board. My direct reports were the ones who told me to eat, to drink less coffee, and to zip up the back of my dress. Periodically I would tell my husband and boss—and father—that I needed a few days away to catch up on work and find my center. I would fly down to Southeast Florida and stay in my father's uninhabited house, work uninterrupted all morning, and then spend afternoons at the beach. My dad's house had fantastic wine, music, art, and rugs. I would return refreshed, centered, caught up on critical projects, and mentally present when physically present with my family, coworkers, and friends.

Several respondents' comments highlight this strategy's importance:

Billie: Scripture, music, [and] friends are encouraging.

Lara: Prayer. Hope. A strong belief that I have the ability to connect with others to be the change that others need.
Leslie: PRACTICE SELF CARE.
Mathilda: My main encouragement comes from God. I know He is in control and has placed me exactly where He wants me to lead. It might not be senior leadership at this time, but I trust him. I also seek counseling, foster friendships, exercise, and read encouraging words.

(3) Personal Support

Leaders should seek to reach consensus on the support they need and can expect from a partner if they have one. My former husband and I crafted our work schedules so we could share in child-rearing. Is your partner willing to move with you for your job or do you need to be place-based? If you have or desire children, what type of flexibility does your partner have? Can you figure out ways to share child-rearing duties? I enrolled in an accelerated doctoral program that required me to be away one weekend a month and one week during the summer—all while I had three children younger than twelve and was working a demanding full-time cabinet-level job. I studied nights and early mornings. Eventually I moved my family of five, and five pets, cross-country for a coveted role. This required support from my spouse (as did my doctoral program and flying to Florida).

A leader can also secure commitments about the role of and support they can expect from extended family and friends. We did not have family in the area, so we relied on our friends who were often our secondary emergency contacts. It's also important to consider and delegate responsibilities. These might include hiring cleaning help, moving closer to family, or creating surrogate family members among friend groups. I once changed a job, which was reliant on me traveling regularly, because my former husband began to travel more frequently. Our children were teenagers at the time but don't let anyone say teenagers need less support than toddlers! Yet, I still found myself out of town when my youngest child had a bad fall in Aikido and a friend ended up taking them to the emergency room. This same friend also took this child and my Labrador for the summer following high-school graduation, because I secured a job in the time zone of aging parents, sold the house, and the role commenced before my youngest was ready to leave for college. I commuted from the East Coast to the West coast every ten days.

(4) Professional Support

A major component of a leader's ever-evolving plan may include identifying what type of professional support is required to meet leadership goals, to deepen knowledge, and to master standards and dispositions. Where can that support be found, or learning procured, and how much will it cost in time, money, relationships, and position? What does a current employer and union (if relevant) offer for leadership development, professional development, conference attendance, conference days, and tuition aid? One can assess the amount of money needed (and available) for travel, lodging, conference registration, and coursework, and mine affiliations to participate in networks and secure mentors. Regardless of whether one's organization provides such support, it may be necessary for a leader to identify their own prospective mentors, coaches, and sponsors. How will you approach them? Who do you know that knows such people if you don't? In what areas do you need to grow and can advisors be most constructive? The same is true for finding educational programs, volunteering for stretch assignments, and diversifying an experience set. How will you let people know you are interested in stretching yourself? What committees might you join? Are there internal and external positions for which you can apply? What volunteering is manageable? Which universities and programs offer the kind of continuing education desired? How can you network at local or national conferences to talk to graduate students attending a program you are considering or with other practitioners in roles you desire?

Respondents acknowledge that because leadership work is challenging, it's important to engage in self-care (spiritually, emotionally, physically, and/or mentally); to find a group of like-minded and safe peers; and to support, recognize, and elevate other women.

> **Avril**: Find a group of colleagues who share your responsibilities in another district/organization and connect with them regularly. Since they are outside of your organization, there is no competitiveness, only support. I met with a group of special education administrators for two hours once monthly for many years and that group became my lifeline. We shared ideas, helped each other problem-solve and interpret special ed. laws and regulations and provide a forum to just vent … stepping away for a brief moment and breathing/running/yoga [also] helped me to refocus and return to face the challenge.
>
> **Catrina**: Other people. When faced with challenges, they would help me put things into perspective and stay the course.

Dedee: Always have a mentor (one or more); these may be dependent on the different situations you find yourself. Models for continuous improvement (depending on the type of staff with whom you are working).

Diedre: Reach out to people you admire and find a collective group of people who want to learn and grow together, but who will also be honest with you about what you need to do differently—these are the people who will tell you when you have kale in your teeth. Treasure these relationships and make them a priority.

Jean: Colleagues and supervisors influenced my professional aspirations, as did my family. When I pursued a district-level leadership position my husband was very supportive and encouraging, as he was when I opted to return to graduate school.

Joan: Networks, strong relationships, educational and professional training, experience in other sectors, ability to speak the language of business (having worked in corporate finance), understanding of philanthropy/politics in this work, recognizing this work is hard and it is not prescriptive [facilitated my ability to implement sound educational leadership practices].

Julie: Find peers in separate but in similar settings that can provide support and advice without coming from a competitive or threatened perspective.

Kelly: Find a group of people that support you and hold you down and help you grow.

Lydia: It is important to find colleagues who have similar values and surround yourself with supportive people. Higher levels of leadership can be more and more isolating as the supports are fewer and the risks larger. Reach out to others for help when needed and be able to separate your life from your work.

Michelle: My own education studies helped to inform my work daily, and my work experience made me feel very confident in all of my academic learning. I feel that I reached a high pinnacle in both my career experience and my academic work, and that makes me very content … "ground[ing] yourself with knowledge, experience, and a support network of caring colleagues."

Nola: It is important to find colleagues who have similar values and surround yourself with supportive people. Higher levels of leadership can be more and more isolating as the supports are fewer and the risks larger. Reach out to others for help when needed and be able to separate your life from your work. Having a supportive family and a professional network helped move me forward when it felt impossible to continue to do the work.

Sharon: Band together and support one another in the quest for equality.

Tang: I have benefited from some key mentoring and also sponsoring relationships, both of which have enabled me to exercise sound leadership practices. The network of professionals I have to rely on as sounding boards, especially those who have more experience in leadership, have supported me in my own growth and development on the job ... The other women of color in educational leadership positions and the retired women of color who once led schools give me hope that I, too, can contribute something to the field of education.

Tanya: Find a good base of likeminded people to surround yourself with and just keep going.

Zelda: Network and find mentors and a tribe who can support you ... [I benefitted from] surrounding myself with other people both within and outside of education who are my cheerleaders has kept me going ... I place a high importance on my own personal professional development both through formal and informal avenues. I believe it is important to have a strong network of mentors and colleagues who can encourage self-reflection along with practical advice and problem-solving skills and knowledge. Being around other leaders provides an opportunity to learn from and reflect on my own practice. In addition, being intentional about inquiry into my own practice is important.

(5) Skills and Experiences

I devote the prior chapter to establishing what women educational leaders should know and be able to do. Think of the standards and dispositions as the espoused leadership skill set women educational leaders need. I've dedicated this chapter's focus to enacting that espoused skill set by leveraging one's organization, creating and following a leadership development plan, taking care of oneself, and building important personal and professional relationships and experiences. I will not revisit the standards and dispositions women can develop to become effective and compassionate educational leaders. I won't repeat the experiences and hardships from which I benefitted to lead in educational settings. Rather this last chapter's last subsection is the opportunity for you to consider all these implementation strategies and the types of experiences that will facilitate your realization of educational leadership.

Multiple respondents report that their experiences in a variety of roles and organizations facilitated their leadership expertise and skill development.

Avril: What is probably most unique about my situation is my longevity in my position. I started teaching special education the same year that the Education for All Handicapped Children Act was enacted and so I "grew up" professionally as the field evolved. I became a special ed. administrator at age 29 and remained in the same district through retirement at age 64 (last week!). I loved what I did and always stayed current—this definitely helped facilitate my ability to implement sound educational leadership practices.

Catrina: I have held various positions within our District: Teacher, Staff Development Coordinator, Assistant Principal, Principal, and Assistant Superintendent. Each position has provided me with not only different perspectives but detailed knowledge of how each person contributes to the overall effectiveness of an organization.

Crystal: Seek out as many cross functional opportunities as possible and stay as close to the work as possible.

Diedre: Be willing to stretch yourself to take on experiences that prepare you for the job you want and to apply for that job as soon as it is available. Do not wait for the "right time" to have more experience, more knowledge, more anything. Applying will teach you a lot about yourself and if you are not selected, it will help you see what you need to do to be ready next time.

Ester: I've worked as a sub for several districts as well as in a charter school before I worked in the district I am in now. I have been able to see what education looks like in different settings. I've been a part of a start up school as well as established schools.

Jackie: My experiences as a charter school teacher, administrator, researcher, board member, and parent have given me a variety of perspectives to draw from to support and assist teams that want to start charter schools, and integrate knowledge when designing programs that support charter school developers.

Julie: Having positions that have allowed me to manage clear, distinct projects has helped [me].

Reese: My early roles in education non-profits, at the associate and coordinator levels, definitely facilitated my strengths as a project manager and systems builder. When you're at the lower levels of an organization, you often are tasked with organizational systems, project trackers, and other tools that facilitate strong project management.

Working. my way up the non-profit ladder has been invaluable in that regard … Seize as many opportunities as are available to you to lead projects, even if and especially if you aren't sure you are the best person for the job. Chances are that you're just more self-critical than a man would be in the same situation, so say yes and be willing to take the risk even if you fear failure.

Zelda: I believe that my experiences in a wide variety of educational sectors has facilitated my ability to implement sound educational practices. Having worked at traditional public, charter public, private, higher Ed, and nonprofit settings has given me unique perspectives on education and leadership. Within my current role as an educational leadership professor I also have the opportunity to interact with educational leaders in a variety of settings also broadening my perspectives. In addition, I've had the privilege to be in settings that have prioritized research and inquiry specifically in leadership … Think broadly about how you can meet your professional goals so that you are not stuck, and these goals do not need to necessarily be positions but what is the work that you really want to do.

Conclusion

We've made it to Oz—the end of the road of twists, turns, stop offs, delays, challenges, dreams, misinformation, realizations, friendships, frenemies, saboteurs, guides, and accomplishments. I share my own story, key concepts I believe are relevant, and perspectives from the thirty-seven respondents in the hopes that readers can benefit and position themselves to navigate their own journeys with ease and insight. As my own and respondents' stories highlight, the road to educational leadership for women is not easy. Yet there are many who've already tread it. With mettle, support, and skill women and others can overcome bias and lead with aplomb.

Yes, there will be challenges but as I and respondents show, there are enumerable women leader allies. With this and earlier chapters' strategies in hand, women educational leaders and YOU can—without compromising your values—have a positive impact on each other, colleagues, communities, the enterprise of education, and most importantly the children we are entrusted with serving and educating. I advise you to listen to your gut and pay attention to red flags. Use what I share to be savvier than I was about formally developing and sharing a leadership development plan, identifying or declining glass cliff roles, and conducting due diligence. Above all, don't allow anyone or any position to knock you off your center! If you temporarily lose touch with your core drivers, be honest with yourself, take time, regroup, recover, and learn from the experience. Leadership is about self-reflection, learning, improving, resilience, and authenticity.

We are well past the time when one should discount, belittle, and dismiss someone merely because that person identifies, values, or is prepared differently. Today there are people on both sides of the culture wars who say they are leading with their values. It is important to live with oneself, know oneself, and understand one's moral compass and purpose—especially while working to ensure that all children have the same access to and outcomes from a quality education. To do so, one may develop understanding of the community context and seek to improve workplace and learning environments. This set of commitments doesn't imply that leaders take a scorched earth approach to leadership. Instead, as respondents and I elucidate through stories, standards, dispositions, identities, and callings, a leader can seize the opportunity to share and distribute power, engage in authentic dialogue, listen to understand, include others in design and decision-making, and adjust strategies based on input.

Now that I've reflected and grown through researching and writing this book, this is your time for reflection and growth—and action! I hereby pass the baton. Remember, you aren't alone on your trek.

> Don't you know I'm still standing better than I ever did
> Looking like a true survivor, feeling like a little kid
> I'm still standing after all this time
> —Elton John and Bernie Taupin, composers (1983)[31]

Reflective Questions

1. In what ways, if any, has your organization, supervisor, or mentor supported your leadership journey?
2. In what ways does your organization support leadership development?
3. What type of information, if any, does your organization make available regarding selection, promotion, and development?
4. What types of evaluation and monitoring systems are in place where you work?
    a. Is the information used, or in what ways could you use it, to inform future practices?
5. In what ways does your organization deliver leadership development?
6. Which of the four learning strategies—Learning by Doing and Reflecting in Context, Learning Alongside and from Others, Learning through Individualized Feedback and Growth Plans, and Learning through Leaders' Preferences and Contexts—does your organization incorporate into leadership development?
    a. Which do you believe are most effective and why?
7. In what ways, if any, has your organization, supervisor, or mentor aligned learning with your own needs?
    a. The organization's?
8. What type of leadership plan have you developed?
    a. Did you let anyone else inform, or know about, it?
9. In what ways, have you attended to you own emotional and physical health and/or sought out deliberate support from family, friends, mentors, colleagues, etc.?
10. Now that you've reached the end of this book, what stands out for you?
11. What, if anything, surprised you?
12. What if anything will you do differently for yourself or for others?

Appendix A

Respondents (Using Pseudonyms for Confidentiality)

Respondent #1, "Angela" ' (2020), age 35–44, identifies as "mixed," possesses a master's degree, and works for an independent school.

Respondent #2, "Tanya" (2020), age 25–34, identifies as black, possesses a bachelor's degree, and works for a third-party education organization.

Respondent #3, "Julie" (2020), age 45–54, identifies as white, possesses a doctorate, and works for a third-party education organization.

Respondent #4, "Rachel" (2020), age 35–44, identifies as black, possesses a master's degree, and works for a school district.

Respondent #5, "Diane" (2020), age 35–44, identifies as black and Hispanic, possesses a master's degree, and works for a third-party education organization.

Respondent #6, "Sonja" (2020), age 25–34, identifies as white, possesses a bachelor's degree, and works for a charter school network.

Respondent #7, "Kelly" (2020), age 25–34, identifies as "other "and Hispanic, possesses a master's degree, and works for a school district.

Respondent #8, "Jackie" (2020), age 45–54, identifies as white, possesses a doctorate, and works for a charter school association.

Respondent #9, "Wilma" (2020), age 25–34, identifies as "other" and Hispanic, possesses a doctorate, and works for an education partnership organization.

Respondent #10, "Ester" (2020), age 25–34, identifies as mixed race, possesses a master's degree, and works for an education partnership organization.

Respondent #11, "Reese" (2020), age 25–34, identifies as white and Hispanic, possesses a master's degree and works for an education partnership organization.

Respondent #12, "Karin" (2020), age 25–34, identifies as white, possesses a master's degree, and works for a charter school network.

Respondent #13, "Jaimie" (2020), age 45–54, identifies as black, possesses a doctorate, and works for a school district.

Respondent #14, "Catrina" (2020), age 55–64, identifies as white, possesses a master's degree, and works for a school district.

Respondent #15, "Joan" (2020), age 25–34, identifies as "other" and Hispanic, possesses a master's degree, and works for a school district.

Respondent #16, "Natalie" (2020), age 35–44, identifies as white, possesses a master's degree, and works for a school district.

Respondent #17, "Ellie" (2020), age 35–44, identifies as white and Hispanic, possesses a master's degree, and works for a state department of education.

Respondent #18, "Avril" (2020), age 55–64, identifies as white, and possesses a doctorate degree, and is retired from a school district.

Respondent #19, "Sharon" (2020), age 55–64, identifies as white, possesses a doctorate, and is a school district superintendent.

Respondent #20, "Tang" (2020), age 35–44, identifies as Asian, possesses a doctorate, and works for an independent school.

Respondent #21, "Michelle" (2020), age 55–64, identifies as white and Hispanic, possesses a doctorate, and is retired from a state department of education.

Respondent #22, "Crystal" (2020), age 35–44, identifies as white, possesses a doctorate, and works for a school district.

Respondent #23, "Bonnie" (2020), age 65 or older, identifies as white, possesses a doctorate, and works for a charter school.

Respondent #24, "Lydia" (2020), age 65 or older, identifies as white, possesses a doctorate, is retired from a school district, and works as an independent education consultant.

Respondent #25, "Mathilda" (2020), age 45–54, identifies as white, possesses a doctorate, and works for a school district.

Respondent #26, "Diedre" (2020), age 55–64, identifies as white and Hispanic, possesses a doctorate, and works for a school district.

Respondent #27, "Billie" (2020), age 55–64, identifies as white, possesses a master's degree, and is a retired school district superintendent.

Respondent #28, "Patty" (2020), age 65 or older, identifies as white, possesses a master's degree, is retired from a school district, and works as an education consultant.

Respondent #29, "Jean" (2020), age 65 or older, identifies as white, possesses a doctorate, and is retired from a school district and VP of a third-party education organization.

Respondent #30, "Georgette" (2020), age 55–64, identifies as black, possesses a doctorate, and is retired from a school district and is serving as an acting superintendent & assistant superintendent.

Respondent #31, "Dionne" (2020), age 55–65, identifies as white, possesses a doctorate, is retired from a school district, and works for a college.

Respondent #32, "Lara" (2020), age 45–54, identifies as black, possesses a doctorate, and works for an education association.

Respondent #33, "DeDee" (2020), age 45–54, identifies as white, possesses a doctorate, and works for an education partnership organization.

Respondent #34, "Nola" (2020), age 55–64, identifies as white, possesses a doctorate, and works for a school district.

Respondent #35, "Zelda" (2020), age 35–44, identifies as Asian possesses a doctorate, and works for a university.

Respondent #36, "Leslie" (2020), age 45–54, identifies as black, possesses a master's degree, and works for a charter school.

Respondent #37, "Lottie" (2020), age 65 or older, identifies as black, possesses a master's degree, and is retired from an education partnership organization.

Appendix B

Abbreviations

Adequate yearly progress	AYP
Advanced placement	AP
African Methodist Episcopal	AME
American Association of School Administrators	AASA
American College Testing	ACT
Associate of Occupational Studies	AOS
Attention deficit hyperactivity disorder	ADHD
Black Lives Matter	BLM
Cambridge Assessment International Education	AICE
Center for Creative Leadership	CFCL
Chief executive officer	CEO
Council of Chief State School Officers	CCSSO
Corporate Leadership Council	CLC
Critical Race Theory	CRT
Diversity, Equity, and Inclusion	DEI
Doctorate in Education	EdD
Frequently asked questions	FAQs
Human Resource Management	HRM
Institutional Review Board	IRB
International Baccalaureate	IB
Kindergarten/prekindergarten to eighth grade	K-8/PreK-8
Kindergarten/prekindergarten to sixteen (end of college)	K-16/PreK-16
Kindergarten/prekindergarten to sixth grade	K-6/PreK-6
Kindergarten/prekindergarten to twelfth grade	K-12/PreK-12
Lessons of Experience framework	LOE
Master of Fine Arts	MFA

Master of Science	MS
Memorandum of understanding	MOU
National Association of Independent Schools	NAIS
National Center for Education Statistics	NCES
National Education Association	NEA
National Educational Leadership Preparation	NELP
National Policy Board for Educational Administration	NPBEA
No Child Left Behind	NCLB
Request for proposal	RFP
Science, Technology, Engineering, and Math	STEM
Seventh to eighth grade	7–8
Sixth to eighth grade	6–8
Socioeconomic status	SES
Synergistic Leadership Theory	SLT

Appendix C

Elements to Support an Audit of Leadership Development Capacity

When the leadership team possesses the commitment to collaboratively develop a leadership/professional development program and plan and the organization has the capacity to conduct an audit, then they may wish to incorporate these elements:

1. Examine organizational recruitment, selection, placement, support, development, promotion, and evaluation structures and practices—and the people presiding over them—for implicit and overt bias against women and women with intersectional identities
2. Consider the ways in which power dynamics, communication, interactions, and culture perpetuate and reinforce the status quo and/or bias
3. Explicate skills and experiences needed by role type
4. Scaffold the standards and dispositions one needs by role type—and those helpful to underrepresented groups
5. Define the leadership development delivery strategies to employ
6. Parse, package, and share critical information about leadership development and selection processes
7. Identify, involve, and target critical audiences
8. Frame objective selection criteria and rubrics for each leadership role
9. Develop job descriptions aligned to selection criteria and rubrics for each leadership role
10. Clarify the feedback loops and supports one will receive along the way and once in a leadership role
11. Create and deliver training for hiring managers, mentors, sponsors, coaches, and supervisors

12. Evaluate hiring managers, mentors, sponsors, coaches, and supervisors on the nature and quality of the support they provide, their interactions with others, and their own openness to feedback
13. Broadly describe various leadership roles (i.e., leaders can be teacher-, support staff-, committee-, department, school-, and system-level leaders)
14. Establish internal goals and measures for leadership development and selection
15. Monitor progress against the goals

Notes

1 Introduction: A Rising Tide Lifts All Boats

1 Clerkin, Cathleen, and Meena S. Wilson (2017), "Gender Differences in Developmental Experiences," in *Handbook of Research on Gender and Leadership*, edited by Susan R. Madsen, Northampton, MA: Edward Elgar Publishing, 385.
2 Eagly, Alice H., and Linda L. Carli (2007a), *Through the Labyrinth: The Truth about How Women Become Leaders*, Leadership for the Common Good, Boston, MA: Harvard Business School Publishing Corporation, 86.
3 Ibid., 86.
4 Kumra, Savita (2017), "Reflections on Glass: Second Wave Feminist Theorizing in a Third Wave Feminist Age?," in *Handbook of Research on Gender and Leadership*, edited by Susan R. Madsen, Northampton, MA: Edward Elgar Publishing, Inc., 52.
5 Moore, Izzy Carlisle (2022), "Glass Escalator Sketch," Author Commissioned.
6 U.S. Department of Education, National Center for Education Statistics (2020), "Characteristics of Public School Principals," in *The Condition of Education*, Washington, DC: IES, Figure 1; U.S. Department of Education, National Center for Education Statistics (2021), "Characteristics of Public School Teachers," in *The Condition of Education*, Washington, DC: IES, Figure 1.
7 AASA (2020b), "AASA Releases Key Findings from American Superintendent 2020 Decennial Study," *Press Release* (blog), (February 10, 2020).
8 ILO Group (2022), "Updated Analysis Shows Leadership Disruption Impacts Almost Half of the Nation's Largest School Districts," *Press Release* (website), (December 12, 2022).
9 Eagly and Carli, *Through the Labyrinth*, 164.
10 Ryan, Michelle K., and S. Alexander Haslam (2007), "The Glass Cliff: Exploring the Dynamics Surrounding the Appointment of Women to Precarious Leadership Positions," *Academy of Management Review*, 32(2), 558–9.
11 Powell, John A. (2017), "Us vs Them: The Sinister Techniques of 'Othering'—and How to Avoid Them," *The Guardian*, November 8, 2017.
12 Ibarra, Herminia, Robin Ely, and Deborah Kolb (2019), "Women Rising: The Unseen Barriers," in *On Women and Leadership*, Cambridge, MA: Harvard Business School Publishing Corporation, 46.

13 Dana, Joyce A., and Diana M. Bourisaw (2006), *Women in the Superintendency: Discarded Leadership*, Lanham, MD: Rowman & Littlefield Education (in partnership with AASA), 188.
14 Hoyt, Crystal L., and Stefanie Simon (2017), "Social Psychological Approaches to Women and Leadership Theory," in *Handbook of Research on Gender and Leadership*, edited by Susan R. Madsen, Northampton, MA: Edward Elgar Publishing, 90–1.
15 Lumby, Jack (2009) citing Amartya Sen (2006), "Disappearing Gender: Choices in Identity," in *Women Leading Education across the Continents: Sharing the Spirit, Fanning the Flame*, edited by Helen C. Sobehart, Lanham, MD: Rowman & Littlefield Education, 29.
16 Aldridge, Michael (2020), "IRB Exempt Determination by Integ Review IRB," August 2020.
17 Creswell, John W., and David J. Creswell (2018), *Research Design: Qualitative, Quantitative, and Mixed Methods Approaches*, 5th ed., Thousand Oaks, CA: Sage, 521.
18 Oregon State University (2022), "Snowball Sampling," Human Research Protection Program, Corvallis, OR: Oregon State University.
19 Ngunjiri, Faith Wambura, Cathy-Ann C. Hernandez, and Heewon Chang (2010), "Living Autoethnography: Connecting Life and Research [Editorial]," *Journal of Research Practice* 6(1), 8.
20 Moustakas, Clark (1994), *Phenomenological Research Methods*, Thousand Oaks, CA: Sage, 13.
21 Creswell and Creswell, *Research Design*, 512.
22 Maxwell, John A. (2005), *Qualitative Research Design: An Interactive Approach*, 2nd ed., Applied Social Research Methods Series 41, Thousand Oaks, CA: Sage, 36.
23 Creswell, John W., and Cheryl N. Poth (2018), *Qualitative Inquiry & Research Design: Choosing among Five Approaches*, 4th ed., Los Angeles, CA: Sage Publications, 26–7.
24 Denith, Audrey M., and Barbara Peterlin (2011), "Leadership Education from within a Feminist Ethos," *Journal of Research on Leadership Education*, 6(2), 40 (emphasis in original).
25 Bierema, Laura L., and Susan R. Madsen (2017), "No Women Left Behind: Critical Leadership Development to Build Gender Consciousness and Transform Organization," in *Handbook of Research on Gender and Leadership*, Northampton, MA: Edward Elgar Publishing, 153.
26 Creswell and Creswell, *Research Design*, 160; Bierema and Madsen, "No Women Left Behind," 153.
27 Young, Michelle D., and Catherine Marshall (2013), "Critical Feminist Theory," in *The Handbook of Educational Theories*, edited by Beverly J. Irby, Genevieve

Brown, Rafael Lara-Alecio, and Shirley Jackson, Charlotte, NC: Information Age Publishing, 977.
28 Marion, Russ, and Leslie D Gonzales (2014), *Leadership in Education: Organizational Theory for the Practitioner*, 2nd edition, Long Grove, IL: Waveland Press, 303.
29 Blackmore, Jill (2013), "Social Justice in Education," in *The Handbook of Educational Theories*, edited by Beverly J. Irby, Genevieve Brown, Rafael Lara-Alecio, and Shirley Jackson, Charlotte, NC: Information Age Publishing, 1005.
30 Creswell and Creswell, *Research Design*, 514.
31 Creswell and Poth, *Qualitative Inquiry*, 21.

2 Leadership Models and Stories: Lean In or Shove Off

1 Grogan, Margaret, and Charol Shakeshaft (2009), "Conscious Leadership in a Political World," *Women Leading Education Across the Continents: Sharing the Spirit, Fanning the Flame*, edited by Helen C. Sobehart, Lanham, MD: Rowman & Littlefield Education (in partnership with AASA), 25.
2 Grogan, Margaret, and Charol Shakeshaft (2013), "A New Way: Diverse Collective Leadership," in *The Jossey-Bass Reader on Educational Leadership*, edited by Margaret Grogan, 3rd edition, San Francisco, CA: Jossey-Bass, 121.
3 Collard, John (2007), "Constructing Theory for Leadership in Intercultural Contexts," *Journal of Educational Administration*, 45(6), 751.
4 Franco, Carmella S., Maria Gutierrez Ott, and Darlene P. Robles (2013), "Lessons Learned: Cultural Assets Inform Actions," in *The Jossey-Bass Reader on Educational Leadership*, edited by Margaret Grogan, 3rd edition, San Francisco, CA: Jossey-Bass, 95.
5 Blackmore, "Social Justice," 997.
6 Melaku, Tsedale M., Angie Beeman, David G. Smith, and Brad W. Johnson (2020), "Be a Better Ally," *Harvard Business Review*, December 2020.
7 Green, Erica L. (2021), "New Leader Pushes Teachers' Union to Take on Social Justice Role," *New York Times*, December 12, 2021.
8 Rice, Joy K. (2007), "Introduction to Part II: Collaboration and Leadership," in *Women and Leadership: Transforming Visions and Diverse Voices*, edited by Jean Lau Chin, Bernice Lott, Joy K. Rice, and Janis Sanchez-Hucles, Malden, MA: Blackwell Publishing, 136; Blackmore, "Social Justice," 1007; Denith and Peterlin, "Leadership Education," 36.
9 Chin, Jean Lau (2007a), "Conclusion," in *Women and Leadership: Transforming Visions and Diverse Voices*, edited by Jean Lau Chin, Bernice Lott, Joy K. Rice, and Janis Sanchez-Hucles, Malden, MA: Blackwell Publishing, 358.

10 Denith and Peterlin, "Leadership Education," 42–43.
11 Chin, "Conclusion," 358.
12 Grogan, Margaret, and Charol Shakeshaft (2011), *Women and Educational Leadership*, San Francisco, CA: Jossey-Bass Leadership Library in Education, 19–20.
   Zepeda, Sally J., Parylo Oksana, and Hans W. Klar (2017), "Educational Leadership for Teaching and Learning," in *The Wiley International Handbook of Educational Leadership*, edited by Duncan Waite and Ira Bogotch, 1st edition, Hoboken, NJ: John Wiley & Sons, 239.
13 Liggins-Moore, Lysa (2016) citing Terry (1993), "Forty-Three African American Women Executives' Perceptions of Challenges and Required Capabilities to Become a Leader," Dissertation, Pepperdine University, 17.
14 Fine, Marlene G. (2007), "Chapter 8: Women, Collaboration, and Social Change: An Ethics-Based Model of Leadership," in *Women and Leadership: Transforming Visions and Diverse Voices*, edited by Jean Lau Chin, Bernice Lott, Joy K. Rice, and Janis Sanchez-Hucles, Malden, MA: Blackwell Publishing, 186.
15 Ibid., 186.
16 Boyatzis, Richard, and Annie McKee (2005), *Resonant Leadership*, Boston, MA: Harvard Business School Press, 4–5.
17 Sergiovanni, Thomas (2013), "Leadership as Stewardship: Who's Serving Who?," in *The Jossey-Bass Reader on Educational Leadership*, 3rd edition, San Francisco, CA: Jossey-Bass, 387.
18 Devnew, Lynne E, Ann M. Berghout Austin, Marlene Janzen Le Ber, and Mary Shapiro (2017), "Women's Leadership Aspirations," in *Handbook of Research on Gender and Leadership*, edited by Susan R. Madsen, Northampton, MA: Edward Elgar Publishing, 167.
19 Irby, Beverly J., Genevieve Brown, and LingLing Yang (2013), "The Synergistic Leadership Theory: An Inclusive Theory in the Twenty-First Century," in *The Handbook of Educational Theories*, edited by Beverly J. Irby, Genevieve Brown, Rafael Lara-Alecio, and Shirley Jackson, Charlotte, NC: Information Age Publishing, 992.
20 Fine, "Chapter 8: Women," 178.
21 Marion and Gonzales, *Leadership in Education*, 244–6.
22 Eagly, Alice H., and Linda L. Carli (2019), "Women and the Labyrinth of Leadership," in *On Women and Leadership*, Harvard Business Review's 10 Must Reads, Cambridge, MA: Harvard Business School Publishing Corporation, 12.
   Harvard Business Publishing (2018), *The 2018 State of Leadership Development: Meeting the Transformation Imperative*, Learning Design, Brighton, MA: Harvard Business Publishing Corporate Learning, 5.
   Shields, Carolyn M. (2017), *Transformative Leadership in Education: Equitable and Socially Just Change in an Uncertain and Complex World*, 2nd edition, New York: Routledge, 19; Marion and Gonzales, *Leadership in Education*, 148.

23 Brooks, Jeffrey S., and Lisa A. W. Kenslar (2011), "Chapter 4: Distributed Leadership and Democratic Community," in *The SAGE Handbook of Educational Leadership: Advances in Theory, Research, and Practice*, edited by Fenwick W. English, 2nd edition, Thousand Oaks, CA: Sage, 56.
24 Leadership Academy (2021), *A Portrait of a Culturally Responsive School System*, Long Island City, NY: The Leadership Academy, 3.
25 Ibid., 4.
26 Grogan and Shakeshaft, "Conscious Leadership," 24; Marion and Gonzales, *Leadership in Education*, 65 and 106.
27 Grogan and Shakeshaft, "Conscious Leadership," 24; Marion and Gonzales, *Leadership in Education*, 65 and 106.
28 Hoyt and Simon, "Social Psychological," 90.
29 Boyatzis and McKee, *Resonant*, 7.

3 Purpose, Identity, and Power: What We Stand For

1 Shields, *Transformative Leadership*, 23.
2 Collard, "Constructing Theory," 751.
   Deal, Terrence E., and Kent D. Peterson (2013), "Eight Roles of Symbolic Leaders," in *The Jossey-Bass Reader on Educational Leadership*, edited by Margaret Grogan, 3rd edition, San Francisco, CA: Jossey-Bass, 276.
3 Leadership Academy, *A Portrait*, 4.
4 Eagly and Carli, *Through the Labyrinth*, 146.
5 Tooms, Autumn K., Catherine A. Lugg, and Ira Bogotch (2010) citing Antonio Gramsci (1971), "Rethinking the Politics of Fit and Educational Leadership," *Educational Administration Quarterly* 46(1), 98.
6 Dwyer, Charles E. (1992), *The Shifting Sources of Power and Influence*, Tampa, FL: American College of Physician Executives, 28–9.
7 Eagly and Carli, *Through the Labyrinth*, 137.
8 Fox-Kirk, Wendy, Constance Campbell, and Chrys Egan (2017), "Women's Leadership Identity: Exploring Person and Context in Theory," in *Handbook of Research on Gender and Leadership*, edited by Susan R. Madsen, Northampton, MA: Edward Elgar Publishing, 195.
9 Sanchez-Hucles, Janis V., and Donald D. Davis (2010), "Women and Women of Color in Leadership: Complexity, Identity, and Intersectionality," *American Psychologist* 65(3), 175; Fox-Kirk, Campbell, and Egan, "Women's Leadership Identity," 195, 197–8.
10 Tooms, Luggs, and Botoch, "Rethinking," 113.
11 Ibarra, Ely, and Kolb, "Women Rising," 49.

12 Ibid., 41–2.
13 Longman, Karen A., and Debbie Lamm Bray (2017), "The Role of Purpose and Calling in Women's Leadership Experiences," in *Handbook of Research on Gender and Leadership*, edited by Susan R. Madsen, Northampton, MA: Edward Elgar Publishing, 218.
14 Feifer, Jason (2022), "Jimmy Fallon Spent Years Chasing a Dream That Wasn't Really His. Finding His 'Why' Changed Everything," *Entrepreneur*, January 4, 2022.
15 Dweck, Carol S. (2006), *Mindset: The New Psychology of Success*. New York: Random House, 18.
16 Ibid., 31–2.
17 Council of Chief State School Officers (2015), *Model Principal Supervisor Professional Standards 2015*, Washington, DC: CCSSO, 9.
18 Boyatzis and McKee, *Resonant*, 8.
19 Maxwell, *Qualitative Research*, 43.
20 Rice, Joy K., and Asunsion Miteria Austria (2007a), "Chapter 7: Collaborative Leadership and Social Advocacy among Women's Organizations," in *Women and Leadership: Transforming Visions and Diverse Voices*, edited by Jean Lau Chin, Bernice Lott, Joy K. Rice, and Janis Sanchez-Hucles, Malden, MA: Blackwell Publishing, 136.
    Grogan and Shakeshaft, "A New Way," 112; Blackmore, "Social Justice," 1007; Denith and Peterlin, "Leadership Education," 36.
21 Fennell, Hope-Arlene (2008), "Feminine Faces of Leadership," *Journal of School Leadership*, 18 (November), 610.
22 Bierema and Madsen, "No Women," 153.
23 Denith and Peterlin, "Leadership Education," 39.
24 Johnson, Norine G., Florence L. Denmark, Dorothy W. Cantor, Diane F. Halpern, and Gwendolyn Puryear Keita (2007), "Leadership through Policy Development: Collaboration, Equity, Empowerment, and Multiculturalism," in *Women and Leadership: Transforming Visions and Diverse Voices*, edited by Jean Lau Chin, Bernice Lott, Joy K. Rice, and Janis Sanchez-Hucles, Malden, MA: Blackwell Publishing, 154.
25 Marion and Gonzales, *Leadership in Education*, 303.
26 Lumby (2009) citing Amartya Sen, "Disappearing Gender," 29.
27 Hall, Ruth L., BraVada Garrett-Akinsanya, and Michael Hucles (2007), "Chapter 13: Voices of Black Feminist Leaders: Making Spaces for Ourselves," in *Women and Leadership: Transforming Visions and Diverse Voices*, edited by Jean Lau Chin, Bernice Lott, Joy K. Rice, and Janis Sanchez-Hucles, Malden, MA: Blackwell Publishing, 282–3; Chin, "Conclusion," 360.
    Sanchez-Hucles, Janis, and Penny Sanchez (2007), "Introduction to Part III: From the Margin to Center: The Voices of Diverse Feminist Leaders," in *Women*

and Leadership: Transforming Visions and Diverse Voices, edited by Jean Lau Chin, Bernice Lott, Joy K. Rice, and Janis Sanchez-Hucles, Malden, MA: Blackwell Publishing, 211 and 214.
28 Rice, "Introduction to Part II," 129.
29 Kendall, Mikki (2021), *Hood Feminism: Notes from the Women That a Movement Forgot*, New York: Penguin Books, 2.
30 Ibid., 3.
31 Young and Marshall, "Critical Feminist," 976.
32 Eagly and Carli, *Through the Labyrinth*, 86.
33 Kumra, "Reflections on Glass," 50.
34 English, Fenwick, Beverly Irby, Genevieve Brown, Rafael Lara-Alecio, and Shirley Jackson (eds.) (2013), "Section 11: Leadership and Management Theory Introduction," in *The handbook on Educational Theories*, Charlotte, NC: Information Age Publishing, 897.
35 Chin, Jean Lau (2007b), "Overview," in *Women and Leadership: Transforming Visions and Diverse Voices*, edited by Jean Lau Chin, Bernice Lott, Joy K. Rice, and Janis Sanchez-Hucles, Malden, MA: Blackwell Publishing, 5.
36 Marion and Gonzales, *Leadership in Education*, 63.
37 Brown, Kathleen M. (2012), "Trait Theory," in *The Handbook of Educational Theories*, edited by Beverly J. Irby, Genevieve Brown, Rafael Lara-Alecio, and Shirley Jackson, Charlotte, NC: Information Age Publishing, 897.
38 Eagly and Carli, *Through the Labyrinth*, 102.
39 Kumra (2017) citing Eagly and Karau, "Reflections on Glass," 50.
40 Irby, Brown, and Yang, "The Synergistic," 985.
41 Thomas, Rachel, Marianne Cooper, Kate McShane Urban, Ali Bohrer, Sonia Mahajan, Lareina Yee, Alexis Krivkovich et al. (2021), *Women in the Workplace: 2021*, Boston, MA, 62. Available online: https://wiw-report.s3.amazon aws.com/Women_in_the_Workplace_2021.pdf.
42 Equity in the Center (2020), *Awake to Woke to Work: Building a Race Equity Culture*, 25. Available online: https://equityinthecenter.org.
43 Forrester, Sarah, David Jacobs, Rachel Zmora, Pamela Schreiner, and Veronica Roger (2019), "Racial Differences in Weathering and Its Associations with Psychosocial Stress: The CARDIA Study," *Population Health*, 7.

4 Navigating Challenges to Women's Leadership: Hummingbird

1 Imbler, Sabrina (2021), "Female Hummingbirds Avoid Harassment by Looking like Males," *New York Times*, August 26, 2021.

2 Harragan, Betty Lehan (1977), *Games Mother Never Taught You: Corporate Gamesmanship for Women*, New York: Grand Central Publishing.
3 Glass, Christy, and Alice Ingersoll (2017), "Sociological Approaches to Women and Leadership Theory," in *Handbook of Research on Gender and Leadership*, edited by Susan R. Madsen, Northampton, MA: Edward Elgar Publishing, 104.
4 Ibid., 105.
5 Ibarra, Ely, and Kolb, "Women Rising," 44.
6 Banaji, Mahzarin R., and Anthony G. Greenwald (2016), *Blind Spots: Hidden Biases of Good People*, New York: Bantam Books, xii.
7 Ibid., 4.
8 Tooms, Lugg, and Botoch, "Rethinking," 121.
9 Ibid., 115.
10 Maranto, Robert, Kristen Carroll, Albert Cheng, and Manuel P. Teodoro (2018), "Boys Will Be Superintendents: School Leadership as a Gendered Profession," *Phi Delta Kappan*, 100(2), 13.
11 AASA, "AASA Releases."
12 Maranto et al., "Boys Will Be," 13.
13 Glass and Ingersoll (2017) citing Smith, "Sociological Approaches," 107.
14 Glass and Ingersoll (2017), "Sociological Approaches," 107.
15 Dana and Bourisaw, *Women in the Superintendency*, 25.
16 Eagly and Carli, "The Female Leadership," 818.
17 Ibid., 818.
18 Powell, "Us vs Them."
19 Glass and Ingersoll, "Sociological Approaches," 105.
20 Eagly and Carli, *Through the Labyrinth*, 157.
21 Glass and Ingersoll, "Sociological Approaches," 106.
22 Ryan and Haslam, "The Glass Cliff," 558.
23 Ibid., 558.
24 Reeves, Arin N. (2015), "Mansplaining, Manterrupting, and Bropropriating: Gender Bias and the Pervasive Interruption of Women," Yellow Paper Series, Nextions. Chicago, IL, 3.
25 Ibid., 10.
26 Dodgson, Lindsay (2018), "What Is Hepeating?", *Business Insider Newsletter*, March 8, 2018.
27 Chemaly, Soraya (2018), *Rage Becomes Her: The Power of Women's Anger*, New York: Atria Books, 202.
28 Fox-Kirk, Campbell, and Egan et al., "Women's Leadership Identity," 202.
29 Hoyt and Simon, "Social Psychological," 90–1.
30 Chemaly, *Rage*, 14.
31 Eagly and Carli, *Through the Labyrinth*, 103.

32 Chemaly, *Rage*, 70.
33 Vanek Smith, Stacey (2021), *Machiavelli for Women: Define Your Worth, Grow Your Ambition, and Win the Workplace*, New York: Gallery Books, 73–4.
34 Meyerson, Debra, and Megan Tompkins (2007), "Tempered Radicals as Institutional Change Agents: The Case of Advancing Gender Equity at the University of Michigan," *Harvard Women's Law Journal* 30(2), 303.
35 Kelan, Elisabeth K. (2009), "Gender Fatigue: The Ideological Dilemma of Gender Neutrality and Discrimination in Organizations," *Canadian Journal of Administrative Sciences*, 26(3), 199.
36 Chemaly, *Rage*, 255.
37 Kay, Katty, and Claire Shipman (2014), *The Confidence Code: The Science and Art of Self-Assurance—What Women Should Know*, 1st edition, New York: Harper Collins Publishers, 51; Kumra, "Reflections on Glass," 55.
   Sandberg, Sheryl, and Nell Scovell (2013), *Lean in: Women, Work, and the Will to Lead*, New York: Alfred A. Knopf, 62.
38 Forrester, Sarah, David Jacobs, Rachel Zmora, Pamela Schreiner, and Veronica Roger (2019), "Racial Differences in Weathering and Its Associations with Psychosocial Stress: The CARDIA Study," *Population Health*, 7.
39 Dweck, *Mindset*, 228.
40 Ibid., 138.
41 Blackmore, "Social Justice," 997.
42 Shields, *Transformative Leadership*, 60, 108, 110.
43 Vanek Smith, *Machiavelli for Women*, 155.
44 Shapiro, Ester E., and Jennifer M. Leigh (2007), "Chapter 4: Toward Culturally Competent, Gender-Equitable Leadership: Assessing Outcomes of Women's Leadership in Diverse Contexts," in *Women and Leadership: Transforming Visions and Diverse Voices*, edited by Jean Lau Chin, Bernice Lott, Joy K. Rice, and Janis Sanchez-Hucles, Malden, MA: Blackwell Publishing, 96.
45 Chemaly, *Rage*, 210.
46 Ibid., 196.
47 Ibid., 196.
48 Bligh, Michelle, and Ali Ito (2017), "Organizational Processes and Systems That Affect Women in Leadership," in *Handbook of Research on Gender and Leadership*, edited by Susan R. Madsen, Northampton, MA: Edward Elgar Publishing, 291.
49 Liggins-Moore, "Forty-Three African," 29.
50 Liggins-Moore (2016) citing Cacioppo, Reis, and Zautra, "Forty-Three African American," 41.
51 Liggins-Moore (2016) citing Keck and Sakdapolrak, "Forty-Three African," 41.
52 Vanek Smith, *Machiavelli for Women*, 48.
53 Clerkin and Wilson, "Gender Differences," 378–9.

54 Ibid., 385.
55 Ibid., 380–1.

5 Leadership Routes and Areas of Knowledge: Yellow Brick Road

1 Moore, "Yellow Brick Road Sketch."
2 Diehl, Amy B., and Leanne Dzubinski (2017), "An Overview of Gender-Based Leadership Barriers," in *Handbook of Research on Gender and Leadership*, Northampton, MA: Edward Elgar Publishing, 276.
3 Tan, Jo-Ann (2016), "For Women of Color, the Glass Ceiling is Actually Made of Concrete," *Huffington Post*, April 20, 2016.
4 Eagly and Carli, *Through the Labyrinth*, 2–3.
5 Chemaly, *Rage*, 206; Ryan and Haslam, "The Glass Cliff," 558–9.
6 Ryan and Haslam, "The Glass Cliff," 559.
7 Kumra, "Reflections on Glass," 52.
8 Kumra, "Reflections on Glass," 52, citing Miller et al. (1999).
9 Eagly and Carli, *Through the Labyrinth*, 4–5.
10 Sandberg and Scovell, *Lean In*, 53.
11 Devnew et al., "Women's Leadership," 167, citing Stead and Elliott (2009).
12 Blair, Dana (2016), "Giving a Voice to Women in K-12 Educational Leadership: A Narrative Analysis," Dissertation, Boston, MA: College of Professional Studies, Northeastern University, 133.
13 Eagly and Carli, *Through the Labyrinth*, 8–9.
14 Eagly and Carli, "Women and the Labyrinth," 2–3.
15 Eagly and Carli, *Through the Labyrinth*, 7.
16 Ibid., 7.
17 Kramer, Kirk, and Preeta Nayak (2013), *Nonprofit Leadership Development: What's Your 'Plan A' for Growing Future Leaders?*, Boston, MA: Bridgespan Group, 56.
18 Murphy, Jerome T. (2013), "The Unheroic Side of Leadership: Notes from the Swamp," in *The Jossey-Bass Reader on Educational Leadership*, edited by Margaret Grogan, 3rd edition, San Francisco, CA: Jossey-Bass, 32 (emphasis in original).
19 Kramer and Nayak, *Nonprofit Leadership*, 55–6.
20 Chin, *Women*, 5.
21 Kramer and Nayak, *Nonprofit Leadership*, 56.
22 Fine, "Chapter 8: Women," 119.
23 Chin, *Women*, 6.
24 Kramer and Nayak, *Nonprofit Leadership*, 56.

25 Leadership Academy (2020), *Culturally Responsive Leadership: A Framework for School & School Systems Leaders*, Long Island City, NY, 1–2, Available online: https://www.leadershipacademy.org/resources/culturally-responsive-leadership-a-framework-for-school-school-system-leaders/.
26 Ibid., 1.
27 Leadership Academy (2021), *A Portrait*, 3–4.
28 National Association of Independent Schools (2020), *NAIS Principles of Good Practice*, Washington, DC: NAIS, 1–34.
29 National Policy Board for Educational Administration (2015), *Professional Standards for Educational Leaders 2015*, Reston, VA: NPBEA, 2.
30 Ibid., 27
31 Ibid., 2.
32 Ibid.
33 National Policy Board for Educational Administration (2018), *National Educational Leadership Preparation (NELP) Program Recognition Standards—Building Level*, Reston, VA: NPBEA. Accessed March 3, 2022. Available online: http://www.npbea.org, 3.
34 Council of Chief State School Officers (2015), *Model Principal Supervisor Professional Standards 2015*, Washington, DC: CCSSO, 8–9.
35 Ibid., 3 and 9.

6 Standards and Dispositions for Women Educational Leaders: The Dance

1 National Policy Board for Educational Administration, *Professional Standards*, 2.
2 AASA (2020a), "AASA's Decennial Study Defines Current State of the Superintendency," *Report Announcement* (blog) (February 2020).
3 Vornberg, James A. (2013), "Systems Theory," in *The Handbook of Educational Theories*, edited by Beverly J. Irby, Genevieve Brown, Rafael Lara-Alecio, and Shirley, Charlotte, NC: Information Age Publishing, 806.
4 Robinson, Viviane (2013), "Three Capabilities for Student-Centered Leadership," in *The Jossey-Bass Reader on Educational Leadership*, 3rd edition, San Francisco, CA: Jossey-Bass, 298.
5 Bierema and Madsen, "No Women," 155.
6 Tienken, Christopher, ed. (2021), *The American Superintendent Decennial Study*, London: Rowman & Littlefield Education (in partnership with AASA), 27.
7 Maranto et al., "Boys Will Be," 13.
8 Marion and Gonzales, *Leadership in Education*, 60.
9 Ibarra et al., "Women Rising," 63.

10 Moore, "Yellow Hat Sketch."
11 Mindell, Phyllis (2001), *How To Say It for Women: Communicating with Confidence and Power Using the Language of Success*, Hoboken, NJ: Prentice Hall Press.
12 Bligh and Ito, "Organizational Processes," 290; Chears, Edith Coleman (2017), "Advancing Women's Leadership: Women Navigating Persisting Perceptions of Their Leadership and the Potential Impact of Awareness," Dissertation, The Chicago School of Professional Psychology, 149; Eagly and Carli, *Through the Labyrinth*, 48; Kay and Shipman, *The Confidence Code*, 6.
13 Kay and Shipman, *The Confidence Code*, 49–50.
14 Meyerson and Tompkins, "Tempered Radicals," 310.
15 Meyerson, Debra E. (2004), "The Tempered Radicals: How Employees Push Their Companies—Little by Little—to Become Socially Responsible," *Stanford Social Innovation Review*, Fall, 16.
16 Eagly and Carli (2007a) citing Judge et al., *Through the Labyrinth*, 40.
17 Eagly and Carli, *Through the Labyrinth*, 43.
18 Eagly and Carli (2007a) citing Martell et al., *Through the Labyrinth*, 95.
19 Bishop, Russel (2011), *Workarounds That Work: How to Conquer Anything That Stands in Your Way at Work*, New York: McGraw Hill, 2 and 12.
20 Tienken, *The American Superintendent*, Preface xv.
21 Chears, "Advancing Women's," 50.
22 Kairiene, Aida (2018), "Toward a Broader Understanding: A Formal Concept Analysis of the Micropolitics of a School," *Acta Paedagogica Vilnensia*, 400, 134.
23 Council of Chief State School Officers, *Model Principal*, 9.
24 Porter, Natalie, and Jessica Henderson Daniel (2007), "Chapter 11: Developing Transformational Leaders: Theory to Practice," in *Women and Leadership: Transforming Visions and Diverse Voices*, edited by Jean Lau Chin, Bernice Lott, Joy K. Rice, and Janis Sanchez-Hucles, Malden, MA: Blackwell Publishing, 250.
25 Chemaly, *Rage*, 18.
26 Reeves, "Mansplaining," 3.
27 Smith, Amy E., and Deneen M. Hatmaker (2017), "Individual Stress and Strains in the Ascent to Leadership: Gender, Work, and Family," in *Handbook of Research on Gender and Leadership*, edited by Susan R. Madsen, Northampton, MA: Edward Elgar Publishing, 309.
28 Gardner, John W. (2013), "The Nature of Leadership," in *The Jossey-Bass Reader on Educational Leadership*, edited by Margaret Grogan, 3rd edition, San Francisco, CA: Jossey-Bass, 20.
29 Wagner, Thomas, and Robert Kegan (2013). "Conclusion," in *Bringing the Outward Inward Focus Together*, edited by Margaret Grogan, 3rd edition, San Francisco, CA: Jossey-Bass, 238.

30 Denith and Peterlin, "Leadership Education," 53; Shields, *Transformative Leadership*, 23.
31 Creswell and Creswell, *Research Design*, 514.

7 Strategies and Supports: Still Standing

1 Leberman, Sarah, and Jane Hurst (2017), "The Connection between Success, Choice, and Leadership During Women's Careers," in *Handbook of Research on Gender and Leadership*, edited by Susan R. Madsen, Northampton, MA: Edward Elgar Publishing., 259.
2 Gallardo-Gallardo, Eva, and Marian Thunnissen (2016) citing Piansoongnern et al (2011), "Standing on the Shoulder of Giants? A Critical Review of Empirical Talent Management Research," *Employee Relations*, 38 (1), abstract.
3 Kramer and Nayak, *Nonprofit Leadership*, 11–12.
4 Ibid., 15.
5 Eagly and Carli, *Through the Labyrinth*, 156.
6 Kramer and Nayak, *Nonprofit Leadership*, 15–16.
7 Bierema and Madsen, "No Women," 153.
8 Ibid., 155.
9 DeSmet, Jeff, Louise Axon, and John Alsbury (2016), *Accelerate Leadership Development with Optimal Design: Six Key Principles*, Learning Design, Brighton, MA: Harvard Business Publishing Corporate Learning, 7.
10 Chemaly, *Rage*, 206.
11 Glass and Ingersoll (2017) citing Smith, "Sociological Approaches," 107.
12 Rhodes, Deborah L. (2017), "Gender Stereotypes and Unconscious Bias", in *Handbook of Research on Gender and Leadership*, edited by Susan R. Madsen, Northampton, MA: Edward Elgar Publishing, 322.
13 Kramer and Nayak, *Nonprofit Leadership*, 82.
14 DeSmet, Axon, and Alsbury, *Accelerate Leadership*, 4.
15 Ibid., 3.
16 Ibarra, Ely, and Kolb, "Women Rising," 46.
17 Collard, "Constructing Theory," 751.
18 Davut Göker, Süleyman, and Kıvanç Bozkuş (2017), "Reflective Leadership: Learning to Manage and Lead Human Organizations," *IntechOpen*, February, 1.
19 DeSmet, Axon, and Alsbury, *Accelerate Leadership*, 6.
20 Aguilar, Elena (2017), "What's the Difference between Mentoring and Coaching?," July 31, 2017. Accessed April 17, 2021. Available online: https://blogs.edweek.org/teachers/coaching_teachers/2017/07/whats_the_difference_between_c.html.
21 Carter and Silva, "Mentoring," 2.

22 Myers "Foreword," in *Handbook*, xxiii.
23 Aguilar, "What's the Difference."
24 Ibid.
25 Ibid.
26 Dana and Bourisaw, *Women in the Superintendency*, 188.
27 DeSmet, Axon, and Alsbury, *Accelerate Leadership*, 5.
28 Harvard Business Publishing, *The 2018 State*, 13.
29 Sanchez-Hucles and Davis, "Women and Women of Color," 172.
30 Theoharis, George (2007), "Social Justice Educational Leaders and Resistance: Toward a Theory of Social Justice Leadership," *Educational Administration Quarterly*, 43(2), 221–58.
31 John, Elton, and Bernie Taupin, composers (1983), "Still Standing," on *Too Low for Zero*, Santa Monica, CA: Geffen Records.

References

AASA (2020a), "AASA's Decennial Study Defines Current State of the Superintendency," *Report Announcement* (blog) (February 2020). Accessed November 23, 2020. Available online: https://nce.aasa.org/aasas-decennial-study-defines-current-state-of-the-superintendency/.

AASA (2020b), "AASA Releases Key Findings from American Superintendent 2020 Decennial Study," *Press Release* (blog) (February 10, 2020). Accessed November 23, 2020. Available online: https://nce.aasa.org/.

Aguilar, Elena (2017), "What's the Difference between Mentoring and Coaching?," July 31. Accessed April 17, 2021. Available online: https://blogs.edweek.org/teachers/coaching_teachers/2017/07/whats_the_difference_between_c.html.

Aldridge, Michael (2020), "IRB Exempt Determination by Integ Review IRB," August 2020.

Banaji, Mahzarin R., and Anthony G. Greenwald (2016), *Blind Spots: Hidden Biases of Good People*, New York: Bantam Books.

Bierema, Laura L., and Susan R. Madsen (2017), "No Women Left Behind: Critical Leadership Development to Build Gender Consciousness and Transform Organization," in *Handbook of Research on Gender and Leadership*, Northampton, MA: Edward Elgar Publishing, 145–62.

Bishop, Russel (2011), *Workarounds That Work: How to Conquer Anything That Stands in Your Way at Work*, New York: McGraw Hill.

Blackmore, Jill (2013), "Social Justice in Education," in *The Handbook of Educational Theories*, edited by Beverly J. Irby, Genevieve Brown, Rafael Lara-Alecio, and Shirley Jackson, Charlotte, NC: Information Age Publishing, 1001–9.

Blair, Dana (2016), "Giving a Voice to Women in K-12 Educational Leadership: A Narrative Analysis," Dissertation, Boston, MA: College of Professional Studies, Northeastern University.

Bligh, Michelle, and Ai Ito (2017), "Organizational Processes and Systems That Affect Women in Leadership," in *Handbook of Research on Gender and Leadership*, edited by Susan R. Madsen, Northampton, MA: Edward Elgar Publishing, 287–303.

Boyatzis, Richard, and Annie McKee (2005), *Resonant Leadership*, Boston, MA: Harvard Business School Press.

Brooks, Jeffrey S., and Lisa A. W. Kenslar (2011), "Chapter 4: Distributed Leadership and Democratic Community," in *The SAGE Handbook of Educational Leadership: Advances in Theory, Research, and Practice*, edited by Fenwick W. English, 2nd edition, Thousand Oaks, CA: Sage, 55–66.

Brown, Kathleen M. (2012), "Trait Theory," in *The Handbook of Educational Theories*, edited by Beverly J. Irby, Genevieve Brown, Rafael Lara-Alecio, and Shirley Jackson, Charlotte, NC: Information Age Publishing, 897–901.

Cacioppo, John T., Harry T. Reis, and Alex J. Zautra (2011), "Social Resilience: The Value of Social Fitness with an Application to the Military, *American Psychologist*, 66(1), 43–51. Available online: https://pubmed.ncbi.nlm.nih.gov/21219047/. (Cited in Liggins-Moore below.)

Chears, Edith Coleman (2017), "Advancing Women's Leadership: Women Navigating Persisting Perceptions of Their Leadership and the Potential Impact of Awareness," Dissertation, The Chicago School of Professional Psychology.

Chemaly, Soraya (2018), *Rage Becomes Her: The Power of Women's Anger*, New York: Atria Books.

Chin, Jean Lau (2007a), "Conclusion," in *Women and Leadership: Transforming Visions and Diverse Voices*, edited by Jean Lau Chin, Bernice Lott, Joy K. Rice, and Janis Sanchez-Hucles, Malden, MA: Blackwell Publishing, 355–62.

Chin, Jean Lau (2007b), "Overview," in *Women and Leadership: Transforming Visions and Diverse Voices*, edited by Jean Lau Chin, Bernice Lott, Joy K. Rice, and Janis Sanchez-Hucles, Malden, MA: Blackwell Publishing, 1–17.

Clerkin, Cathleen, and Meena S. Wilson (2017), "Gender Differences in Developmental Experiences," in *Handbook of Research on Gender and Leadership*, edited by Susan R. Madsen, Northampton, MA: Edward Elgar Publishing, 378–94.

Collard, John, (2007), "Constructing Theory for Leadership in Intercultural Contexts," *Journal of Educational Administration*, 45(6): 740–55.

Council of Chief State School Officers (2015), *Model Principal Supervisor Professional Standards 2015*, Washington, DC: CCSSO.

Creswell, John W., and Cheryl N. Poth (2018), *Qualitative Inquiry & Research Design: Choosing among Five Approaches*, 4th edition, Los Angeles, CA: Sage Publications.

Creswell, John W., and David J. Creswell (2018), *Research Design: Qualitative, Quantitative, and Mixed Methods Approaches*, 5th edition, Thousand Oaks, CA: Sage.

Dana, Joyce A., and Diana M. Bourisaw (2006), *Women in the Superintendency: Discarded Leadership*, Lanham, MD: Rowman & Littlefield Education (in partnership with AASA).

Davut Göker, Süleyman, and Kıvanç Bozkuş (2017), "Reflective Leadership: Learning to Manage and Lead Human Organizations," *IntechOpen*, February. Accessed December 12, 2021. Available online: https://doi.org/10.5772/64968.

Deal, Terrence E., and Kent D. Peterson (2013), "Eight Roles of Symbolic Leaders," in *The Jossey-Bass Reader on Educational Leadership*, edited by Margaret Grogan, 3rd edition, San Francisco, CA: Jossey-Bass, 274–86.

Denith, Audrey M., and Barbara Peterlin (2011), "Leadership Education from within a Feminist Ethos," *Journal of Research on Leadership Education*, 6(2), 36–58.

DeSmet, Jeff, Louise Axon, and John Alsbury (2016), *Accelerate Leadership Development with Optimal Design: Six Key Principles*, Learning Design, Brighton, MA: Harvard Business Publishing Corporate Learning.

Devnew, Lynne E, Ann M. Berghout Austin, Marlene Janzen Le Ber, and Mary Shapiro (2017), "Women's Leadership Aspirations," in *Handbook of Research on Gender and Leadership*, edited by Susan R. Madsen, Northampton, MA: Edward Elgar Publishing, 165–79.

Diehl, Amy B., and Leanne Dzubinski (2017), "An Overview of Gender-Based Leadership Barriers," in *Handbook of Research on Gender and Leadership*, Northampton, MA: Edward Elgar Publishing, 271–86.

Dodgson, Lindsay (2018), "What Is Hepeating?," *Business Insider Newsletter*, March 8, 2018. Accessed June 9, 2021. Available online: https://www.businessinsider.com/what-is-hepeating-2017-9.

Duckworth, Angela (2016), *Grit: The Power of Passion and Perseverance*, New York: Scribner.

Dugan, Brian (2021), "Gaslighting," *Encylopaedia Britannica*. Accessed April 7, 2021. Available online: https://www.britannica.com/topic/gaslighting.

Dweck, Carol S. (2006), *Mindset: The New Psychology of Success*, New York: Random House.

Dwyer, Charles E. (1992), *The Shifting Sources of Power and Influence*, Tampa, FL: American College of Physician Executives.

Eagly, Alice H., and Linda L. Carli (2003), "The Female Leadership Advantage: An Evaluation of the Evidence," *The Leadership Quarterly*, 14(6), 807–34.

Eagly, Alice H., and Linda L. Carli (2007a), *Through the Labyrinth: The Truth about How Women Become Leaders*, Leadership for the Common Good, Boston, MA: Harvard Business School Publishing Corporation.

Eagly, Alice H., and Linda L. Carli (2007b), "Women and the Labyrinth of Leadership," *Women and the Labyrinth of Leadership* (blog), September 2007.

Eagly, Alice H., and Linda L. Carli (2019), "Women and the Labyrinth of Leadership," in *On Women and Leadership*, Brighton, MA: Harvard Business Review's 10 Must Reads, Cambridge, MA: Harvard Business School Publishing Corporation, 1–20.

Eagly, Alice H., and Steven J. Karau (2002), "Role Congruity Theory of Prejudice toward Female Leaders," *Psychological Review*, 109, 573–98. doi:10.1037/0033-295X.109.3.573. (Cited in Kumra below.)

English, Fenwick, Beverly Irby, Genevieve Brown, Rafael Lara-Alecio, and Shirley Jackson (eds.) (2013), "Section 11: Leadership and Management Theory Introduction," in *The Handbook on Educational Theories*, Charlotte, NC: Information Age Publishing, 887–90.

Equity in the Center (2020), *Awake to Woke to Work: Building a Race Equity Culture*. Accessed October 19, 2021. Available online: https://equityinthecenter.org.

Feifer, Jason (2022), "Jimmy Fallon Spent Years Chasing a Dream That Wasn't Really His. Finding His 'Why' Changed Everything," *Entrepreneur*, January 4, 2022.

Accessed January 6, 2022. Available online: https://apple.news/ADD27k333Q5ipzA8Q-Rs42g.

Fennell, Hope-Arlene (2008), "Feminine Faces of Leadership," *Journal of School Leadership*, 18 (November): 603–33.

Fine, Marlene G. (2007), "Chapter 8: Women, Collaboration, and Social Change: An Ethics-Based Model of Leadership," in *Women and Leadership: Transforming Visions and Diverse Voices*, edited by Jean Lau Chin, Bernice Lott, Joy K. Rice, and Janis Sanchez-Hucles, Malden, MA: Blackwell Publishing, 175–91.

Forrester, Sarah, David Jacobs, Rachel Zmora, Pamela Schreiner, and Veronica Roger (2019), "Racial Differences in Weathering and Its Associations with Psychosocial Stress: The CARDIA Study," *Population Health*, 7: 8. Accessed October 29, 2022. Available online: https://doi.org/10.1016/j.ssmph.2018.11.003.

Fox-Kirk, Wendy, Constance Campbell, and Chrys Egan (2017), "Women's Leadership Identity: Exploring Person and Context in Theory," in *Handbook of Research on Gender and Leadership*, edited by Susan R. Madsen, Northampton, MA: Edward Elgar Publishing, 193–206.

Franco, Carmella S., Maria Gutierrez Ott, and Darlene P. Robles (2013), "Lessons Learned: Cultural Assets Inform Actions," in *The Jossey-Bass Reader on Educational Leadership*, edited by Margaret Grogan, 3rd edition, San Francisco, CA: Jossey-Bass.

Gallardo-Gallardo, Eva, and Marian Thunnissen (2016), "Standing on the Shoulder of Giants? A Critical Review of Empirical Talent Management Research," *Employee Relations*, 38(1): 31–56.

Gardner, John W. (2013), "The Nature of Leadership," in *The Jossey-Bass Reader on Educational Leadership*, edited by Margaret Grogan, 3rd edition, San Francisco, CA: Jossey-Bass, 17–27.

Glass, Christy, and Alice Ingersoll (2017), "Sociological Approaches to Women and Leadership Theory," in *Handbook of Research on Gender and Leadership*, edited by Susan R. Madsen, Northampton, MA: Edward Elgar Publishing, 100–26.

Gramsci, Antonio (1971), *Selections from the Prison Notebooks*, London: Lawrence Wishart. (Cited in Tooms below.)

Green, Erica L. (2021), "New Leader Pushes Teachers' Union to Take on Social Justice Role," *New York Times*, December 12, 2021. Accessed December 14, 2021. Available online: https://www.nytimes.com/2021/12/12/us/politics/teachers-union-becky-pringle.html?searchResultPosition=1.

Grogan, Margaret, and Charol Shakeshaft (2009), "Conscious Leadership in a Political World," in *Women Leading Education Across the Continents: Sharing the Spirit, Fanning the Flame*, edited by Helen C. Sobehart, Lanham, MD: Rowman & Littlefield Education (in partnership with AASA), 21–8.

Grogan, Margaret, and Charol Shakeshaft (2011), *Women and Educational Leadership*, San Francisco, CA: Jossey-Bass Leadership Library in Education.

Grogan, Margaret, and Charol Shakeshaft (2013), "A New Way: Diverse Collective Leadership," in *The Jossey-Bass Reader on Educational Leadership*, edited by Margaret Grogan, 3rd edition, San Francisco, CA: Jossey-Bass, 111–30.

Gupta, Avina (2013), "Employee Perceptions of Managers who Express Anger: Could High Quality Relationship Buffer Women from Backlash," Dissertation, Columbia University Graduate School of Arts and Sciences. (Cited in Chears above.)

Hall, Ruth L., BraVada Garrett-Akinsanya, and Michael Hucles (2007), "Chapter 13: Voices of Black Feminist Leaders: Making Spaces for Ourselves," in *Women and Leadership: Transforming Visions and Diverse Voices*, edited by Jean Lau Chin, Bernice Lott, Joy K. Rice, and Janis Sanchez-Hucles, Malden, MA: Blackwell Publishing, 281–96.

Harragan, Betty Lehan (1977), *Games Mother Never Taught You: Corporate Gamesmanship for Women*, New York: Grand Central Publishing.

Harvard Business Publishing (2018), *The 2018 State of Leadership Development: Meeting the Transformation Imperative*, Learning Design, Brighton, MA: Harvard Business Publishing Corporate Learning.

Hoyt, Crystal L., and Stefanie Simon (2017), "Social Psychological Approaches to Women and Leadership Theory," in *Handbook of Research on Gender and Leadership*, edited by Susan R. Madsen, Northampton, MA: Edward Elgar Publishing, 85–99.

Ibarra, Herminia, Robin J. Ely, and Deborah M. Kolb (2013), "Women Rising: The Unseen Barriers," *Harvard Business Review*, Cambridge, MA: Harvard Business Publishing, September 2013. Accessed November 23, 2020. Available online: https://hbr.org/2013/09/women-rising-the-unseen-barriers.

Ibarra, Herminia, Robin Ely, and Deborah Kolb (2019), "Women Rising: The Unseen Barriers," in *On Women and Leadership*, Cambridge, MA: Harvard Business School Publishing Corporation, 39–50.

ILO Group (2022), "Updated Analysis Shows Leadership Disruption Impacts Almost Half of the Nation's Largest School Districts," *Press Release* (website) (December 12, 2022). Accessed December 14, 2022. Available online: https://www.ilogroup.com/news/press-release-updated-analysis-shows-leadership-disruption-impacts-almost-half-of-nations-largest-school-districts/.

Imbler, Sabrina (2021), "Female Hummingbirds Avoid Harassment by Looking like Males," *New York Times*, August 26, 2021. Accessed April 20, 2022. Available online: https://www.nytimes.com/2021/08/26/science/hummingbirds-female.html?action=click&module=card&pageType=theWeekenderLink.

Irby, Beverly J., Genevieve Brown, and LingLing Yang (2013), "The Synergistic Leadership Theory: An Inclusive Theory in the Twenty-First Century," in *The Handbook of Educational Theories*, edited by Beverly J. Irby, Genevieve Brown, Rafael Lara-Alecio, and Shirley Jackson, Charlotte, NC: Information Age Publishing, 985–95.

John, Elton, and Bernie Taupin, composers (1983), "Still Standing," on *Too Low for Zero*, Santa Monica, CA: Geffen Records. Accessed April 20, 2022. Available online: https://www.azlyrics.com/lyrics/eltonjohn/imstillstanding.html.

Johnson, Norine G., Florence L. Denmark, Dorothy W. Cantor, Diane F. Halpern, and Gwendolyn Puryear Keita (2007), "Leadership through Policy Development: Collaboration, Equity, Empowerment, and Multiculturalism," in *Women and Leadership: Transforming Visions and Diverse Voices*, edited by Jean Lau Chin, Bernice Lott, Joy K. Rice, and Janis Sanchez-Hucles. Malden, MA: Blackwell Publishing, 140–6.

Judge, Timothy, A., Joyce E. Bono, Remus Ilies, and Megan W. Gerhardt (2002), "Personality and Leadership: A Qualitative and Quantitative Review, *Journal of Applied Psychology*, 87(40), 765–80. (Cited in Eagly Carli 2007a above.)

Kairiene, Aida (2018), "Toward a Broader Understanding: A Formal Concept Analysis of the Micropolitics of a School," *Acta Paedagogica Vilnensia*, 40, 127–41. Accessed March 17, 2022. Available online: https://doi.org/10.15388/ActPaed.2018.0.11892.

Kay, Katty, and Claire Shipman (2014), *The Confidence Code: The Science and Art of Self-Assurance—What Women Should Know*, 1st edition, New York: Harper Collins Publishers.

Keck, Marcus, and Patrick Sakdapolrak (2013), "What is Social Resilience? Lessons Learned and Ways Forward," *Erdkunde*, 67(1), 5–19. (Cited in LIggins-Moore below.)

Kelan, Elisabeth K. (2009), "Gender Fatigue: The Ideological Dilemma of Gender Neutrality and Discrimination in Organizations," *Canadian Journal of Administrative Sciences*, 26: 197–210. Accessed November 29, 2020. Available online: https://doi.org/10.1002/CIAS.106.

Kendall, Mikki (2021), *Hood Feminism: Notes from the Women That a Movement Forgot*, New York: Penguin Books.

Kramer, Kirk, and Preeta Nayak (2013), *Nonprofit Leadership Development: What's Your "Plan A" for Growing Future Leaders?*, Boston, MA: Bridgespan Group.

Kumra, Savita (2017), "Reflections on Glass: Second Wave Feminist Theorizing in a Third Wave Feminist Age?," in *Handbook of Research on Gender and Leadership*, edited by Susan R. Madsen, Northampton, MA: Edward Elgar Publishing, 49–62.

Leadership Academy (2020), *Culturally Responsive Leadership: A Framework for School & School Systems Leaders*, Long Island City, NY. Accessed March 7, 2022. Available online: https://www.leadershipacademy.org/resources/culturally-responsive-leadership-a-framework-for-school-school-system-leaders/.

Leadership Academy (2021), *A Portrait of a Culturally Responsive School System*, Long Island City, NY: Leadership Academy. Accessed October 19, 2021. Available online: https://www.leadershipacademy.org/resources/portrait-of-a-culturally-responsive-school-2/.

Leberman, Sarah, and Jane Hurst (2017), "The Connection between Success, Choice, and Leadership during Women's Careers," in *Handbook of Research on Gender and Leadership*, edited by Susan R. Madsen, Northampton, MA: Edward Elgar Publishing, 254–67.

Liggins-Moore, Lysa (2016), "Forty-Three African American Women Executives' Perceptions of Challenges and Required Capabilities to Become a Leader," Dissertation, Pepperdine University. Accessed November 20, 2020. Available online: https://digitalcommons.pepperdine.edu/etd/736.

Longman, Karen A., and Debbie Lamm Bray (2017), "The Role of Purpose and Calling in Women's Leadership Experiences," in *Handbook of Research on Gender and Leadership*, edited by Susan R. Madsen, Northampton, MA: Edward Elgar Publishing, 207–22.

Lumby, Jack (2009), "Disappearing Gender: Choices in Identity," in *Women Leading Education Across the Continents: Sharing the Spirit, Fanning the Flame*, edited by Helen C. Sobehart, Lanham, MD: Rowman & Littlefield Education, 29–38.

Maranto, Robert, Kristen Carroll, Albert Cheng, and Manuel P. Teodoro (2018), "Boys Will Be Superintendents: School Leadership as a Gendered Profession," *Phi Delta Kappan*, 100(2): 12–15.

Marion, Russ, and Leslie D. Gonzales (2014), *Leadership in Education: Organizational Theory for the Practitioner*, 2nd edition, Long Grove, IL: Waveland Press.

Martell, R.F., C. Parker, C.G. Emrich, and M.S. Crawford (1998), "Sex Stereotyping in the Executive Suite: "Much ado about something," *Journal of Social Behavior and Personality*, 13: 127–38. (Cited in Eagly and Carli 2007a above.)

Maxwell, John A. (2005), *Qualitative Research Design: An Interactive Approach*, 2nd edition, Applied Social Research Methods Series 41, Thousand Oaks, CA: Sage.

Melaku, Tsedale M., Angie Beeman, David G. Smith, and Brad W Johnson (2020), "Be a Better Ally," *Harvard Business Review*, December 2020. Accessed April 28, 2022. Available online: https://hbr.org/2020/11/be-a-better-ally.

Meyerson, Debra E. (2004), "The Tempered Radicals: How Employees Push Their Companies—Little by Little—to Become Socially Responsible," *Stanford Social Innovation Review*, 14–23.

Meyerson, Debra, and Megan Tompkins (2007), "Tempered Radicals as Institutional Change Agents: The Case of Advancing Gender Equity at the University of Michigan," *Harvard Women's Law Journal*, 30(2): 303–22.

Miller, Will, Brinck Kerr, and Margaret Reid (1999), "A National Study of Gender-Based Segregation in Municipal Bureaucracies: Persistence of Glass Walls?," *Public Administration Review*, 59(3), 218–30. (Cited in Kumra above.)

Mindell, Phyllis (2001), *How To Say It for Women: Communicating with Confidence and Power Using the Language of Success*, Hoboken, NJ: Prentice Hall Press.

Moore, Izzy Carlisle (2022), "Three Sketches (Glass Escalator, Yellow Brick Road, Yellow Hat)," Commissioned by Author.

Moustakas, Clark (1994), *Phenomenological Research Methods*, Thousand Oaks, CA: Sage.

Murphy, Jerome T. (2013), "The Unheroic Side of Leadership: Notes from the Swamp," in *The Jossey-Bass Reader on Educational Leadership*, edited by Margaret Grogan, 3rd edition, San Francisco, CA: Jossey-Bass.

Myers, Betsy (2017), "Foreword," in *Handbook of Research on Gender and Leadership*, edited by Susan R. Madsen, Northampton, MA: Edward Elgar Publishing, xxii–xxiii.

National Association of Independent Schools (2020), *NAIS Principles of Good Practice*, Washington, DC: NAIS.

National Policy Board for Educational Administration (2015), *Professional Standards for Educational Leaders 2015*, Reston, VA: NPBEA.

National Policy Board for Educational Administration (2018), *National Educational Leadership Preparation (NELP) Program Recognition Standards—Building Level*, Reston, VA: NPBEA. Accessed March 3, 2022. Available online: http://www.npbea.org.

Ngunjiri, Faith Wambura, Cathy-Ann C. Hernandez, and Heewon Chang (2010), "Living Autoethnography: Connecting Life and Research [Editorial]," *Journal of Research Practice*, 6(1), 17.

O'Neill, Olivia A., and Charles A. O'Reilly III (2011), "Reducing the Backlash Effect: Self-monitoring and Women's Promotions," *Journal of Occupational and Organizational Psychology*, 84(4), 82. Accessed November 19, 2020. Available Online: https://doi.org/10.1111/j.2044-8325.2010.02008.x. (Cited in Chears above.)

Oregon State University (2022), "Snowball Sampling," Human Research Protection Program, Corvallis, OR: Oregon State University. Accessed March 19, 2022. Available online: https://research.oregonstate.edu/irb/policies-and-guidance-investigators/guidance/snowball-sampling

Piansoongnern, Opas, P. Anurit, and Sureeporn Kuiyawattananonta (2011), "Talent Management in Thai Cement Companies: A Study of Strategies and Factors Influencing Employee Engagement," *African Journal of Business Management*, 5(5), 1578–83. (As cited in Gallardo-Gallardo and Marian Thunnissen above.)

Porter, Natalie, and Jessica Henderson Daniel (2007), "Chapter 11: Developing Transformational Leaders: Theory to Practice," in *Women and Leadership: Transforming Visions and Diverse Voices*, edited by Jean Lau Chin, Bernice Lott, Joy K. Rice, and Janis Sanchez-Hucles, Malden, MA: Blackwell Publishing, 245–63.

Powell, John A. (2017), "Us vs Them: The Sinister Techniques of "Othering'—and How to Avoid Them," *The Guardian*, November 8, 2017. Accessed October 5, 2021. Available online: https://www.theguardian.com/inequality/2017/nov/08/us-vs-them-the-sinister-techniques-of-othering-and-how-to-avoid-them.

Reeves, Arin N. (2015), "Mansplaining, Manterrupting, and Bropropriating: Gender Bias and the Pervasive Interruption of Women," Yellow Paper Series, Chicago, IL: Nextions. Accessed May 31, 2021. Available online: hhttps://nextions.com/wp-content/uploads/2017/05/manterruptions-bropropriation-and-mansplaining-2-yellow-paper-series.pdf.

Rhodes, Deborah L. (2017), "Gender Stereotypes and Unconscious Bias," in *Handbook of Research on Gender and Leadership*, edited by Susan R. Madsen, Northampton, MA: Edward Elgar Publishing, 316–27.

Rice, Joy K. (2007), "Introduction to Part II: Collaboration and Leadership," in *Women and Leadership: Transforming Visions and Diverse Voices*, edited by Jean Lau Chin, Bernice Lott, Joy K. Rice, and Janis Sanchez-Hucles, Malden, MA: Blackwell Publishing, 127–39.

Rice, Joy K., and Asunsion Miteria Austria (2007a), "Chapter 7: Collaborative Leadership and Social Advocacy among Women's Organizations," in *Women and Leadership: Transforming Visions and Diverse Voices*, edited by Jean Lau Chin, Bernice Lott, Joy K. Rice, and Janis Sanchez-Hucles, Malden, MA: Blackwell Publishing, 157–76.

Robinson, Viviane (2013), "Three Capabilities for Student-Centered Leadership," in *The Jossey-Bass Reader on Educational Leadership*, 3rd edition, San Francisco, CA: Jossey-Bass, 297–316.

Ryan, Michelle K., and S. Alexander Haslam (2007), "The Glass Cliff: Exploring the Dynamics Surrounding the Appointment of Women to Precarious Leadership Positions," *Academy of Management Review*, 32(2): 549–72.

Sanchez-Hucles, Janis V., and Donald D. Davis (2010), "Women and Women of Color in Leadership: Complexity, Identity, and Intersectionality," *American Psychologist*, 65(3): 171–81.

Sanchez-Hucles, Janis, and Penny Sanchez (2007), "Introduction to Part III: From the Margin to Center: The Voices of Diverse Feminist Leaders," in *Women and Leadership: Transforming Visions and Diverse Voices*, edited by Jean Lau Chin, Bernice Lott, Joy K. Rice, and Janis Sanchez-Hucles, Malden, MA: Blackwell Publishing, 211–27.

Sandberg, Sheryl, and Nell Scovell (2013), *Lean in: Women, Work, and the Will to Lead*, New York, NY: Alfred A. Knopf.

Sen, Armatya (2006), *Identity and Violence: The Illusion of Destiny*, New York: W.W. Norton & Company. (Cited in Lumby above.)

Sergiovanni, Thomas (2013), "Leadership as Stewardship: Who's Serving Who?," in *The Jossey-Bass Reader on Educational Leadership*, 3rd edition, San Francisco, CA: Jossey-Bass, 372–89.

Shapiro, Ester E., and Jennifer M. Leigh (2007), "Chapter 4: Toward Culturally Competent, Gender-Equitable Leadership: Assessing Outcomes of Women's Leadership in Diverse Contexts," in *Women and Leadership: Transforming Visions and Diverse Voices*, edited by Jean Lau Chin, Bernice Lott, Joy K. Rice, and Janis Sanchez-Hucles, Malden, MA: Blackwell Publishing, 88–105.

Shields, Carolyn M. (2017), *Transformative Leadership in Education: Equitable and Socially Just Change in an Uncertain and Complex World*, 2nd edition, New York: Routledge.

Smith, Amy E., and Deneen M. Hatmaker (2017), "Individual Stress and Strains in the Ascent to Leadership: Gender, Work, and Family," in *Handbook of Research on Gender and Leadership*, edited by Susan R. Madsen, Northampton, MA: Edward Elgar Publishing, 304–15.

Smith, Valerie, ed., (2013), *Sociology of Work: An Encyclopedia*, Los Angeles, CA: Sage. (Cited in Glass and Ingersoll above.)

Stead, Valerie, and Carole Elliott, C. (2009), *Women's Leadership*, London: Palgrave Macmillan. (Cited in Devnew above.)

Tan, Jo-Ann (2016), "For Women of Color, the Glass Ceiling Is Actually Made of Concrete," *Huffington Post*, April 20, 2016.

Tannen, Deborah (2019), "The Power of Talk: Who Gets Heard and Why," in *On Women and Leadership*, Brighton, MA: Harvard Business School Publishing, 67–90.

Terry, Robert (1993), *Authentic Leadership: Courage in Action*, San Francisco, CA: Jossey Bass. (Cited in Liggins-Moore above.)

Theoharis, George (2007), "Social Justice Educational Leaders and Resistance: Toward a Theory of Social Justice Leadership," *Educational Administration Quarterly*, 43(2): 221–58. Available online: https://doi.org/10.1177/0013161X06293717.

Thomas, Rachel, Marianne Cooper, Kate McShane Urban, Ali Bohrer, Sonia Mahajan, Lareina Yee, Alexis Krivkovich, Jess Huang, Ishanaa Rambachan, and Tiffany Burns (2021), *Women in the Workplace: 2021*, Boston, MA. Accessed September 30, 2021. Available online: https://wiw-report.s3.amazonaws.com/Women_in_the_Workplace_2021.pdf.

Tienken, Christopher, ed. (2021), *The American Superintendent Decennial Study*, London: Rowman & Littlefield Education (in partnership with AASA).

Tooms, Autumn K., Catherine A. Lugg, and Ira Bogotch (2010), "Rethinking the Politics of Fit and Educational Leadership," *Educational Administration Quarterly*, 46(1): 96–131. Accessed March 15, 2021. Available online: https://doi.org/10.1177/1094670509353044.

U.S. Department of Education, National Center for Education Statistics (2020), "Characteristics of Public School Principals," *The Condition of Education*, Washington, DC: IES. Accessed January 21, 2022. Available online: https://nces.ed.gov/programs/coe/indicator/cls.

U.S. Department of Education, National Center for Education Statistics (2021), "Characteristics of Public School Teachers," *The Condition of Education*, Washington, DC: IES. Accessed January 25, 2022. Available online: https://nces.ed.gov/programs/coe/indicator/clr.

Vanek Smith, Stacey (2021), *Machiavelli for Women: Define Your Worth, Grow Your Ambition, and Win the Workplace*, New York: Gallery Books.

Vornberg, James A. (2013), "Systems Theory," in *The Handbook of Educational Theories*, edited by Beverly J. Irby, Genevieve Brown, Rafael Lara-Alecio, and Shirley, Charlotte, NC: Information Age Publishing, 805–13.

Wagner, Thomas, and Robert Kegan (2013). "Conclusion," *Bringing the Outward Inward Focus Together*, edited by Margaret Grogan, 3rd edition, San Francisco, CA: Jossey-Bass.

Walters, Gae (2017), *Solving for X in the Y Domain: Strategies for Overcoming Gender Barriers to Leadership*, Bloomington, IN: Archway Publishing. (Cited in Chears above.)

Young, Michelle D., and Catherine Marshall (2013), "Critical Feminist Theory," in *The Handbook of Educational Theories*, edited by Beverly J. Irby, Genevieve Brown, Rafael Lara-Alecio, and Shirley Jackson, Charlotte, NC: Information Age Publishing, 975–84.

Zepeda, Sally J. (2015), *Job Embedded Professional Development: Support, Collaboration, and Learning in Schools*, Eye on Education, New York: Routledge.

Zepeda, Sally J., Parylo Oksana, and Hans W. Klar (2017), "Educational Leadership for Teaching and Learning," in *The Wiley International Handbook of Educational Leadership*, edited by Duncan Waite and Ira Bogotch, First, Hoboken, NJ: John Wiley & Sons, 227–52. Accessed March 16, 2021. Available online: https://eclass.uowm.gr/modules/document/file.php/NURED425/Waite%20%26%20Bogotch%20-%20The%20Wiley%20International%20Handbook%20of%20Educational%20Leadership%20%282017%29%20book.pdf#page=247.

Index

abuse
  author definition of 70
  in chapter 4 summary 18
  11 respondents experienced abuse 69, 78
  table summarizing respondents' experience with 79
  ways respondents addressed 79
adaptive leadership
  description 30
  using Rafael's to describe 29
administration & operations (as standard)
  discussion and rationale 120–2
administrative leadership
  definition 33
  using Bud to describe 33
African Methodist Episcopal (AME)
  description of principal's background 21–2
agentic
  characteristics 3
  contrasted with communal 52
  definition 3
  misperception of author based on 41
Aguilar, Elena, "What's the Difference between Mentoring and Coaching?," (2017)
  coaching definition 179
  mentoring definition 178
  sponsor definition 179
American Association of School Administrators (AASA), "AASA Releases Key Findings," (2020b)
  referenced in description of Women's underrepresentation in superintendency/AASA data 5–6
Angela (Respondent #1 pseudonym)
  profile description in Appendix 197
  quotation about exceptional competence 6
  quotation about harassment 71
  quotation about intersectionality 56

  quotation about softeners 69
angry woman/angry black woman 16, 68, 154
antiracism/anti-racism/antiracist/ anti-racist
  definition 85
antisexist
  definition 85
allyship/ally/allies
  definition 24
  as important to support change agents 7
American Dream
  as linked to meritocracy or advancement 2, 24, 75, 166
American Superintendent Decennial Study (2021)
  quotation about instructional focus 132
authentic leadership
  using Jeff to describe 28
auto-ethnography/auto-ethnographical
  definition 13
  study type 10, 13
Avril (Respondent #18 pseudonym)
  profile description in Appendix 198
  quotation about administration and operations standard 122
  quotation about collaboration and engagement disposition 139
  quotation about resilience 158
  quotation about route to leadership 102
  quotation about skills and experiences 192
  quotation about support networks 189
  quotation on gendered issues 53

background/backgrounds
  author's 9
  for author to consider when interpreting data 11
  author's and respondents' background in driving leadership 58

in relationship to fit 63
respondents 9
backlash
   against racial, gender, social movements 9
   trade offs 9
barriers/challenges
   and abuse in chapter 4 summary 18
   as part of author's chapter 4 summary 18
   as referencing racism, sexism, harassment,
   summary of barriers and challenges 62
   as theme author identifies and describes 16
behaviors
   expected of women 4
benevolent sexism
   Glass Cliff," (2007) discussion 65–6
   Michelle Ryan and Alexander Haslam, "The
Bierema, Laura and Susan Madsen, "No Woman Left Behind," (2017)
   on the job development strategies 125
   leadership development monitoring 171
Bill (pseudonym)
   Profile used to describe heroic leadership 31–3
Billie (Respondent #27 pseudonym)
   profile description in Appendix 198
   quotation about organizational strategies to redress/prevent bad behavior 84
   quotation about political savvy 151
   quotation about resilience 158
   quotation about reflection and continuous learning disposition 161
   quotation about emotional supports 187
   on upbringing's influence on identity and beliefs 43
Bishop, Russell *Workarounds That Work*, (2011)
   workaround definition 147
Black feminism/Black feminist leadership
   purpose 49–50
   role 50
Black Lives Matter
   as linked to Critical Race Theory 51
   referenced as movement 8

blind spot
   definition 63
Bob (pseudonym)
   Profile used to describe heroic leadership 31–3
Bonnie (Respondent #23 pseudonym)
   profile description in Appendix 198
   quotation about collaboration and engagement disposition 139
   quotation about defining educational leadership 26
   quotation about political savvy 152
   quotation about purpose for leading 43
   quotation about teaching and learning standard 134
Boyatzis, Richard and Annie McKee, "Resonant Leadership," (2005)
   quoted defining resonant leadership 29
broken rung
   definition 53
Brooks, Jeffrey and Lisa Kenslar, "Educational Leadership and Globalization," (2011)
   quoted defining distributive leadership 30
bropropriate/bropropriating
   definition 66
Bud (pseudonym)
   profile describing administrative leadership 33
   profile used to describe underminer 74
bully/bullied/bullying
   author definition of 70
   Carol Dweck, *Mindset*, (2006) quote about bullying 73
   discussion about and table summarizing respondents' experience with 73
   28 respondents experienced bullying 69
   ways respondents addressed 79
bureaucracy (bureaucratic)

calling/callings—*see also* purpose, drivers
   author's call to educational leadership 38
   See also drivers and purpose
Catrina (Respondent #14 pseudonym)
   profile description in Appendix 198

quotation about Competence standard 124
quotation about skills and experiences 192
quotation about support networks 189
quotation about vision 137
quotation on gendered issues 53
Center for Creative Leadership (in xxx mix of training strategies 175–6
characteristics
Chemaly, Soraya, *Rage*, (2018)
    discussion about de-escalation 88
    discussion of harassment and social tolerance 70
    discussion about women talking too much 87
Chin, Jean Lau, "Overview," in *Women and Leadership*, (2007b)
    quote about style approach 104
coach, coaches, coaching
    benefits to women 19, 31
    Elena Aguilar, "What's the Difference between Mentoring and Coaching?," (2017) definition 179
    preparation for superintendency 63
    reference to author 87, 125, 142
    reference to women's style 3
    as support strategy 109, 168, 171, 173, 176, 178
collaboration and engagement disposition discussion 138–40
collective endorsement
    Definition 67
collectivist leadership
    definition 23
    as driver for author 23
    as leadership model 23
colorblind/color blindness
communal
    characteristics of 3
    contrasted with agentic 52
communication disposition
    discussion 140–4
    Mindell, Phyllis *How to Say it for Women*, (2001), on communication 142
competence
    Corporate Leadership Council definition as cited in Kirk Kramer and Preeta Nyack, *Nonprofit Leadership Development*, (2013) 104
    definition 104
    as standard 122–3
concrete
    as metaphor group 99
concrete ceiling
    Jo-Ann Tan, (2016), "For Women of Color," (2016), description of 99
concrete wall
    description of 99
confidence
    confidence as disposition 144–6
    ways in which women must demonstrate (as element of survey design) 11
conformity
    Glass, Christy and Alice Ingersoll, "Sociological Approaches," (2017) on relationship to leader profile 64
contextual leadership
    description 29
continuous learning (reflection and continuous learning) as disposition 120, 123, 159, 165
continuous learning (as standard) 111, 112, 120
Corporate Leadership Council (CLC) (in Kirk Kramer and Preeta Nyack, *Nonprofit Leadership Development*, (2013))
    definition of knowledge 104
Council of Chief State School Officers (CCSSO), *Model Principal Supervisor*, (2015)
    instructional leader and transformational educational leader practices 110
    quoted about reflection 44
    referenced in chapter 5 summary of standards 18
    summary, table, and figure 109–10
    transformational education leaders 153
Coverer
    description 154
creativity & innovation disposition
    discussion 146–9
critical feminist theory

defined and its purpose 49, 51
critical leadership
　defined 49
Critical Race Theory (CRT)
　definition 51
　linked to Black Lives Matter 50
　misunderstandings about 57
　purpose described 49–50
critical theories
　justice theory 49
　purpose of critical social theory/social as study's framework for analysis 14
crystal (Respondent #22 psuedonym)
　quotation about administration and operations standard 122
　quotation about collaboration and engagement disposition 139–40
　quotation about confidence and competence 145
　quotation about development and support standard 126
　quotation about performance management standards 131
　quotation about reflection and continuous learning disposition 162
　quotation about skills and experiences 192
　profile description in Appendix 198
cultural competence
　author definition 52
cultural leadership
　definition 24
　as driver for author 24
　as leadership model 24
culture/cultural
　definition 39
　as an influence on leadership, leadership identity, and beliefs and behaviors 41
culturally responsive leadership
　description by Leadership Academy, *A Portrait of a Culturally Responsive School System, (2021)* 30–1
　Leadership Academy (2020) Culturally Responsive Leadership framework and actions 105–6
culturally responsive practice
　definition by Leadership Academy (2021) 106

Dedee (Respondent #33 pseudonym)
　profile description in Appendix 199
　quotation about Competence standard 124
　quotation about equity 40
　quotation on gendered issues 53
　quotation about resilience 158
　quotation about support networks 190
deescalation/escalation
　Sally (pseudonym) used to highlight 88
　Soraya Chemaly, *Rage*, (2018), to highlight early conditioning 88
DeSmet, Jeff, Louise Axon, and John Alsbury, *Accelerate Leadership Development*, (2016)
　learning in context 176
　learning with others 178
　learning through teaching definition 173
development & support standard
　discussion about 124–6
development
　organizational and individual strategies as in chapter 7 summarized 9
Diane (Respondent #5 pseudonym)
　profile description in Appendix 197
　quotation about equitable culture standard 128
　quotation about how handled harassment 80
Diedre (Respondent #26 pseudonym)
　profile description in Appendix 198
　quotation about addressing harassment 81
　quotation about collaboration and engagement disposition 140
　quotation about competence standard 124
　quotation about creativity and innovation disposition 148
　quotation about equitable culture standard 128
　quotation about intersectionality 56
　quotation about leadership development 172
　quotation about political savvy 152
　quotation about skills and experiences 192
　quotation about support networks 190
　quotation about vision 138

Dionne (Respondent #31 pseudonym)
    profile description in Appendix 199
    quotation about addressing bullying 81
    quotation about bullying 80
    quotation about creativity and innovation disposition 149
    quotation about defining educational leadership 26
    quotation on professionalism and ethics 155
    quotation about reason for leading 47
disposition/dispositions
    Corporate Leadership Council definition as cited in Kirk Kramer and Preeta Nyack, *Nonprofit Leadership Development*, (2013) 104
    description of quoting Kirk Kramer and Preeta Nyack, *Nonprofit Leadership Development*, (2013) 104
    summary of author's proposed dispositions for women 119
disproportionate representation of women in educational leadership 5, 63
disproportionate outcomes for students of color 127, 128, 184
distributive leadership
    using Gabriella profile to define 30
diversifying perspectives
    as potential area for further study for black and brown women's reasons for leading 48
diversity, Equity, and Inclusion
    debate about 57
diversity
    definition 85
domains as area of focus for knowledge development 11, 18, 87, 96, 119, 123, 132
    as referenced by Dionne 126
    as referenced by NPBEA regarding standards domains 107, 108
dominant culture 38, 50, 54, 63, 94, 147
    Leadership Academy, *A Portrait of a Culturally Responsive School System*, (2021), definition 39
double bind
    definition 68
double Jeopardy
    definition 67
drivers/reasons for pursuing educational Calling, purpose, drivers for leadership
    author's 2, 45–6
    author's call to educational leadership 38
    as part of author chapter 3 summary 17
    as part of author's chapter 3 summary of Herminia Ibarra, Robin Ely, and Deborah Kolb, "Women Rising," (2019) on leadership drivers/purpose for women 41–3
    Karen Longman and Debbie Lamm Bray "The Role of Purpose and Calling," (2017) on purpose/drivers 43
    respondents' reasons for pursuing leadership: (1) forwarding social justice/improving educational outcomes, (2) improving teaching and learning, (3) making changes to bureaucratic management and leadership structures and approaches, and (4) diversifying perspectives 38, 45–7
    respondents' reasons for leading 18
    as theme author identifies and describes 17
Dweck, Carol, *Mindset* (2006)
    continuous learning as definition for success 44
    definition of bullying 73
    definition of fixed mindset and relationship to bullying 74
    growth mindset 44
Dwyer, Charles, *Shifting Sources of Power*, (1992)
    quoted describing power, authority, and responsibility 41

Eagly, Alice and Linda Carli
    communal and agentic description, "Women and the Labyrinth of Leadership," (2007a) 51
    "The Female Leadership Advantage," (2003), discussion of prejudice and stereotype 64

glass ceiling, "Women and the Labyrinth
of Leadership," (2007a) 100
Labyrinth, "Women and the Labyrinth
of Leadership," (2007a) 101
respecting women as leaders, "Women
and the Labyrinth of Leadership,"
(2007a) 170
role theory, "Women and the Labyrinth
of Leadership," (2007a) 51
egalitarian
author's perspective 2
Ellie (Respondent #17 pseudonym)
profile description in Appendix 198
quotation about defining educational
leadership 26
quotation about imposter syndrome 69
emotional intelligence
enact/enacted/enacts
epistemology
as part of paradigm description 14
equitable culture (as standard)
discussion of 126–9
equity/equitable
definition 85
espouse/espoused/espouses
Ester (Respondent #10 pseudonym)
profile description in Appendix 197
quotation about collaboration and
engagement disposition 140
quotation about performance
management standards 131
quotation about skills and experiences
192
ethical leadership
definition 29
using Matt to describe 29s
Evelyn (Respondent #10 pseudonym)
profile description in Appendix 197
exceptional competence/unexpected
excellence/Superior task knowledge
description 6
as element of survey design 11
expertism
description 4

fair practices
necessary to address bullying,
harassment, racism, and abuse at a
structural/organizational level 72

Fallon, Jimmy
his why described by Jason Feifer,
Entrepreneur (2022) 44
Feifer, Jason *Entrepreneur* (2022)
Jimmy Fallon's why 44
feedback
author on 4
feminism/feminist leadership
description 14, 25
driver for author 25
element of study's paradigm 14
leadership model 25
fit
Autumn Tooms, Catherine Lugg,
and Ira Botoch, "Rethinking
the Politics of Fit," (2010),
re: community role in defining
fit 63
definition 63
relationship to gatekeeping 63
fixed mindset
Carol Dweck, *Mindset*, (2006) quote
about relationship to bullying 74

Gabriela (pseudonym)
profile used to describe distributive
leadership 30
profile used to highlight shaming 87
Gallardo-Gallardo, Eva and Marian
Thunnissen, "Standing on the
Shoulder of Giants?," (2016)
talent management definition 167
gatekeeping
create barriers to entry 63, 65
gender
respondents' – Avril, Dedee, Jaimie,
Joan, Kelly, Natalie, Nola, Sharon,
Sonja, Reese, Wilma – quotations
about, gender 53–4
Georgette (Respondent #30 pseudonym)
profile description in Appendix 199
quotation about Development and
Support standard 126
quotation about intersectionality 56
quotation about Performance
Management standards 131
quotation about reflection and
continuous learning disposition
162

quotation about resilience 159
quotation about type of organization to look for 186
Glass, Christy and Alice Ingersoll, "Sociological Approaches," (2017)
   conformity and leader profiles 64
   token definition 65
glass metaphors
   Glass cliff
      description 6, 99
      Michelle Ryan and Alexander Haslam, "The Glass Cliff," (2007) discussion 99
   glass cushion
      description 99
   glass escalator
      description 4, 100
      dketch 4
   glass ceiling
      Eagly, Alice and Linda Carli "Women and the Labyrinth of Leadership," (2007a), description 100, 101
   as group of metaphors 99
good woman
   description 68
growth mindset
   definition 44
   as defined by Carol Dweck, *Mindset* (2006) 44

hardships
   Center for Creative Leadership Lesson's of Experience framework element 91
   definition 3
   definition 91
harassment
   discussion summarizing respondents' experience with 77
   referenced in chapter 4 summary 18
   16 respondents experienced harassment
   author definition of 70
   table summarizing respondents' experience with 78
   ways respondents addressed 79
Harvard Business School, *The 2018 State of Leadership Development: Meeting the Transformation Imperative*, (2018)
   reference to relevance of learning 181–2
hegemonic/hegemony
   definition 40
hepeating
   definition 66
heroic leadership
   description 32
   profiles of bill and Bob used in description 31–3
homosocial reproduction
   definition 64
hood feminism
   definition 50
   as contrasted with traditional feminism 50
humor
   in reference to author's 16, 17, 20, 77, 92, 157, 165, 187

Ibarra, Herminia, Robin Ely, and Deborah Kolb, "Women Rising," (2019)
   on purpose/drivers 42
identity
   as driver for leadership 42
   as influenced by power, culture, and organizational practices 41
   as part of author chapter 3 summary 17
   role of vis a vis power 38
   as theme author identifies and describes 16
implicit
   bias 54, 62–3, 171, 174, 203
   leadership 17, 29
imposter syndrome
   definition 69
ILO Group, "Updated Analysis," (2022)
   reference to superintendent's research project data 6
inclusion
   definition 85
influencers to one's leadership
   summary of respondents' influencers 46–7
in-group favoritism 99, 174
   description 99
innovation (as standard)
instructional leadership
   definition 27
   as part of author chapter 2 summary 17

quote about in *The American Superintendent Decennial Study* (2021) 132
as referenced by respondents as important to their practice 26
instructional leader and transformational educational leader practices described by Council of Chief State School Officers 110
intersectional/intersectionality
  Challenges and barriers relating to 66
  definition 50
  discussion 55
  respondents' mitigation strategies 55
  respondents – Angela, Diedre, Georgette, Lara, Leslie, Lottie, Michelle, Reese, Tanya, Tang – quotations about 56–57
Irby, Beverly, Genevieve Brown, and LingLing Yang, "The Synergistic Leadership Theory," (2013)
  reference to synergistic leadership theory 52

Jackie (Respondent #8 pseudonym)
  Profile description in Appendix 197
  quotation about creativity and innovation disposition 149
  quotation about principal's role in bullying 81
  quotation about reflection and continuous learning disposition 162
  quotation about skills and experiences 192
  quotation about teaching and learning standard 134
Jaimie (Respondent #13 pseudonym)
  profile description in Appendix 198
  quotation about defining educational leadership 26
  quotation about double jeopardy 68
  quotation about equitable culture standard 128
  quotation on gendered issues 53
  quotation about organizational strategies to redress/prevent bad behavior 84
  quotation about political savvy 152
  quotation on professionalism and ethics 155
  quotation about type of organization to look for 187
  quotation about verbal abuse 81
Jean (Respondent #29 pseudonym)
  profile description in Appendix 199
  quotation about bullying and mistreatment 71
  quotation about her comments being ignored 67
  quotation about equitable culture standard 128
  quotation about route to leadership 102
  quotation about support networks 190
Jeff (pseudonym for leader)
  profile used to describe authentic leadership 28
Joan (Respondent #15 pseudonym)
  profile description in Appendix 198
  quotation about addressing bullying 82
  quotation about collaboration and engagement disposition 140
  quotation about confidence 146
  quotation about defining educational leadership 26
  quotation about equitable culture standard 128
  quotation on gendered issues 53
  quotation about intersectionality 56
  quotation about performance management standards 131–2
  quotation about purpose for leading/why 43
  quotation about resilience 158
  quotation about support networks 190
  quotation about vision 137
John, Elton and Bernie Taupin, composers, "Still Standing," (1983)
  reference to chapter subtitle 194
Julie (Respondent #3 pseudonym)
  profile description in Appendix 197
  quotation about support networks 190
  quotation about skills and experiences 192
Julie (pseudonym for colleague)
  profile used to highlight silencing 87
Jungle gym
  leadership 100
  as metaphor for women's route to

Karin (Respondent #12 pseudonym)
   profile description in Appendix 198
   quotation about defining educational leadership 26
   quotation about keeping good people in education 187
   quotation about purpose and her privilege 43
   quotation about resilience 158
Kay, Katty and Claire Shipman, *The Confidence Code* (2014)
   link between confidence and action 145
Kelly (Respondent #7 pseudonym)
   profile description in Appendix 197
   quotation about bullying 80
   quotation about collaboration and engagement disposition 140
   quotation about creativity and innovation disposition 149
   quotation about equitable culture standard 129
   quotation on gendered issues 54
   quotation about identity and community 67
   quotation about political savvy 152
   quotation about support networks 190
knowledge
   Corporate Leadership Council definition as cited in Kirk Kramer and Preeta Nyack, *Nonprofit Leadership Development*, (2013) 104
   types of knowledge described by Murphy, Jerome, "The Unheroic Side of Leadership, (2013) 104
Kramer, Kirk and Preeta Nyack, *Nonprofit Leadership Development*, (2013)
   CEO role in development 170
   competence definition 104
   definition of knowledge 104
   dispositions definition 104
   leadership development definition 167
   skills definition 104
   trait definition 104
Kumra, Savita, "Reflections on Glass," (2017)
   women's roles, trait theory, and stereotypes 51

labyrinth
   definition 101
   Eagly and Carli, "Women and the Labyrinth of Leadership," (2019) 101
   as resonates with author 97
Lara (Respondent #32 pseudonym)
   profile description in Appendix 199
   quotation about defining educational leadership 26
   quotation about double jeopardy 68
   quotation about emotional supports 188
   quotation about intersectionality 56
   quotation about organizational strategies to redress/prevent bad behavior 84
   quotation about political savvy 152
   quotation about reason for leading 47
   quotation on professionalism and ethics 155
Leadership Academy, *A Portrait of a Culturally Responsive School System*, (2021)
   quoted in defining culturally responsive leadership 30–1
   quoted defining dominant culture and white dominant culture 39
   referenced in chapter 5 summary 18
Leadership Academy, *Culturally Responsive Leadership*, (2020)
   culturally Responsive Leadership actions 105–6
   culturally Responsive Leadership framework 105
   definition of culturally responsive leadership practice 106
   quote about minoritized communities 105
leadership development
   author summary of support for 167
   Bierema, Laura and Susan Madsen, "No Woman Left Behind," (2017), leadership development monitoring 171
   Content priorities as transparent 183
   Individual strategies: (1) planning your leadership development, (2) attending to emotional and

physical well-being, (3) negotiating personal support, (4) identifying professional support, and (5) engaging in due diligence 184–93
Kirk Kramer and Preeta Nyack, *Nonprofit Leadership Development*, (2013), definition 167
Kirk Kramer and Preeta Nyack, *Nonprofit Leadership Development*, (2013), CEO role 170
organizational strategies – 1) Coherent Selection and Development, (2) Varied Delivery Techniques, and (3) Aligned Content and Figure 7.1) – 168–84
responsibility for in Sarah Leberman and Jane Hurst, "The Connection between Success, Choice, and Leadership," (2017) 166–7
strategies 168
leadership equation
 referenced by author as purpose 9–10
leadership identity
 how formed 41
 Autumn Tooms, Catherine Lugg, and Ira Botoch, "Rethinking the Politics of Fit," (2010) on identity formation 42
leadership models
 as focus of chapter 2 summary 17
 overview to chapter 2 describing models based on author's experience with particular leaders 23
 as theme author identifies and describes 16
leadership path
 as referenced to author's circuitous path 2
 referenced as strategy in chapter 7 summarized 19
leadership profiles
 shaped by 97
leadership routes
 complicated and veiled as problem author is addressing 10, 96
 as referenced in chapter 5 summary 18

 convoluted 97
 Steps 166
 Yellow Brick Road description and figure as evocative of author's route 97–8
leadership standards
 discussion of standards as starting point 118
 proposal that women need their own standards 118
 respondents' standards'
  priorities: Communication (thirty-one respondents), People and Relationships (thirty people), Culture as well as Vision (twenty-eight people), Resilience (twenty-five people), and Teamwork (twenty-four respondents) 97, 111–12
 summary of author's revised standards for women 119
 as theme author identifies and describes 17
 author summary of her proposed standards to test 111
leadership style
 as element of survey design 11
 as referencing women's styles 3, 11
learning experiences
 Relevant in Harvard Business School, *The 2018 State of Leadership Development: Meeting the Transformation Imperative*, (2018) 181–2
leadership for teaching and learning
 definition 27
 as model
 as part of author chapter 2 summary 17
 as referenced by respondents as important to their practice 26
Learning through Individual Feedback and Growth Plans
 author proposed strategy 176
Learning Alongside and from Others
 author proposed strategy 176, 177–8
Learning by Doing and Reflecting in Context
 author proposed strategy 176
learning in context

DeSmet, Jeff, Louise Axon, and John Alsbury, *Accelerate Leadership Development*, (2016) 176
Learning through Leaders' Preferences and Contexts
  Author proposed strategy 176, 180–1
learning through teaching
  DeSmet, Jeff, Louise Axon, and John Alsbury, *Accelerate Leadership Development* (2016) 173
learning with others
  DeSmet, Jeff, Louise Axon, and John Alsbury, *Accelerate Leadership Development*, (2016) 178
  Leberman, Sarah and Jane Hurst, "The Connection between Success, Choice, and Leadership," (2017)
  Responsibility for leadership development 166–7
Leslie (Respondent #36 pseudonym)
  profile description in Appendix 199
  quotation about addressing racism and bullying 82
  quotation about emotional supports 188
  quotation about intersectionality 56
  quotation about leadership development 172
  quotation on professionalism and ethics 156
  quotation about servant leadership 29
Longman, Karen and Debbie Lamm Bray, "The Role of Purpose and Calling," (2017)
  purpose/drivers 43
Lottie (Respondent #37 pseudonym)
  Profile description in Appendix 199
  quotation about confidence 146
  quotation about handling harassment 82
  quotation about intersectionality 56
  quotation about leadership development 172
  quotation about reason for leading 48
  quotation about teaching and learning standard 134
  quotation about understanding others 40
Lydia (Respondent #24 pseudonym)
  profile description in Appendix 198
  quotation about Development and Support standard 126
  quotation about experience as teacher 177
  quotation about her ideas being usurped 67
  quotation about her why 43
  quotation about race and white privilege 40
  quotation about support networks 190

macro-aggression
  respondents' experience with 69
  women's encounter with as element of survey design 11
Making Changes to Bureaucratic Management & Leadership Structures and Approaches 18, 38, 45, 46, 58
manels
  description 99
manimization
  definition 66
mansplain
  description 154
marathon
  as leadership route metaphor 101
Maranto, Robert, Kristen Carroll, Albert Chengy, and Manuel Teodoro, "Boys Will be Superintendents," (2018)
  on secondary schools as training ground for superintendents 64
marginalized/marginalize
Mariana (pseudonym)
  used to describe Queen Bee 86
Mathilda (Respondent #25 pseudonym)
  profile description in Appendix 198
  quotation about confidence 146
  quotation about creativity and innovation disposition 149
  quotation about culture 174
  quotation about Development and Support standard 126
  quotation about emotional supports 188
  quotation describing ethical stance 33
  quotation about equitable culture standard 129

quotation about handling harassment 82
quotation about leadership development 172
quotation about performance management standards 132
quotation about political savvy 152
quotation about reason for leading 47
quotation about reflection and continuous learning disposition 162
quotation about resilience 159
quotation about teaching and learning standard 134
quotation about vision 137
Mathilda Effect
 definition 67
Matt (pseudonym)
 profile used to describe ethical and resonant leadership 29
John Maxwell, *Qualitative Research Design*, (2005)
 definition of theory 49
Me Too
 referenced as movement 8
mentor
 Elena Aguilar, "What's the Difference between Mentoring and Coaching?," (2017) definition 178
 referenced as strategy in chapter 7 summarized 19
meritocracy
 as linked to American Dream 2
metaphor
 as theme author identifies and describes 16
Meyerson, Debra and Megan Tompkins, "Tempered Radicals as Institutional Change Agents," (2007)
 tempered radicals and entrepreneurship 147
Michelle (Respondent #21 pseudonym)
 quotation about Competence standard 124
 quotation about confidence 146
 quotation about defining educational leadership 26
 quotation about harassment 78
 quotation about intersectionality 56
quotation about organizational strategies to redress/prevent bad behavior 84
quotation about purpose for leading 43
quotation about resilience 159
quotation about route to leadership 102
quotation about support networks 190
quotation about vision 137
profile description in Appendix 198
micro-aggression
 definition of 55
 quotation about light bullying being a micro-aggression 73
 respondents' experience with 69
 women's encounter with as element of survey design 11
micro-politics
 description 150
mindbug
 definition 63
Mindell, Phyllis *How to Say it for Women*, (2001)
 on Communication 142
mindful/mindfulness
 definition of 44
minoritized communities
 Leadership Academy (2020) description 105
Model Principal Supervisor Professional Standards 2015
 eight standards referenced in Council of Chief State School Officers summary and table 109
motivation/motivate/motivational/ motivations
movements/Reckonings
 Black Lives Matter 8
 MeToo 8
 Times Up 8
 treatment they seek to reflect 8
moves and related lessons
 author's experience and flags 89–90
Murphy, Jerome, "The Unheroic Side of Leadership," (2013)
 description of types of knowledge 104

Nancy (pseudonym)
 profile used to highlight silencing 87

Natalie (Respondent #16 pseudonym)
  profile description in Appendix 198
  quotation about defining educational leadership 27
  quotation about ideas being ignored 67
  quotation on gendered issues 54
National Association of Independent Schools (NAIS), *NAIS Principles of Good Practice*, (2020)
  as referenced in chapter 5 summary 18
  as referenced Principles of Good Practice 106–7
National Educational Leadership Preparation (NELP) accreditation
  reference to 107
National Policy Board for Educational Administration (NPBEA), *Professional Standards for Educational Leaders* (2015)
  Professional Standards for Educational Leaders 2015, 106–7
  as referenced in chapter 5 summary 18
  as referencing National Educational Leadership Preparation (NELP) and summary table 107–8
navigation/navigated/navigate
  definition 150
  women having much to share to help others navigate referenced 19
neo-liberalism/neo-liberal
  definition of 76
  discussion of reforms on which author has worked 76
Network/networker/networks/networking
  referenced as strategy in chapter 7 summarized 19
Nola (Respondent #34 pseudonym)
  profile description in Appendix 199
  quotation about collaboration and engagement disposition 140
  quotation on gendered issues 54
  quotation about resilience 159
  quotation about route to leadership 102
  quotation about support networks 190
  quotation about vision 137
Norm (pseudonym)
  profile used to describe silencing 87

on-the-job training
  quotation by Lara Bierema and Susan Madsen, "No Woman Left Behind," (2017) 125
  referenced as strategy in chapter 7 summarized 19
ontology
  part of paradigm description 14
oppress/oppression
other/others
  description 6
  discussion 6, 8, 9, 10, 13, 14, 32, 41, 50, 51, 65, 87, 91, 93, 99, 166, 169
  John Powell, "Us versus Them," (2017) 65
outsider status
  author's 4, 74, 76, 182
  reference to 64, 146, 147

paradigm
  author's study's paradigm 14
  description 14
Patty (Respondent #28 pseudonym)
  profile description in Appendix 198
  quotation on professionalism and ethics 156
  quotation about reason for leading 48
  quotation about reflection and continuous learning disposition 162
  quotation about teaching and learning standard 134
people & relationships (as standard) 18, 97, 111–12, 120, 138
performance evaluation
performance management standard
  discussion 129–32
phenomenology
  definition of 13
  type of study 10, 13
poisoned chalice
  in reference to chapter subtitle 22
political savvy as disposition
  discussion 149–52
Powell, John, "Us versus Them," (2017)
  Others and othering 65
power
  as theme author identifies and describes 16
  as part of author chapter 3 summary 17

role of vis a vis identity 38
preservation and reproduction 40
as an influence on leadership, leadership identity, and beliefs and behaviors 41
influencers on identity 41
Power stress
  description 33
pragmatic/pragmatism
  description 14
  as element of study's paradigm 14
prejudice
  Alice Eagly and Linda Carli, "Female Leadership Advantage," (2003) definition 64
principles of good practice
  National Association of Independent Schools (NAIS), *NAIS Principles of Good Practice* (2020) 106–7
private apology
  discussion 88
privilege/privileges/privileged
  author's reference to her own 8
  reference in contrast to women of color 8, 50, 52
Professional Standards for Educational Leaders 2015
  Overview, description, and table 106–8
professionalism & ethics disposition
  discussion 152–6
public education
  as a right as part of author's beliefs 24
purpose
  author's reasons for writing 9–10
  driver for leading 41–3
  fill hole/gap 9
  provide navigation tools to women 62

qualitative study
  author's study type 10, 13
  definition 13
Queen Bee
  description 86
  profile of mariana used to highlight 86

race/racism/racist
Rachel (Respondent #4 pseudonym)
  profile description in appendix 197
  quotation about handling harassment 82
  quotation about resilience 159
racism
  author definition of 70
  discussion of elements of racism 30, 48, 51, 62, 69, 75
  discussion about and table summarizing respondents' experience with 75–8
  ways respondents addressed 79
  as referenced in chapter 4 summary 18
  19 respondents experienced racism
Rafael (pseudonym)
  profile used to describe servant, implicit, contextual, situational, adaptive, and transformational leadership 29
Rager
  description 154
Reese (Respondent #11 pseudonym)
  profile description in Appendix 197
  quotation about Administration and operations standard 122
  quotation about bullying 73
  quotation about confidence 146
  quotation about defining educational leadership 27
  quotation on gendered issues 54
  quotation about intersectionality 57
  quotation about leadership development 172
  quotation about reflection and continuous learning disposition 162–3
  quotation about skills and experiences 192–3
  quotation about vision 138
reflection/reflective
  Defined by Council of Chief State School Officers (CCSSO), *Model Principal Supervisor*, (2015) 44
  as learning strategy 177
reflexive/reflexivity
  definition of 15
  as used by author in analysis 15
research framework (author's)
  elements of 10–16
  overview 10
resilience
  author's attempts at 91, 157–8

author's strategies for resilience 92
disposition discussion 156–9
definition of 90–1
necessary to overcome challenges as element of survey design 11
resonant leadership
definition 29
description using matt 29
quoting Richard Boyatzis and Annie McKee, *Resonant Leadership*, (2005) 29
role congruity theory
description 52
Ryan, Michelle and Alexander Haslam, "The Glass Cliff," (2007)
discussion about benevolent sexism 65–6

Sally (pseudonym)
profile used to describe escalation/de-escalation 88
savior myth
description of 4
second generation bias
definition 62–3
secondary schools
complexity 64
Robert Maranto, et al, "Boys Will be Superintendents," (2018) discussion of high schools as training grounds for superintendency 64
self-reflection & continuous learning disposition
discussion 159–62
sexism
as referenced in chapter 4 summary 18
Shapiro, Ester and Jennifer Leah, "Chapter 4: Toward Culturally," (2007)
Preservation of status quo 87
Sharon (Respondent #19 pseudonym)
profile description in Appendix 198
quotation about administration and operations standard 122
quotation about collaboration and engagement disposition 140
quotation about double bind 68

quotation about harassment and bullying 71
quotation about support networks 191
quotation on gendered issues 54
Shields, Carol, *Transformative Leadership*, (2017)
on misuse of power and addressing it 83
silencing
Soraya Chemaly, *Rage*, (2018), on silencing 87
use of Julie to describe 87
use of Norm to describe 87
use of Nancy to describe 87
situational leadership
description 29
skills
Corporate Leadership Council definition as cited in Kirk Kramer and Preeta Nyack, *Nonprofit Leadership Development* (2013) 104
social justice
definition 24–5
as driver for author 24–5
as leadership model 24–5
social role theory
description of 52
Savita Kumra, "Reflections on Glass," (2017) discussion of 51
softeners
Vanek-Smith, Stacey, *Machiavelli for Women*, (2021) defintion 69
Sonja (Respondent #6 pseudonym)
profile description in appendix 197
quotation about administration and operations standard 122
quotation about defining educational leadership 27
quotation about handling grievance 82
quotation about own positionality in black and brown district 40
quotation about reason for leading 47
quotation about resilience 159
quotation on gendered issues 54
quotation on professionalism and ethics 155
sponsor
definition 7, 24, 179

Elena Aguilar, "What's the Difference between Mentoring and Coaching?," (2017) definition 179
  referenced as strategy in chapter 7 summarized 19
  as strategy for author 165, 166, 179, 180
  as strategy for leadership 170, 178, 182, 184, 185, 189, 203
standards
  proposal that women should have their own set of standards and dispositions as included in summary of chapter 6, 18
  as referenced in chapter 5 summary 18
  as summary of respondents' priorities communication; people and relationships; culture and vision; resilience; and teamwork 18
status quo
  preservation of as discussed by Shapiro, Ester and Jennifer Leah, "Chapter 4: Toward Culturally," (2007) 87
stereotype
  Alice Eagly and Linda Carli, "Female Leadership Advantage," (2003) definition 64
strategies
  author's strategies for resilience 92
  respondents' strategies for leadership standards 113
  respondents' – Billie, Jaimie, Lara, Michelle, Tang, and Wilma – comments about organizational strategies for combatting bad behavior 84
  summary of potential organizational strategies to redress/prevent bad behavior 84–5
  summary of those that support women 7
stress
  as a barrier to women in leadership 70
stretch assignments
  definition 7
  as experienced by author 28, 29, 165
  as strategy 102, 168, 176, 177, 180, 182
study justification
  author's summary of 11
style approach
  description by Chin, Jean Lau, "Overview," in *Women and Leadership*, (2007b) 104
success
  as Carol Dweck, *Mindset*, (2006) defines as continuous learning 44
superintendent profile
  white male as norm 63
synergystic leadership theory
  developed by Beverly Irby, Genevieve Brown, and LingLing Yang, "The Synergistic Leadership Theory," (2013) 52
superwoman
  definition 90
talent management
  definition by Eva Gallardo-Gallardo and Marian Thunnissen, "Standing on the Shoulder of Giants?," (2016) 167
  referenced as strategy in chapter 7 summarized 19
talent development
  definition 166, 167–8, 169
  referenced as strategy in chapter 7 summarized 19
Tan, Jo-Ann, (2016), "For Women of Color," (2016)
  description of concrete ceiling 99
Tang (Respondent #20 pseudonym)
  profile description in Appendix 198
  quotation about defining educational leadership 27
  quotation about double bind 68
  quotation about intersectionality 57
  quotation about leadership development 172
  quotation about organizational strategies to redress/prevent bad behavior 84
  quotation about reflection and continuous learning disposition 163
  quotation about silencing self 82
  quotation about support networks 191
Tanya (Respondent #2 pseudonym)
  quotation about confidence 146

quotation about creativity and
    innovation disposition 149
quotation about handling harmful
    person 83
quotation about intersectionality 57
quotation about reflection and
    continuous learning disposition
    163
quotation about support networks
    191
profile description in appendix 197
teaching & learning (as standard)
    discussion 132–4
teamwork (as standard)
tempered radicals
    Meyerson, Debra and Megan Tompkins,
        "Tempered Radicals as Institutional
        Change Agents," (2007) 147
terminology
    reference to unpacking of myriad of
        terms from literature 16
themes/theme
    identified by author through
        coding 15–16
    as summarized by author 16–17
theory/theories
    as defined by John Maxwell (2005) 48
    purpose of critical social theory/social
        justice theory 49
    as method for understanding leadership
        introduced 39, 48
    as study's framework for analysis 14
        critical theory 14, 49
        social justice theory 14, 49
theory of change
    definition 95
thirty-seven women in study
    introduction to 9
    overview of respondents'
        backgrounds 12–13
    reasons for including them for teaching
        purposes 10
token/tokenism
    Christy Glass and Alice Ingersoll,
        "Sociological Approaches," (2017)
        discussion 65
    Tooms, Autumn, Catherine Lugg, and Ira
        Botoch, "Rethinking the Politics of
        Fit," (2010)

On school community and leader
    identity 42
toxic/toxicity
trait/traits
    Corporate Leadership Council
        definition as cited in Kirk Kramer
        and Preeta Nyack, *Nonprofit
        Leadership Development*, (2013)
        104
trait theory
    discussion of 51–2
transactional leadership
    definition 33–4
    using profile of bud to describe 33–4
transformational leadership
    Council of Chief State School Officers
        (CCSSO), *Model Principal
        Supervisor*, (2015) 152–3
    description 30
transformationally resilient
    author's use of 90

unconscious bias
    definition 62
underminer
    bud profile used to describe
        underminer 74
    definition of 74
underrepresented / underrepresentation
    data 5
    women's underrepresentation in
        leadership/U.S. Department of
        Education National Center for
        Education Statistics (NCES),
        "Characteristics of Public
        School Principals," (2020) and
        "Characteristics of Public School
        Teachers," (2021) 5
    Women's underrepresentation in
        superintendency/American
        Association of School
        Administrators, (AASA), "AASA
        Releases Key Findings," (2020b)
        data 5–6
    As problem author is addressing 10
    U.S. Department of Education National
        Center for Education Statistics
        (NCES), "Characteristics of Public
        School Principals," (2020) and

"Characteristics of Public School Teachers," (2021)
  data on women in teaching versus leadership 5

value/values
Vanek-Smith, Stacey, *Machiavelli for Women*, (2021)
  definition of softeners 69
vision standard
  discussion 134–7
  Yellow Hat sketch about 136

web
  leadership web as route 100
weather/weathering
  description of 55, 72
white dominant culture
  Definition by Leadership Academy, *A Portrait of a Culturally Responsive School System*, (2021) 39
why
  see purpose and drivers
Wilma (Respondent #9 pseudonym)
  profile description in Appendix 197
  quotation about defining educational leadership 27
  quotation about equitable culture standard 129
  quotation about imposter syndrome 69
  quotation about leadership development 173
  quotation about organizational strategies to redress/prevent bad behavior 84
  quotation about not handling harassment directly 83
  quotation about reason for leading 47
  quotation on gendered issues 54–5

Wonder Woman T Shirt
  as referenced by author as mitigation strategy 7, 93, 157
workaround
  author's use of 148, 158
  description 146–7
  Russell Bishop, *Workarounds That Work*, (2011) definition 147
worldview
  definition of 10
  as part of author chapter 3 summary 17
  as referenced to author's foundational beliefs 10

Zelda (Respondent #35 pseudonym)
  profile description in Appendix 199
  quotation about addressing toxic work environments and people 72
  quotation about exceptional competence 6
  quotation about leadership development 173
  quotation about organization not handling micro-aggressors 83
  quotation about organizational strategies to redress/prevent racism, bullying, harassment 84
  quotation about political savvy 152
  quotation about reflection and continuous learning disposition 163
  quotation about route to leadership 102
  quotation about skills and experiences 193
  quotation about support networks 191
  quotation about teaching and learning standard 134
  quotation about vision 138

www.ingramcontent.com/pod-product-compliance
Lightning Source LLC
Chambersburg PA
CBHW071817300426
44116CB00009B/1350